1 ~ 316

p 67
EGALITARIAN
as a word for
paper of hierarchy

APOCALYPTICISM
pp 81-98

✗ p 46
look up

do this written by a believer? e.g.: BCE + CE

psychological ⓟ p 92 + 95   101   BURIAL 113

ⓟ 94-5   DEVELOPMENT 09, 11?11

99

100

MESSAGE OF THE SACRAMENTS

Monika K. Hellwig, Editor

Volume 6

Mission and Ministry

History and Theology
in the
Sacrament of Order

by

Nathan Mitchell, O.S.B.

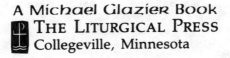
A Michael Glazier Book
THE LITURGICAL PRESS
Collegeville, Minnesota

Typography by Peg McCormick

Printed in the United States of America.

3	4	5	6	7	8	9

Library of Congress Cataloging-in-Publication Data

Mitchell, Nathan.
  Mission and ministry : history and theology in the sacrament of order / by Nathan Mitchell.
      p.   cm.
  Reprint. Originally published: Wilmington, Del. : M. Glazier, 1982. (Message of the sacraments ; 6).
  "A Michael Glazier book."
  Includes bibliographical references.
  ISBN 0-8146-5292-1
  1. Ordination—Catholic Church. 2. Catholic Church—Clergy. 3. Mission of the church. 4. Clergy—Office.   I. Title. II. Series: Message of the sacraments ; 6.
BX2240.M57   1990
234'.164—dc20   90-38450
                                                                          CIP

For Nancy and Michael,
and for
Kristen, Sean, Kirk and Jennifer

Contents

CHAPTER TWO: THE EARLIEST PATTERNS
OF CHRISTIAN MINISTRY

CHAPTER THREE: MINISTRY IN THE LATER
NEW TESTAMENT PERIOD

CHAPTER FOUR: A CHRISTIAN PRIESTHOOD

CHAPTER FIVE: A THEOLOGY OF
HOLY ORDERS

10

EDITOR'S PREFACE

This volume is one of the series of eight on *The Message of the Sacraments*. These volumes discuss the ritual practices and understanding and the individual sacraments of the Roman Catholic community. Each of the eight authors has set out to cover five aspects of the sacrament (or, in the first and last volumes, of the theme or issue under discussion). These are: first of all, the existential or experiential meaning of the sacrament in the context of secular human experience; what is known of the historical development of the sacrament; a theological exposition of the meaning, function and effect of the sacrament in the context of present official Catholic doctrinal positions; some pastoral reflections; and a projection of possible future developments in the practice and catechesis of the sacrament.

There is evident need of such a series of volumes to combine the established teaching and firm foundation in sacramental theology with the new situation of the post-Vatican II Church. Because the need is universal, this series is the joint effort of an international team of English-speaking authors. We have not invited any participants whose writing would need to be translated. While we hope that our series will be useful particularly to priests, permanent deacons, seminarians, and those professionally involved in sacramental and catechetical ministries, we also address ourselves confidently to the educated Catholic laity and to those outside the Roman Catholic communion who are interested in learning more about its life and thought. We have all tried to write so as to be easily understood by readers with little or no specialized preparation. We have all tried to deal with the tradition imaginatively but within the acceptable bounds of Catholic orthodoxy, in the firm conviction that that is the way in which we can be most helpful to our readers.

The Church seems to be poised today at a critical juncture in its history. Vatican II reopened long-standing questions about collegiality and participation in the life of the Church, including its sacramental actions, its doctrinal formulations and its government. The Council fostered a new critical awareness and raised hopes which the Church as a vast and complicated institution cannot satisfy without much confusion, conflict and delay. This makes ours a particularly trying and often frustrating time for those most seriously interested in the life of the Church and most deeply committed to it. It seems vitally important for constructive and authentically creative community participation in the shaping of the Church's future life, that a fuller understanding of the sacraments be widely disseminated in the Catholic community. We hope that many readers will begin with the volumes in this series and let themselves be guided into further reading with the bibliographies we offer at the ends of the chapters. We hope to communicate to our readers the sober optimism with which we have undertaken the study and thereby to contribute both to renewal and to reconciliation.

Monika K. Hellwig

INTRODUCTION

My aim in writing this book can be simply stated: I hope to help Christians, especially those of the Roman Catholic communion, understand more fully the origins, evolution and theological interpretation of ordained ministry in the church. This is not, therefore, a book about pastoral strategies for ministry today, nor is it a manifesto for new ministries, whether ordained or non-ordained. Readers who are interested in these latter topics may want to consult recently published works such as David Power's *Gifts That Differ* (New York: Pueblo Publishing Company, 1980), or James and Evelyn Whitehead's *Method in Ministry* (New York: Seabury Press, 1980).

A primary goal of this volume is to make available to the nonspecialist the results of recent biblical research as these affect our understanding of the world into which the Christian movement was born and out of which the Christian ministry grew. To that end, the first three chapters are devoted. We begin with an account of the priesthood in Israel, from its earliest appearance to its development at the time of Jesus' ministry (Chapter One). Chapter Two attempts, first, to situate the Christian movement itself within the broader context of the many "religious renewal movements" that were popular in first-century Palestine.

From there, the chapter moves to a discussion of ministry in the earliest Christian congregations: the "wandering charismatics" in Palestine; the Jerusalem church, where the parties of James and Stephen came into conflict; the communities established by the missionary apostle Paul. Chapter Three continues the New Testament story by drawing attention to the crisis of leadership Christians faced in the second and third generations. We shall see how these Christians dealt with such serious issues as the fall of Jerusalem (70 C.E.), the delay of Jesus' return, and the death of those "first witnesses" (the apostles) who had enjoyed special intimacy with Jesus. We shall also see how the response to these issues helped shape patterns of Christian ministry in the later-first and early-second centuries. Chapter Four examines the evolution of "priesthood" in the Christian church. Of particular interest will be the development of a specialized vocabulary of ordained ministry ("orders", "holy orders"), as well as the growth of the notion that ordination is a "sacrament", parallel in nature and effects, to baptism and eucharist. In the fifth and final chapter, a theology of holy orders will be sketched.

This book is offered, then, in the hope that it will enrich the historical and theological understanding of Christians who are engaged in ministry today. Most of all, the author hopes that it will deepen the desire of all who serve the church to follow the lead of Jesus, the "high priest of a new and everlasting covenant."

Nathan Mitchell, OSB
St. Meinrad Archabbey
Lent, 1982

CHAPTER ONE
A KINGDOM OF PRIESTS

Introduction

For many Christian readers of the Bible, "priest" is a resonant word that evokes images of sacrifice, altars, vestments and mysteriously powerful communion with God. Human but exotically "different"; a devil or an angel; a servant who rules and ruler who serves; leader-listener-healer-companion: these are some of the conflicting signals linked with priesthood. Even today, almost twenty years after the II Vatican Council began, "priest" is a word that can raise questions, instill confidence, provoke anger or offer hope.

Attitudes toward priesthood usually reflect the combined influence of history, culture, church and personal experience; and the priesthood itself is subject to the same influences. Today's Christian priests are thus products of a long evolution punctuated by success and failure, forgotten truths and remembered falsehoods, historical accident and (a believer would say) divine plan. During the course of that evolution the priesthood has absorbed a vast amount of practical wisdom and theological interpretation; it has also experienced a profound metamorphosis. Even though we use "priest" to identify ordained christian leaders of various ages, we must remember that it is a word whose meaning has shifted through the centuries.

The same thing can be said about priest and priesthood in the religion of Israel. A Jewish priest of Jesus' day was a religious figure quite different from the Elide family about whom we read in the First Book of Samuel. Similarly, King David's priests, Zadok and Abiathar, differed from those priests we hear about during the time of Israel's settlement in Canaan after the exodus.

This chapter offers a sketch of the Israelite priesthood from its earliest appearance until its collapse in the year 70 C.E. It is a complex history, one that will require careful attention to the literature of the Hebrew Bible. For the reader's convenience I have divided the material into two sections, each containing several subdivisions. Section I will discuss the emergence of priesthood in Israel, the era of the biblical patriarchs, the age of exodus and settlement in Canaan, the "levitical" priests, the tribal confederacy, and developments from the rise of the monarchy to the exile. In Section II, the post-exilic priesthood is discussed: the "priesthood of Aaron," the appearance of "high priests", the crisis of hellenism, and priests in the Roman-Herodian period. The student who is unfamiliar with the basic details of Israel's history may want to consult one or another of the works mentioned in the footnotes to Chapter One.

I

From The Beginnings to the Exile

THE EMERGENCE OF A PRIESTHOOD IN ISRAEL

The Hebrew Scriptures, like the later Christian New Testament, did not suddenly materialize, fully-developed, from the mists of ancient history. Over many centuries and after much sifting and editing the biblical literature took shape. What we today call the Bible is precisely that: a library of

books and pamphlets (Greek: *ta biblia*) that span broad
epochs of cultural history and offer a distillation of varied
— sometimes conflicting—histories, theologies, collections
of poetry, sermons, liturgical fragments, perhaps even
"short stories" (e.g. Jonah) or "historical novels" (e.g., I and
II Chronicles). To speak of the Bible in this way is not to
deny its historical value or its inspired character as God's
Word; it is merely to acknowledge that its writers were
skillful artists and inventive theologians — and that they did
not necessarily share the twentieth century's compulsion for
"accurate reporting" or "the news almost before it
happens." We must remember, further, that written literature is usually the product of a settled people who have
developed some form of "urban" civilization. In Israel's
history this process of settling in took centuries: bedouin
/nomadic and rural agricultural phases preceded the
appearance of urban centers of cult and government like the
Jerusalem of King David's day (ca. 1010-970 B.C.E.).

The beginnings of a written literature in Israel probably
cannot be dated before the time of David and Solomon.
This is important to remember when we discuss the development of religious institutions like the priesthood or the
Temple. By the time the earliest Hebrew authors wrote, an
official cult, with temple and priesthood under royal
patronage, had already come into existence. When they
spoke of priests, therefore, these writers naturally registered
their own contemporary experiences: regular liturgies carried out by a band of religious professionals (priests) at a
centralized national sanctuary (Solomon's Temple). Centuries later, after the Exile and the construction of a Second
Temple, these earlier literary traditions about the priesthood were re-edited and sometimes extensively rewritten.
As a result, the Bible's information about the Israelite
priesthood often reflects the liturgical customs and popular
traditions of a post-exilic age: the period of the Second
Temple (after 515 B.C.E.).

An example may be useful here. In Exodus 28 and 29 we
are given detailed descriptions of the priestly vesture and

"ordination" of Aaron and his sons. The final edition of this section of the book of Exodus comes from the post-exilic period — long after institutions like the desert "tent of meeting", the monarchy and Solomon's temple had disappeared. The post-exilic author-editor tells us that both Aaron (29:7) and his sons (cf. 28:41) should be anointed with oil at their consecration to priestly service. In point of fact, however, there is no evidence that the custom of anointing Israelite priests existed prior to the Exile.[1] Further, in the earlier narratives of the Pentateuch, Aaron is not depicted as a priest at all.[2] Clearly, the post-exilic redactor of these chapters, commonly identified by scholars as a member of a priestly circle of writers ("P"), is more concerned about scoring a theological point than about reporting things "as they actually happened." His point, of course, is that the anointed priesthood of the post-exilic (Second Temple) period is in faithful continuity with Israel's most ancient and hallowed traditions. Since in Exodus the traditions come from *Moses,* who receives them from *God,* they must represent divine will for Israel. In short, "P" wants to show that the relatively "new" custom of anointing priests — appropriated, doubtless, from the pre-exilic custom of anointing kings — faithfully reflects God's way and will. Implicitly, too, "P" defends the anointed *high priest* (another post-exilic development) as a legitimate successor to Aaron and to the royal prerogatives that once were linked in Israel's history with the monarchy.

Our knowledge of the Israelite priesthood in its earliest stages of development thus resembles a collage constructed of literary scraps, archaeological remains and educated guesses. The Bible provides no eyewitness account of precisely how and when priests emerged in the religious life of Israel. Like a wall coated with several layers of paint, the

[1] See John J. Castelot, "Religious Institutions of Israel," in *The Jerome Biblical Commentary.* Edited by Raymond Brown, Joseph Fitzmeyer, and Roland Murphy. Englewood Cliffs, New Jersey: Prentice-Hall, Inc., Vol. II, p. 705 (76:12).
[2] See Aelred Cody, *A History of Old Testament Priesthood.* Analecta Biblica 35; Rome: Pontifical Biblical Institute, 1969, p. 150.

biblical texts allow us to glimpse some of the stages through which the priesthood passed, provided we are willing to chip at the paint in order to uncover both earlier and later strata of development. Sometimes, when we hit the final layer, little more than a riddle appears on the wall. When that happens, we must often rely upon archaeological information or upon comparisons between the religious institutions of Israel and those of its Near Eastern neighbors. A history of the early Israelite priesthood is thus a somewhat hypothetical reconstruction.

THE PATRIARCHAL ERA (ca. 2000-1700 B.C.E.)

Biblical scholars do not agree on how much historical value ought to be attributed to the stories of Israel's patriarchs as they are narrated in the book of Genesis. Some, like Martin Noth and his disciples, argue that these sagas are primarily *religious* texts that convey a theological message: the unique God of Israel calls "Abraham" and his heirs to abandon all human security and to entrust their future to a mysterious divine promise. While this religious message is clearly present, it need not exclude the possibility that "Abraham, Isaac and Jacob" were real historical personalities. Documents recovered from the ancient royal palace of Mari, on the middle Euphrates, indicate that in the first quarter of the second millennium B.C.E. there was, in fact, a migration of "proto-Aramaean" (Amorite) peoples from the Syro-Arabian desert.[3] It is altogether plausible that the distant ancestors of the Hebrews were among these migrants.

Significantly, the patriarchal stories in Genesis contain numerous examples of sacrificial offerings, but none of them are linked with a "priesthood." Sacrifice seems, instead, to have been a function of family or tribal leadership. The familiar story of Abraham and Isaac found in Gen 22:1-19 offers a convenient illustration. After Abraham passes God's test of his faith by raising his knife to slaughter

---

[3] See *ibid.*, pp. 8-9.

Isaac, he spies a ram with its horn caught in a thicket; the animal is then offered "as a holocaust" and the place is named "Yahweh-yireh" ("the Lord will see;" Gen 22:13-14). Nowhere in the story is Abraham identified as a priest (Hebrew: *kohen*). Later in Genesis, Abraham's grandson Jacob is also depicted as offering sacrifice (Gen 31:54). Here, the sacrifice appears to seal an agreement between Jacob and his father-in-law Laban, and it concludes with the sharing of a ritual meal; but there is no evidence that Jacob's action was regarded as "priestly."

Examples could be multiplied (e.g., Gen 4:3ff — Cain and Abel; Gen 8.20 — Noah), but the ones just cited suffice to show that in the patriarchal sagas no explicit connection is made between sacrifice and "priesthood." In the Abraham cycle there is, however, the mysterious story of Melchizedek (Gen 14:18-20). Since in later Christian tradition Melchizedek's offering of bread and wine has been linked with priesthood and eucharist, it is worth spending a few moments analyzing this story. First, while Melchizedek is identified as both king and priest, he is not a Hebrew; his name, which means "My king is justice," is probably of Canaanite origin. Secondly, Melchizedek serves "God Most High" (Hebrew: *el-elyon*): a name used for a deity in some Aramean and Phoenician sources and later adopted as an epithet for Israel's unique God, Yahweh.[4] Thirdly, the writer of this story probably wants the reader to identify Salem, of which Melchizedek is king, with *Jerusalem*. Finally, no priestly genealogy is provided for Melchizedek — a point about which later Israelite priests were rather sensitive. In short, Melchizedek appears to fulfill none of the conditions for priesthood as these might have been understood by a Hebrew author of the monarchic period (when the story achieved written form): he is neither a Hebrew, nor a worshipper of Yahweh nor, obviously, a member of the priestly tribe of Levi.

---

[4]See Eugene Maly, "Genesis," in *The Jerome Biblical Commentary*, Vol. I, p. 19 (2:57).

What, then, is the point of the story? If we remember that the Melchizedek legend was given *written* shape after the rise of the monarchy, then we have some clues. The literary artist, familiar with institutions like kingship and a centralized national sanctuary in Jerusalem, wants us to understand first that Melchizedek, as king of "Salem" (= Jerusalem), has a right to receive spoils from a military expedition. (Note that in Gen 14:20, Abram is depicted as giving Melchizedek "a tenth of everything.") The king's right to a "tithe" of this sort is not merely a royal prerogative, but a *priestly* one as well. Further, the author suggests, whoever is king in Jerusalem possesses the priesthood not from Levitical descent, but "according to the order of Melchizedek"(cf. Psalm 110:4). Reading this story, the author's contemporaries would have found justification for a number of royal prerogatives: 1) Israel's king may be accorded priestly status, even though he is not from the tribe of Levi; 2)The king's royal priesthood is an ancient privilege, going back to the age of the patriarchs (Abraham); 3) The king, as priest, has a right to support from tithes (since Abraham, the prototypical Hebrew man of faith, gave Melchizedek a tenth of everything).

Given this interpretation, the "priesthood of Melchizedek" is something specifically — and exclusively — *royal.* This does not mean that Israel's kings acted, or were expected to act, as professional priests in the later sense of that term (presiding at temple liturgies, offering grain and animal sacrifices). As we shall see in a later section of this chapter, it is unlikely that Israel's monarchs functioned as priests on precisely "cultic" occasions.[5] They did, however, act as *administrators,* overseeing worship and its performance — and controlling revenues from the cult. This last point fits in well with the interpretation of the Melchizedek legend given above. As a "priest according to the order of Melchizedek," the king possessed ultimate authority over temple, cult and priesthood — especially in fiscal matters.

[5]See Cody, *A History of Old Testament Priesthood, pp. 100-102.*

This too matches Israel's image of the perfect monarch: one who takes responsibility for the well-being of all the people in all aspects of life, including their relation with God. It is not difficult to see how in the post-exilic period, when Israel had no monarch of its own, the "high" priest could absorb prerogatives formerly linked with the king's status as "Melchizedek" (administrative responsibility for the cult, control of temple finances). This linkage between high priesthood and Melchizedek is reflected in chapter 7 of the Letter to the Hebrews. There, Jesus is called "high priest"(Heb 7:26) because, like Melchizedek, he has no Levitical lineage yet can lay claim to a priesthood that transcends both time and physical descent.

The story of Melchizedek cannot, then, be used as evidence for an early connection between priesthood and sacrifice in Israel. Its inclusion among the stories of the Abraham cycle in Genesis seems directed toward legitimating the "priestly" prerogatives of the king in his dealings with the cult, personnel and finances of the Jerusalem temple. It thus betrays the concerns of a later phase in Israel's history: the monarchy, with its urban culture and centralized sanctuary. Nothing in the Melchizedek incident provides us with accurate information about what Israelite priests may have done in the patriarchal period. Nor, in this case, are comparisons with Israel's ancient neighbors very helpful. The civilizations of Sumer, Babylonia, Assyria and Egypt possessed highly developed religious institutions, but they reflect an organized urban culture rather than the semi-nomadic conditions of Israel's roaming patriarchs. Similarly, the ancient Phoenician civilization, which included the people living in Canaan when Israel began penetrating that territory after the exodus, possessed an elaborate pantheon; but we know little about how the Phoenician clergy and its work were organized.[6] About all we can say with confidence of the patriarchal era is that functions *later* regarded as "priestly" — e.g., offering sacrifice — were in the hands of family or

[6]*See ibid.*, pp. 8-10.

tribal leaders. No professional class of Israelite clergy can be discerned in the sagas attached to the patriarchs.

THE PERIOD OF EXODUS AND CONQUEST (ca. 1300-1050 B.C.E.)

Scholars today generally agree that Israel's long stay in Egypt probably began during the Hyksos period (ca. 1720-1550 B.C.E.). The Hyksos appear to have been a family of Canaanite or Amorite rulers whose origins can be traced to Palestine and southern Syria. These rulers would thus have originated in a geographical area not terribly distant from the region that produced Israel's tribal ancestors. This may help to explain why the Hyksos originally welcomed Hebrew immigrants from Canaan like Joseph and his family (cf. Gen 37-47). But the Hyksos dynasty fell, after about 200 years, to a "new kingdom" created by native Egyptians. This changed political situation, which occurred ca. 1580-1550 B.C.E., may be reflected in the opening chapter of Exodus: "Then a new king, who knew nothing of Joseph, came to power in Egypt" (Ex 1:8).

It can hardly be doubted that under the new Egyptian rule the situation of immigrant peoples like the Hebrews deteriorated badly. We know, for example, that the dynasty of the "new kingdom" in Egypt gained a reputation for its extensive building projects, especially under Rameses II (1290-1224). And it is reasonable to believe that ethnic minorities would have provided a cheap and convenient labor force. This lends plausibility to the Bible's complaint that the Egyptian ruler forced the Hebrews to work under extremely unfavorable conditions (see e.g., Ex 5). In any event, the explosive potential of oppressed minorities is an amply documented fact for twentieth century readers.

For Israelites in Egypt the breaking point seems to have been reached by the 13th century B.C.E., the rough date most scholars assign to the Exodus. The biblical description of the event is highly dramatic and heavily theologized (see Ex 13-15), as are the descriptions of the desert sanctuary, its furnishings and priestly ministers (see Ex 25-30). As we have seen, the account of Aaron's "ordination" as priest (Ex 29) reflects liturgical details from the monarchic and even post-exilic periods. We cannot assume, therefore, that in the time immediately following Israel's departure from Egypt there was an organized clergy led by "Aaron" or his sons.

But what about the figure of Moses, the hero to whom so many of Israel's legal and religious institutions were attributed: was he in any sense a "priest"? In the minds of later editors of the Pentateuch the answer to this question was clearly "no". The "P" circle mentioned earlier was overwhelmingly concerned to justify the exclusive right of "Aaron's descendants" to the priesthood — and thus the texts of the Pentateuch edited by "P" never call Moses a priest. Still, there are pentateuchal traditions — some of them quite ancient — which depict Moses performing "priestly" acts: he appears, for example, to "preside" at Aaron's "ordination" and to manipulate the sacrificial blood at the liturgy which follows (see Ex 29). Are these simply passages that slipped by the "P" censors — or do they hint at an ancient tradition in which Moses is portrayed as a priest?

One's answer to this question depends on how "priest" should be defined in Israel's history immediately following the exodus. Moses is clearly presented in the Pentateuch as a *leader*, a *go-between* in matters affecting Israel's relation with God, a *person who received divine communications* and transmits them to the people. He is also portrayed as the one responsible for establishing the authentic worship of Yahweh — a point the editors of the Pentateuch may have wanted to emphasize in the account of Moses's presidency at Aaron's ordination. If tribal leadership, mediation between God and people, and transmission of divine commands constitute "priestly" activities, then we can say that Moses acts as a priest in the transition period between exodus from Egypt and the beginnings of Hebrew settlement in Canaan.

Israel's "conquest" of Canaan was not immediate. In the traditional style of epic literature, the Book of Joshua telescopes events, leaving the reader with the impression that what actually took about 200 years (ca. 1300-1050 B.C.E.) was accomplished in a hero's magnificent lifetime. In actual fact, Israel took possession of Palestine only gradually, through a series of tribal migrations and, eventually, through the formation of a loose tribal confederacy (an "amphictyony"). It is during this period that we begin to see evidence for the emergence of a recognizable class of Israelite "priests". Who were these priests and what were their functions? Some answers to this question are suggested by the narratives contained in Judges 17-18. In Judges 18, a party of scouts from the tribe of Dan has been set to reconnoiter a new district in Palestine, with an eye to a possible migration there. While on this mission the scouts meet a certain Micah who lives in the mountain region of Ephraim and who has hired a young Levite to act as his priest in exchange for food, clothing, shelter and salary (see Judg 17:7-13). The Danite scouts order the Levite to "Consult God, that we may know whether the undertaking we are engaged in will succeed " (Judg 18:5). The Levite replies: " 'Go and prosper: the Lord is favorable to the undertaking you are engaged in' " (Judg 18:6).

What we have here is possibly the earliest "job description" of an Israelite priest: they are oracles to be consulted for discerning God's judgment ("yes" or "no") on a crucial venture that is about to be undertaken. In addition to their work as oracular consultants, priests also seem to serve as sanctuary attendants hired by a family or household. That is how the "Levite" mentioned in Judges 17-18 landed his job at Micah's place. We are told that originally Micah had consecrated one of his own sons as priest to care for his household idols (Judg 17:5). Later, a Levite emigrating from Bethlehem of Judah arrived at Micah's home and was offered the job of priest at a salary of ten silver shekels a year (Judg 17:7-13). The episode seems to have embarrassed the later editor of Judges; he comments drily that Micah's original arrangement (his son as priest to care for the household idols) was one of those bizarre things that happen when people lack a king: "In those days there was no king in Israel; everyone did what he thought best" (Judg 17:6). We can also see the editor's hand at work in 17:7-13, where the objectionable priest (Micah's son) is replaced by a *Levite*. In its edited version the "moral" of the story is clear: the correct person to have as a *priest* (= "oracular consultant" and "sanctuary attendant") is a *Levite*. This, of course, reflects a later stage in the evolution of Israelite priesthood, when the tribe of Levi was popularly linked with priestly functions — a point to be discussed later in this chapter.

The priest's job of consulting Yahweh and transmitting divine decisions appears to have been accomplished by the manipulation of the *"urim* and *thummim"* (The "lots"). What these were is not precisely known; they may have been sticks, stones or dice. They were, in any case, a device used for ascertaining God's "yes" or "no" to particular questions: e.g., will the Danites enjoy success in their proposed migration to the north of Palestine (Judg 18)? When we speak of the early Israelite priest as an oracular consultant, this is the practice implied. The priest "asked" God by casting lots; it was a mechanical procedure, not a mystical encounter between a sacred minister and a divine being.

The earliest Israelite priests thus appear to have been caretakers of household sanctuaries and consultors of the divine will through the casting of lots. They were not originally cultic specialists charged with offering a regular round of sacrifices, nor were they "professionals" in the strict sense of that word. Their teaching (Hebrew: *"torah"*), at this period, seems to have been restricted to the limited information derived from the *urim* and *thummim*.[7] The stories in Judges 17-18 suggest that in the early stages of Israel's settlement in Palestine priests wre not necessarily Levites. At the same time, it is clear that the Levites gradually did emerge as a professional class of priests. We need to ask how this happened—and why.

THE RISE OF A "LEVITICAL" PRIESTHOOD

We have noted that Israel's conquest of Canaan was

---

[7]See *ibid.,* p. 25.

neither automatic nor immediate. Hebrew tribes did not always settle in one place and stay there, as is illustrated by the story of Dan's migrations in Judges 17-18. Moreover, the list of tribes that settled in Canaan is not absolutely consistent. Some of the older lists (e.g., Gen 49:3-27) name twelve tribes and include "Levi" among them, while later lists (e.g., Num 1:5-15, 20-43) differ. Thus, for example, 1:1-5 lists eleven names among Moses' "assistants" in the migration to Palestine; these come from the tribes of Reuben, Simeon, Judah, Issachar, Zebulun, Ephraim, Benjamin, Dan, Asher, Gad and Naphtali. A few verses later (Num 1:20-43), twelve tribes are mentioned at the census taken in the Sinai desert (Manasseh is added: Num 1:34). Neither of the lists in Numbers mentions Levi, and this naturally raises a question about just who the Levites were and what happened to them.

Several hypotheses about the origin of the Levites and their emergence as a class of professional priests have been advanced; perhaps the most plausible one is that proposed by Aelred Cody. The exact origins of the tribe of Levi, Cody notes, are now lost to us, but it is reasonable to assume that it was originally a full secular tribe like the others (Reuben, Simeon, Judah, etc.).[8] For reasons unknown, however, the Levites failed to acquire or maintain land during the period of tribal settlement in Palestine. They became a tribe "reduced in status", its members wandering about the land, taking up residence among other tribes. The levites thus became "*gerim*", i.e., people of the same racial stock who were not members of the tribe among whom they lived.[9] As *gerim,* many (though not all) Levites appear to have "specialized" in priestly jobs such as sanctuary attendant and oracular consultant. Such an hypothesis fits in well with the stories of Judges 17-18: the Levite who becomes Micah's priest had, in fact, been wandering about searching for "another place of residence" (Judg 17:8).

[8]See *ibid.,* pp. 35-37.
[9]See *ibid.,* p. 55.

These levitical priests did not acquire their position through any ritual act such as "ordination." They became priests simply by exercising priestly functions.[10] Theirs was neither a "sacred office" nor a "divine vocation" but rather a practical craft. Since the tribe had no land to serve as an economic base of operations, it is understandable that the Levites began to guard their priestly status jealously. (Note that in the story of Micah's Levite, an annual salary of ten silver shekels is promised: Judg 17:10.) In a very real sense the economic security of an individual Levite might well rest upon his ability to secure and maintain regular employment as a priest.

But not all Levites were priests, nor were all priests Levites. Again, the story of Micah the Ephraimite in Judges 17 is illustrative: initially, his sanctuary was served by one of his own non-levitical sons. By the time this story achieved final written form, however, Levites were the *preferred* kind of priest to have (see Judg 17:13). The editor of the story found Micah's earlier arrangement objectionable, not to say incomprehensible; the edited version thus concludes with an expression of Micah's confidence that having a Levite as priest will guarantee prosperity for his household.

PRIESTHOOD IN THE LATER AMPHICTYONY

Prior to the monarchy there was no single centralized sanctuary in Israel to which all the tribes gave unqualified allegiance. Prominent local sanctuaries were the places where priests functioned. At an earlier stage of Israel's settlement in Palestine some of these sanctuaries may simply have been maintained by individual households (e.g., Micah's sanctuary in Judges 17). Others achieved importance either because they were traditionally associated with the patriarchs (e.g., the sanctuaries of Bethel, Shechem, Mamre and Beer-sheba) or the events during the period of conquest in Canaan (e.g., Gilgal, Shiloh, Mizpah,

[10]See *ibid.*, p. 59.

Ophrah, Dan, Jerusalem). Some of the sanctuaries were probably Canaanite in origin and were adapted to the religion of Yahwism by their later Hebrew patrons. Prestige among these rival sanctuaries was determined above all by the presence of the Ark of the Covenant. Earlier, during the time of exodus and the desert wandering that followed, the Ark was kept in the Tent or Tabernacle, a portable sanctuary described in Exodus 26-27. It is clear, however, that this description, edited by the "P" circle, has used the later *temple* as a model.[11] The actual desert sanctuary (Tent) was probably rather small, of the size and shape that could be conveniently carried on camelback. Once Israel began to settle down in Canaan, however, the Tent would no longer have been used as a dwelling for the Ark. Instead, the Ark was kept at one or another of the local sanctuaries. In the later years of the amphictyony Shiloh was clearly the most prestigious sanctuary — not only because the Ark rested there, but because it had become an important political center as well. It served, for example, as a meeting place for all the tribes (see Josh 18:1) and as a pilgrimage center.

For our purposes Shiloh is also important because, according to the First Book of Samuel, it was under the control of a single family of priests: Eli and his sons (1 Sam 1-2). As its story is narrated in the Bible, the family of Eli comes across quite badly; the author is intent on contrasting the utter goodness of Samuel with the shamelessness of Eli's sons. Here, we can disregard the author's polemic and focus on the type of priesthood exercized by the Elides. They were, first of all, Levites (1 Sam 2:28) — something we might expect, given the emergence of this unpropertied tribe as a class of priestly professionals during the time of settlement in Palestine. One gathers, too, that the Elides were firmly entrenched at Shiloh, and that their economic survival was closely linked with its prestige as a pilgrimage center where

[11]See Roland de Vaux, *Ancient Israel,* (2 Vols.; translated by John McHugh; New York: McGraw-Hill Book Company, 1965, paperback edition), Vol. 2, p. 296.

Israelites came to offer sacrifices. One of the charges laid against Eli's sons by the author-editor of the stories was greed: they grabbed choice portions of the sacrificial meat even before it was properly offered (1 Sam 2:13-17). These allusions prompt us to ask whether sacrifice was a central or exclusive function of the Elide priests. The answer appears to be no. One gets the impression from reading 1 Samuel 2 that individual Israelites themselves offered the sacrifices — but that a portion was customarily set aside for support of the priests. If this is the case, the levitical priests at Shiloh would fit the earlier description, "oracular consultant" and "sanctuary attendant." It is possible that by the time of Samuel the priestly function of oracular consultation had undergone development and included the giving of *torah* ("teaching") in legal or judicial matters.[12] In any case, one should not romanticize Shiloh or its priesthood since at this time the sanctuary was probably quite modest in size, its priests little more than "simple country clergymen."[13]

If the Elides were country parsons, who and what was Samuel? According to the genealogy provided in 1 Sam 1:1-2, Samuel's family was Ephraimite, not Levite. But a later genealogical list found in 1 Chron 6:7-13 includes Samuel among the sons of Levi. Further, both 1 Sam 7:9-17 and 1 Sam 2:18 appear to attribute priestly activities to Samuel. In the first passage he is depicted as offering a holocaust on Israel's behalf and presiding at a ritual meal; in the second, he wears a linen ephod while serving at Shiloh. According to the criteria of later generations of Israelites, these actions would mark Samuel as a priest. But we need to remember, once again, that these later criteria do not give us an accurate picture of the pre-monarchic priesthood. Samuel would probably not have been considered a priest by his contemporaries, though he may have been a "servant" at the disposal of the priests.[14] By placing him at

---

[12]See Cody, *A history of Old Testament Priesthood,* p. 72.
[13]See *ibid.,* p. 69.
[14]See *ibid.,* pp. 78-79.

Shiloh during his childhood, Samuel's "biographer" subtly
hints that the prophet began his career at the very heart of
Yahwistic religion — the sanctuary where the Ark rested.

PRIESTHOOD AND MONARCHY

It was Samuel's career as *prophet,* rather than priest, that
interested those who collected the traditions about him.
Called by God and acknowledged by the people as prophet
(1 Sam 3), Samuel played a central role in the establishment
of the monarchy. It is he who anoints Saul (1 Sam 10:1) and
subsequently acts as the king's conscience (see 1 Sam 13:10-
14). He is also pictured as the *grise eminence* behind David's
rise to royal power (see 1 Sam 16). Priesthood plays no
discernible role in Samuel's relations with either Saul or
David.

One gets the impression, in fact, that the *priest's role* as
one who proclaims God's will through manipulation of the
urim and *thummim* was gradually being absorbed, in the
later amphictyony, by the *prophet.* Thus Samuel the
prophet reveals God's choice of David as king, and Nathan
(another prophet) discloses God's displeasure at David's sin
(2 Sam 11-12). One could say, perhaps, that as the monarchic era dawned priests were regularly upstaged by prophets
in the revelation of God's plans for Israel and its leaders.

But the Israelite priests had an uncanny instinct for survival. Even though Shiloh was destroyed (1 Sam 4) by the
Philistines at the battle of Aphek, the priesthood continued.
After the Ark was returned (1 Sam 6), it was taken first to
Beth-shemesh, then to Kiriath-jearim. There, the people
decided that a sanctuary attendant (= "priest") was needed
and Eleazar was chosen (1 Sam 7:1), even though he was not
a Levite. The Elide family, which was levitical, apparently
survived the disaster of Shiloh's fall, it reappears, in the
person of Ahijah, in 1 Sam 14. Ahijah was part of the group
that accompanied Saul in his campaign against the Philistines (1 Sam 14:3), and his function appears to have been
that of oracular consultant. These two priests — Eleazar at

Kiriath-jearim and Ahijah the Elide — are among the last examples of the "old-fashioned" priests (sanctuary attendants, oracular consultants) that existed prior to the monarchy. Before we leave these "country parsons", one other figure needs to be mentioned: Ahimelech, a brother of Ahijah and thus a levitical Elide. According to 1 Sam 22, Ahimelech was leader of a band of priests at Nob, not too far from Jerusalem (still a Canaanite city). He committed the grave political error of consulting God at David's request, thereby enraging Saul, who dispatched a band of mercenaries under Doeg to massacre the priests of Nob. The massacre was not a complete success: Abiathar, one of Ahimelech's sons, escaped (1 Sam 22, 20-23).

It was the same Abiathar, an Elide and thus a Levite, who became David's priest in Jerusalem once it had become the political and religious capital of the monarchy. Closely associated with Abiathar was Zadok (see, e.g., 2 Sam 15-24), a figure who appears on the scene almost as mysteriously as Melchizedek did in Genesis. 2 Sam 8:17 seems to make Zadok a descendant of the Elide family and thus a Levite and relative of Abiathar, but the passage is not reliable. Perhaps he was already a priest in *Jebusite* Jerusalem, but we have no way to prove this.[15]

One might assume, in theory, that Abiathar's descendants would become the established royal priesthood under the monarchy. They had, after all, the proper credentials: levitical lineage and long-standing connections with the important pre-monarchic sanctuary at Shiloh. Their attendance on the Ark at Jerusalem, where David had brought it, would have made for a smooth transition from the pre-monarchic era of local sanctuaries to the new Davidic centralized sanctuary. But Abiathar committed a serious political blunder. In the quarrel over who should succeed David as king, Abiathar supported Adonijah — a mistake, as it turned out (1 Kings 1:7). Zadok supported Solomon, who in fact

[15]See *ibid.*, p. 92.

became heir (1 Kings 1:8). The stage was thus set for a Zadokite line of priests in the royal establishment at Jerusalem; it was also set, as we shall see, for future conflict between Zadokite "newcomers" and the old-fashioned "country parsons" of the levitical Elide line of Abiathar. This conflict comes to a head later, after the monarchy split into two kingdoms (i.e., after Solomon's death in 922 B.C.E.).

Before we study this conflict, however, some questions need to be asked about the king's role in the development of Israelite priesthood. Some ancient civilizations, such as the Egyptian, regarding the king (pharaoh) as a sacral figure; he alone had the right to enter God's presence in the Temple. Pharaoh's priests thus functioned only as delegates "deputized" to represent the monarch.[16] But this union of royal and priestly power in the person of the king was not a universal phenomenon in the ancient Near East. In Israel, the relation between king and priest seems to have adhered more closely to the Assyrian model.[17] Some Assyrian monarchs were "*sange*" (singular: *sangu*); i.e., they possessed ultimate authority over matters of liturgy and priesthood but did not function as priests themselves. They were cultic administrators rather than servants of the sanctuary. The influence of this Assyrian model may help explain why the Hebrew Bible is reluctant to call an Israelite king "*kohen*" (priest). For one thing, *kohen* is a term that suggests subordinate relationship: a priest is always *attached to somebody* (e.g., the Levite who was *Micah's* priest; Abiathar and Zadok who were *David's* priests). Given this suggestion of subordinate attachment, *kohen* would have seemed inappropriate as a title for the king, whose authority over matters of worship was supreme. This does not mean, of course, that Israel's kings never performed actions that were later reserved to a professional priesthood. In 2 Sam 6.13, for example, David is pictured as offering sacrifices on

16See *ibid.*, p.98.
17See *ibid.*, pp. 100-102.

the occasion of the Ark's being brought to Jerusalem; he also blesses the people—an activity later restricted to priests (see Num 6:22-27, from the "P" circle of writers).

Should we, then, think of Israel's kings as priests? The answer depends upon how one defines "priest" at this juncture of Israel's history. If one takes the old-fashioned model — the priest as a "country clergyman" who served a local sanctuary and acted as oracular consultant — the answer is no. But if one takes the model of priesthood that evolved in Jerusalem under royal patronage — the priest as one who presides at sacrifices and blesses the people — then it can be said that early Israelite kings (David, Solomon) occasionally functioned in a priestly role. Later, as the priesthood of the royal establishment grew in power and prestige, it reserved more and more functions exclusively to itself.

COUNTRY CLERGY AND URBAN PRIESTS

We should not underestimate the dramatic impact the rise of a monarchy had on Israel's life. In many respects, kingship represented the triumph of an emerging urban culture over the older, rural and tribal pattern of life in Palestine. Not everyone believed this was a change for the better. In 1 and 2 Samuel, for instance, one can identify both pro-monarchic and anti-monarchic strains. On the one hand, the king is "the Lord's anointed," object of divine favor and protection; on the other, Israel's request for a king shows that the people have rejected God as their sole ruler (cf. 1 Sam 8:6-9). The "conservative" view regarded the king as an anointed interloper who compromises the ancient beauty of Israel's unique relation with Yahweh, while the "liberal" one saw the monarchy as central to the victory of Yahwistic religion over the dangerous tribal particularism associated, for example, with local sanctuaries and their priests.

During Solomon's reign (961-922 B.C.E.), the conservatives' fears were probably intensified. Solomon's "open policy" with people of other cultures, which led to things like inter-racial marriages, probably offended rural adherents of the old tribal ways (see 1 Kings 10-11). And the construction of a single temple in Jerusalem designed to displace all other Yahwistic sanctuaries would also have sent shock waves through the countryside. The temple would have created serious economic hardships for country clergy who had no "pull" at Jerusalem. After all, who needs to hire a priest when the king's clergy can function for *all* Israel in a centralized sanctuary? Besides, it was difficult for ancient cult centers like Shiloh to compete once the Ark rested, under royal patronage, in Jerusalem.

The split into northern (Israel) and southern (Judah) kingdoms further aggravated the resentment between "conservatives" and "liberals", country clergy and urban priests. As we have seen, the royal priesthood in Jerusalem had become Zadokite. These newcomers were surely resented by the older line of professional clergy — the Levites — who had emerged during the period of the amphictyony. The Levites did not lose out entirely. They appear to have functioned at Dan, a sanctuary of the northern kingdom — but not at Bethel, the central sanctuary of the north established by Jeroboam (922-901) to rival Jerusalem (1 Kings 12:31).[18] The situation in the divided monarchy was further complicated by the survival (or, in some cases, revival) of Baal worship at various sanctuaries in Israel and Judah. The Second Book of Kings is littered with complaints against monarchs who apostasized from the authentic worship of Yahweh and "went after Baal." Even Jerusalem is accused of supporting a temple of Baal (2 Kings 11:18).

The "old-fashioned" view that Levites had a divine claim to priestly status persisted, despite the Zadokites' entrenchment at Jerusalem in the southern kingdom. Even the literature edited during the monarchic period often admits, though somewhat grudgingly, that the Levites had a legitimate point in their favor (see, e.g., 1 Sam 2:27-36). But once the northern kingdom fell (721 B.C.E.), the Levites lost the little they had managed to maintain. The Zadokites refused

---

[18]See *ibid.,* pp. 111-112.

to budge from the royal sanctuaries, and the Levites, who had no ancestral lands, were widely scattered. This situation seems to have lasted throughout the seventh and sixth centuries B.C.E.[19]

THE DEUTERONOMIC REFORM

It is well known that a nation threatened by internal and external pressure will often look nostalgically to its past in order to make sense of its present. And if the nation's identity has a strong religious component, this political nostalgia will frequently be buttressed by a theological conservatism: "Things were better when..." We have already noted that for many Israelites the monarchy (and, by implication, its established cult and priesthood) was an impious innovation, a dangerous departure from the authentic Yahwism rooted in God's revelation to Moses and continued under the old tribal confederacy. Flashes of this nostalgic spirit are already found in the eighth-century prophet Hosea, who bitterly denounces the failure of the monarchy (Hos 7:3-7). Other voices, too, called for social and religious reform. Amos, whose career as prophet dates from the prosperous reign of Jeroboam II (786-746 B.C.E.), attacked the northern kingdom's complacency and greed in bold language (see, e.g., Amos 8:4-14).

Amos's ministry provides an intriguing example of conflict between prophet and priest. He prophesied, initially, at the royal (northern) sanctuary of Bethel, but his increasing boldness was apparently more than the priests there could bear. One can see why:

> I hate, I spurn your feasts,
> I take no pleasure in your solemnities;
> Your cereal offerings I will not accept,
> nor consider your stall-fed peace-offerings....
> (Amos 5:21-22).

---

[19]See *ibid.*, pp. 123-125.

Significantly, Amos singles out the important northern sanctuaries for special condemnation: not only Bethel, but Dan, Gilgal and Beer-sheba as well (Amos 5:5; 8:14). There is more than a little of the "rural conservative" in Amos's call for a worship based on justice and integrity, rather than on the greed of religious professionals (the priests at the royal sanctuaries). And there is explicit nostalgia in Amos 5.25: "Did you bring me sacrifices and offerings for forty years in the desert, O house of Israel?" Things were better when....!

The rural conservatism and political nostalgia of prophets like Amos were probably vindicated, in the opinion of many, after the northern kingdom's fall to Assyria in 721 B.C.E. Perhaps things really were better before Israel had a king — and implicitly, before she had a professional priestly establishment under royal patronage. This growing conviction seems to have touched off serious reform movements in the surviving southern kingdom (Judah), especially during the reigns of Hezekiah (716-687) and Josiah (640-609). These movements were aimed not at removing the monarchy and the centralized sanctuary (Jerusalem), but at reforming them on the basis of Mosaic Yahwism. What is usually called the "Deuteronomic Reform", reflected especially in Deut 12-26, probably took shape sometime prior to Josiah's reign.

Two aspects of this reform are of interest to us here: the attempt to centralize sacrificial worship in a single sanctuary and to reform the priesthood. It is reasonably clear that not even David or Solomon had complete success in their efforts to centralize Jewish worship in Jerusalem. As we have noted, resentment between old country clergy and new urban priests lingered long after David and Solomon had passed from the scene. Nor is there any reason to believe that the country parsons simply closed shop and capitulated to their rivals in Jerusalem. We have to remember that Solomon's temple, for all its reputed glory, did not put an end to worship and sacrifice at other ancient sanctuaries (e.g., Bethel, Dan, Shechem, Beer-sheba, Gilgal). Nor did the emergence of the royal Zadokite priests silence the Levites' claim to the priesthood.

It is in light of these continuing conflicts between rival sanctuaries and rival priesthoods that the Deuteronomic Reforms need to be understood. In principle, the reform recognized the legitimacy of the Levites' claim to priesthood. Dt. 18:1-8 reads like a "bill of rights" that spells out what the "priestly tribe of Levi" may expect to receive from the people in return for their service. It should be noted, however, that this passage implies a distinction between "priest" and "Levite".[20] All Levites are priests, have a right to a priest's share of the sacrifices, and may function at the altar if they wish; *but* Deut 18:3 implies that other, non-levitical, priests also have rights (the word "Levite" is absent from this verse). Elsewhere, Deuteronomy recognizes the ancestral claims of Levites to special priestly functions: e.g., custody of the Ark (Deut 10:8).

What we have here is obviously a compromise that attempts to support the Levites while it safeguards the prerogatives of the Zadokite "newcomers". Ironically, the compromise was doomed by the good intentions of Josiah. The king was eager to eliminate all pagan worship and to centralize the Yahwistic cult in Jerusalem (see 2 Kings 23). Among other things, this meant bringing country priests from the local shrines of Judah into Jerusalem and executing priests from the old northern Kingdom. In theory, Josiah's action matched Deuteronomy's recognition that any Levite who wished could serve at the altar as priest (Deut 18:6-8). But the centralization of cult in Jerusalem meant that only one sanctuary and altar were available--and it was firmly in the hands of the Zadokites! In effect, Josiah's effort to implement Deuteronomic ideals resulted in an empty victory of principle for the Levites and a strategic triumph of practice for the Zadokites. The only kind of temple work available for Levites coming to Jerusalem was rather mediocre; we might even think of it as "janitorial" (cleaning up after sacrifices, gathering wood and water,

---

[20]See *ibid.*, pp. 130-132.

etc.). Unintentionally, Josiah's reform robbed country priests (Levites) of their living at local shrines and provided them with work vastly inferior to that of the Zadokites in Jerusalem.

SACRIFICE AND TEACHING

Josiah died at Megiddo in 609, less than 25 years before Jerusalem fell to the Babylonians (587). On the eve of the Exile, therefore, the Israelite priesthood consisted of a rather tenuous coalition of Levites and Zadokites. The Deuteronomic Reform movement had vindicated levitical claims to priestly status but left the Zadokites firmly in control of worship in Jerusalem, now considered the exclusive legitimate Yahwistic sanctuary. What sort of work did these priest do?

The earliest Israelites priests, as we have seen, were sanctuary servants and oracular consultants. But increasingly, after the rise of the monarchy, the priest's job of "consulting God" was usurped by prophets. Our discussion of figures like Hosea and Amos indicates that this caused tensions. Interestingly, the priests' "bill of rights" contained in Deut 18:1-8 is followed immediately by a "prophets' bill of rights" in verses 9-22. Characteristically, Deuteronomy attributes both priests' and prophets' rights to *Moses,* who receives his instructions directly from *God.* According to the ideals of the Deuteronomic reform, therefore, both priestly and prophetic work are divine institutions legitimated by the Sinai covenant between Yahweh and Israel.

But if the *prophet* has God's "words in his mouth" (Deut 18:18) what is left for the priest to do? Two things, according to Deut 33:9-10: teaching *(torah)* and sacrifice. At this point in Israel's history, *torah* has begun to take on a more precise meaning. Earlier, it was a rather general term for instruction or decisions about matters of right or wrong, liturgical practice or sabbath observance.[21] But under the influence of

[21]See *ibid.,* p. 116.

the Deuteronomic reform movement, *torah* took on new significance. *The* teaching par excellence is what was revealed to "Moses" by "God" at "Sinai." I have placed these words in quotation marks because the "*torah*" contained in the Deuteronomic Code is obviously from an era much later than that of Moses. The Code reflects, however, what Jews stoutly loyal to their ancestral traditions believed about the covenant during the 600's B.C.E. Deut 33:9 indicates that it is the special responsibility of Levites (= priests) to uphold this covenant with all its regulations.

Another new wrinkle also appears in Deut 33: *sacrifice* as a work specially reserved to priests. Once again, this is a departure from earlier Israelite custom, even though the Deuteronomic Code would have us believe that sacrifice as *priests'* work goes back to Moses. Formerly, as we observed in our discussion of the patriarchal era, sacrifice was a feature of family or tribal leadership and had no essential connection with a priesthood. Deut 33, however, suggests that anything involving *contact with the altar* (e.g., sacrificial offerings of animals, grain, incense) belongs to the work of a priest.

Space does not permit a discussion of sacrificial ritual in the preexilic Temple of Solomon. Ample detail about this may be found in Roland de Vaux's classic work *Ancient Israel*.[22] The important point to notice here is that on the eve of the Exile the Israelite priesthood had developed a distinctive shape:

1. Earlier priestly activities had either disappeared or been taken over by others. Political events (like the fall of the northern kingdom) or religious reforms (like that of Deuteronomy) had pretty well effaced the image of a priest as "sanctuary attendant", while prophets had progressively usurped the role of oracle expressing God's will.

2. The rise of Levites as a "professional class" of priests during the period of settlement in Palestine had been over-

---

[22]See de Vaux, *Ancient Israel,* Vol. 2, pp. 312-386.

shadowed by the Zadokite priesthood of the royal establishment in Jerusalem. The Deuteronomic Reform's effort to create a coalition of these two groups was not very successful. In fact, if not in principle, Levites became priests of inferior status.

3. Finally, priests came to be associated, increasingly, with those functions that involved contact with the altar (sacrificial cult). They may also have had limited responsibility for teaching ("*torah*" in the Deuteronomic sense).

As it had evolved by the time of the Exile, therefore, the Israelite priesthood was a functional activity closely linked with altar and sacrifice. It was neither "office" nor "vocation," but a matter of a genealogical lineage (Levite or Zadokite) — nor, probably, did it involve any special ordination or consecration.

II
From the Exile to 70 B.C.E.

THE PRIESTHOOD OF AARON

One of the consequences of the Deuteronomic Reform was, as we have noted, the recognition that all Levites are priests and thus have a right to function at the altar. In fact, however, *Zadokite* supremacy over the cult in Jerusalem was strengthened by this reform. The Exile temporarily halted the conflict between Levites and Zadokites. A month after Jerusalem fell in 587, the temple was destroyed and its highest officials were taken to Riblah in Syria, where they were executed (2 Kings 25:18-21). The Zadokite clergy of the royal establishment appear to have been among the first groups deported to Babylon. Though some of them may have remained behind in Jerusalem, there is no evidence that they attempted to continue any elements of the temple liturgy there. Nor is there evidence that the exiled priests tried to carry on the cult in Babylon.

Far fewer Levites appear to have been deported. Most of them lived in the countryside and would have been less valuable than the established Zadokites to the Babylonian conquerors. After Cyrus's edict of 539 allowed Jews to return home, however, the tensions between Levites and Zadokites were renewed. And once a new temple (the Second Temple or Temple of Zerubbabel) had been built, about 515, some way of resolving these tensions had to be found. From the biblical literature it appears that a solution was hit upon through the theory that all Israelite priests were "sons of Aaron."[23]

The earliest Hebrew literature does not speak of Aaron as a priest. Exodus 4:10-17, for example, depicts Aaron as spokesman for a Moses who lacks eloquence, but the passage does not mention any "priestly" status for Aaron. (This passage is compiled from the "Yahwist" (J) and "Elohist" (E) sources in the Pentateuch; it thus dates, in its original form, from the early monarchic period.) But in passages that have been redacted by the "P" circle after the exile, careful attention is paid to Aaron's "priestly" genealogy. Thus Ex 6:14-27 lists Moses and Aaron among Levi's descendants and Ex 28-29 portrays an elaborate "ordination" ceremony for Aaron and his sons. The authors of these later passages were obviously intent on proving two things: that Aaron was a priest, and that his priesthood was levitical. Further, these passages suggest, Aaron's levitical priesthood was sanctioned by Moses himself and thus by God.

This genealogical/theological theory of the "Aaronic" priesthood played an important role in the post-exilic resolution of conflict between Levites and Zadokites. It reaffirmed the legitimacy of levitical claims to priesthood while it permitted the Zadokites to claim that they too were "sons of Levi." We see this theory working itself out in Ezek 44:6-31, where the Zadokites are explicitly called "levitical priest" (Ezek 44:15). In this passage the Levites are accused of having departed from God when Israel strayed to pursue

[23]See Cody, *A History of Old Testament Priesthood*, p. 146.

idolatry (Ezek 44:10); as punishment for their infidelity they are permitted to carry out only the *inferior* duties of the temple liturgy (keeping the gates of the temple, slaughtering the animals for sacrifices). But the Zadokites of Ezek 44:15-31 are presented as faithful ministers of the sanctuary and thus the proper ones to function in those priestly activities that involve contact with the altar. As priests in the proper (i.e., post-exilic) sense, the Zadokites wear linen vestments, fall under strict rules for marriage, and receive the priestly portions of the cereal and animal offerings (see Ezek 44:17-31). The Zadokites evidently wasted little time in reasserting their hegemony over the temple and its priesthood after the return from exile. The leader of the priests in the restored temple was Jeshua (Zech 6:11; Ezra 3:2); his grandfather, Seraiah, had been the last Zadokite chief priest before the deportation to Babylon in 587.

In the restored post-exilic community, therefore, both Levites and Zadokites claimed priesthood through a common ancestor, Aaron. But if Zadokite supremacy was to be maintained, other reasons had to be developed that would show why Levites, though priests of Aaronic lineage, were actually inferior. One such reason is provided in Ezek 44:6-31: God has reduced the priestly status of Levites because they proved to be unreliable in their care of the sanctuary. Another reason was provided through the genealogical linkage established in Num 20:24-29. There, we are told that Aaron's role in the rebellion of the Israelites at Meribah caused God to transfer the priesthood to Eleazar, Aaron's son. This Eleazar is portrayed in 1 Chron 6:50-53 as the direct ancestor of *Zadok* who, as we have seen, was David's priest. At the same time, Eleazar's younger brother Ithamar (Ex 6:23) was also head of the levitical clan (Num 4:28). But Ithamar's descendants are pictured as having inferior duties: they supervise construction of the desert tent (Ex 28:21) and see to its transportation (Num 7:8). Through such genealogical manipulations the Zadokites of the Second Temple period were able to "prove" that while all priests are levitical, not all are equal in status. Similarly,

while all priests can claim Aaron as ancestor, only Zadokites descend from *Eleazar,* to whom the Lord transferred
the priesthood. Non-Zadokite priests stem from *Ithamar*
and are thus inferior.

The tenuous coalition between Levites and Zadokites
established by the Deuteronomic Reform was carried on in
the post-exilic community through the ideology of an
Aaronic priesthood composed of superior and inferior
classes. The superior (Zadokite) class reserved to itself the
most important aspects of the temple's management and
worship. They controlled its finances and its altar-rituals.
The inferior (Levite) class assumed lesser duties: they were
gatekeepers, singers, instrumentalists, "janitors" and
maintenance-men. Though both classes were "sons of
Aaron", only the Zadokites were linked with Eleazar. As we
shall see, the Zadokite priesthood remained firmly
entrenched in the Jerusalem temple until the second century
B.C.E., when Antiochus IV Epiphanes interrupted the
legitimate succession of Zadokite high priests.

THE HIGH PRIESTHOOD

In the restored Israelite community after the exile there
was no king. Zerubbabel, hailed by Zechariah as the
"Shoot" who would build the Lord's temple (Zech 6:12),
claimed Davidic lineage but was a civil governor under
Persian supervision rather than a sovereign monarch. In his
work as a national leader, he was assisted by Jeshua, who is
consistently given the title "high priest" in post-exilic literature (see Hag 1:1,12,14; Zech 3:1,8). Pre-exilic sources do
not speak of a high priest in Jerusalem, though some of the
Zadokites doubtless achieved special prominence among
the temple clergy. Moreover, the lingering "royalist" hopes
of someone like Zechariah, who hoped to see Zerubbabel
crowned, faded after his hero disappeared from the scene.
Zechariah's optimistic vision of "two anointed ones" ruling
Israel in concert — Jeshua the priest and Zerubbabel the
prince — gave way to a more realistic sense of the restored

community's status. Israel was now a people subject to Persian rule; Judah was part of a province whose capital was Samaria; Jerusalem was no longer the uncontested center of a political and religious universe. Some Jews had not even bothered to return to their homeland; they were content to remain in the "diaspora".

Post-exilic Israel was thus an ethnic and religious minority within a large empire over which it had no control. Unquestionably, this situation contributed to the emergence of priests as the supreme leadership of the Jewish people. Israel became a theocracy, a "kingdom ruled by priests" (see Ex 19:6). Not until Nehemiah appeared (perhaps as late as 398 B.C.E.) did Israel once again have a native civil authority distinct from the priest-rulers. Even then, it is almost impossible to say how long this distinction of roles — "civil governor" and "high priest" lasted. [24] By the second century B.C.E. the high priesthood seems to have absorbed both civil and religious leadership. That may be one reason why Antiochus IV's tampering with the legitimate succession of Zadokite high priests caused such bitter resentment and contributed to the outbreak of the Maccabean revolt (ca. 166 B.C.E.).

The priests of post-exilic Jerusalem were primarily cultic functionaries responsible for the daily round of sacrifices, morning and evening, together with the offerings brought for sacrifice by individuals. They were not necessarily esteemed for their abilities as teachers or "doctors of the Law"; their power was linked to their lineage (Aaronic/ Zadokite) rather than to personal charism or "vocation". Leviticus 1-6, a collection of "P" texts, provides an account of the daily holocaust and cereal offerings as these were offered in the ritual of the Second Temple (Lev 6); detailed descriptions of peace offerings and sin offerings are also given (Lev 3-4). These texts reveal that any action requiring contact with the altar was reserved to the (Zadokite) priests:

[24]See *ibid.*, pp. 178-179.

sprinkling of blood to the altar, libations, expiatory rites, offering of the daily sacrifices.

Despite his social and religious standing the high priest was not required to function in the temple on a regular basis. His "great moment" was the annual Day of Atonement, a feast that seems not to have existed in pre-exilic times.[25] According to Leviticus 16, three elements are combined in the liturgy for this day: sin offerings of bull and goat for the priests' and the people's transgressions; the sprinkling of blood and offering of incense in the Holy of Holies (again, to atone for transgressions); and rites of purification involving the application of blood in the sanctuary and at the altar. To these were added the well-known ritual of the scapegoat (Lev 16:20-28). Of these rites, that of entering the Holy of Holies to sprinkle blood and burn incense was most sacred. Reserved exclusively to the high priest this ritual was performed but once a year. Since the Ark itself had never been recovered after the exile, only the propitiatory (the "covering" of the Ark indicated in Ex 25:17-22) was to be found in the post-exilic Holy of Holies. Still, the solemnity of this moment must have made a deep impression on those who witnessed it, as we can gather from Sirach's description of the high priest Simon on the Day of Atonement (Sir 50:5-21).

A RIVAL TEMPLE: SAMARIA

Post-exilic Judah was not, as we have seen, an independent political entity; it was part of a Persian-controlled province whose capital was Samaria. Ironically, Samaria had once been the ancient heart of the land of Israel; still, Jews who resettled in Palestine after the exile did not regard the Samaritans as genuine Israelites. A population of mixed ethnic background, the Samaritans included both Israelites who had survived the Assyrian deportations (721 B.C.E.) and various Mesopotamian peoples. Negative attitudes toward them can be detected as early as the time of the

---

[25]See de Vaux, *Ancient Israel*, Vol. 2, pp. 507-510.

prophet Hosea, who speaks of the wickedness of Samaria (Hos 7:1). Samaritans were commonly accused of abandoning the authentic worship of Yahweh and of reverting to Canaanite cults. Tensions between Samaria and the restored post-exilic community are evident in the books of Ezra and Nehemiah. When they showed interest in helping rebuild the Temple during the time of Zerubbabel and Jeshua the high priest, the Samaritans were rebuffed: "It is not your responsibility to build with us a house for our God, but we alone must build it for the Lord..." (Ezra 4:3). We are told that the Samaritans reacted ungracefully by interfering with the Temple's construction (Ezra 4:4-6). Later on, they are accused of plotting to prevent Nehemiah from finishing the temple walls (Neh 4; 6:1-13).

In Ezra and Nehemiah, therefore, the Samaritans are portrayed as troublemakers whose malice is directed explicitly against the Second Temple. This evil reputation was still vivid in the New Testament era (see Jn 4, the story of the Samaritan woman). In fact, of course, the roots of conflict between Samaria and Jerusalem go back to pre-exilic times —and possibly stretch all the way back to the division of the monarchy into northern and southern kingdoms. We know that eventually the Samaritans constructed a temple of their own on Mt. Gerizim, possibly as early as the time of Nehemiah (ca. 400 B.C.E.). The great festivals—Passover, Pentecost, Tabernacles—were celebrated there until it was destroyed by John Hyrcanus I, one of the Jewish high priests (134-104 B.C.E.) during the Maccabean period. The Samaritans possessed both a priesthood and a high priest; both these institutions have continued to exist, in fact, until the present. The traditional Samaritan view of priesthood is very similar to what we saw in the "Zadokite manifesto" contained in Ezek 44:6-31: the tribe of Levi is priestly, but the superior line of priests is to be traced from Aaron through Eleazar and Phineas to Zadok.[26] The priests'

---

[26]On this point see John Macdonald, *The Theology of the Samaritans*, (The New Testament Library; Philadelphia: Westminster Press, 1964), pp. 310-311.

work seems to have included giving instruction (*torah*) and performing sacrifice. It was the special duty of the high priest to determine the precise date of festivals, and like his Jewish counterpart he presided at the liturgy on the Day of Atonement.[27] Ironically, the Samaritan priesthood was the only one to survive in Palestine after the fall of Jerusalem in 70 C.E.

It is more probable, in my opinion, that the conflict between Jews and Samaritans stemmed from ethnic and racial considerations than from disparity over cult and priesthood. That the rivalry between temples played a role is, however, also plausible. We know, for example, that the Samaritans retaliated after their own place of worship had been destroyed by John Hyrcanus ca. 128 B.C.E. During the time of the Roman procurator Coponius (6-9 C.E.), some of them defiled the Temple in Jerusalem by scattering human bones across its porches during the Passover celebration.[28] We know, too, that Samaria was receptive to Hellenistic Christian missionaries of Stephen's party—and that Stephen was considered a vociferous opponent of the Jerusalem temple and priesthood (see Acts 7:45-50).

By the first century C.E., then, the enmity between Jews and Samaritans, Gerizim and Jerusalem, had become proverbial; but the ethnic origins of this conflict reach back to a much earlier period. Though the Samaritan temple was demolished, its priesthood survived as a functioning institution. Despite vigorous Jewish polemic against them in the post-exilic period, the Samaritans were probably not a major threat to Israel's social and religious life. And in spite of the uncomplimentary portraits in Ezra and Nehemiah, it is not even certain that the "Samaritans" (Ezra 4, Neh 6:1-13), were among those who pestered the Jews when they tried to rebuild the temple under Zerubbabel and Jeshua.[29]

---

[27]See *ibid.,* p. 311.

[28]See Joachim Jeremias, *Jerusalem in the Time of Jesus,* translated by F.H. and C.H. Cave from the third German edition (1962), with author's revisions to 1967, (Philadelphia: Fortress Press, 1975 paperback edition), p. 353.

[29]See John Bowman, *The Samaritan Problem.* Studies in the Relationships of

A far more serious challenge to Israel's faith and folkways was represented by Hellenism, and we must now turn our attention to it.

THE CRISIS OF HELLENISM

The conquests made by Alexander the Great between 333 and 323 B.C.E. changed the map of the ancient world. His empire was vast, stretching from Greece, Egypt and Asia Minor in the west to what are now the borders of the Indian Subcontinent in the east. Palestine, Lebanon and Syria were part of Alexander's empire, as were those territories that today include parts of Armenia, Iran, Iraq, Afghanistan and Pakistan. Such far-flung empires are notoriously difficult to unify and administer but during his brief lifetime Alexander managed to consolidate his conquests through a system of provincial governors (satraps) and through a centralized fiscal administration that employed a common currency throughout the empire. After Alexander's death, predictable power-struggles erupted and the empire's internal cohesiveness was diminished. Still, the century between roughly 320 and 220 B.C.E. was a triumphant time for hellenistic civilization. Greek language, culture, religion and political system (the "city-state") spread widely as the fulcrum of power shifted from east (the ancient oriental empires) to west (the new hellenistic empire).

As had become common throughout their long history, Jews in Palestine found themselves faced with a new political and religious crisis. In many respects the impact of hellenistic culture after Alexander's conquests posed a deeper and more abiding problem for Jews than had the exile and its aftermath. The exile, after all, had been relatively brief; Cyrus's edict of 539 allowed deported Jews to return home. The tolerant policy of several Persian rulers

Samaritanism, Judaism, and Early Christianity, translated by Alfred M. Johnson, Jr., (Pittsburgh Theological Monograph Series, Number 4; Pittsburgh: The Pickwick Press, 1975), pp. 4-5.

permitted Israelites to practice their ancient religion and even to introduce reforms that would bring it more strictly into line with ancient tradition. Thus Ezra, toward the latter part of the fifth century B.C.E., succeeded in re-establishing "*torah*" (in the more technical post-exilic sense) as the fundamental rule of life for the restored Jewish community (see Neh 8). Dedication to Torah and Temple became the "official" hallmarks of Jewish piety. At the same time, the priesthood—especially the office of high priest—achieved a prominence that was probably unparalleled in pre-exilic times. Since the post-exilic community had no monarchy of its own, as we have seen, the high priest appropriated paraphernalia formerly associated with kingship. In effect, the post-exilic high priest became a royal figure, head of the nation and its representative before God.[30] It is not insignificant that Jewish writers who reflected on the period of restoration under Nehemiah and Ezra took pains to underscore the priestly character of its chief heroes. The author of the book of Ezra, for instance, carefully traces Ezra's ancestry back to "the high priest Aaron" (Ezra 7:5). Our earlier discussion of the "priesthood of Aaron" alerts us to the historical implausibility of such a genealogy, but popular post-exilic theology stressed the importance of an unbroken succession of priests stretching back to Israel's earliest history as a people. Through such a "theology," the restored community could be seen as touching base with its most primitive roots, its most cherished memories—and it could be seen as firmly founded on Torah (Moses) and Temple (with its "Aaronic" priesthood).

This neat theological program was threatened, however, by the pervasive influence of hellenistic civilization after about 320 B.C.E. On the one hand, Alexander's success brought considerable benefits to the ancient world: new trade routes were opened, money replaced the barter system as a medium of exchange, better methods of farming increased agricultural productivity, new products from the

[30]See de Vaux, *Ancient Israel,* Vol. 2, p. 400.

East became available.[31] Increased trade and commerce resulted in the emergence of a new and wealthy middle class, especially in the city-states (e.g., Alexandria, Tyre, Corinth, Ephesus, Antioch). But prosperity also brought a rub. Social conflict intensified, pitting rich against poor and city-dwellers against inhabitants of the countryside. New tensions arose, too, between the aristocracy (the "old money") and the *nouveau riche*. Elements of these conflicts are reflected, as we shall see, in Jewish literature written during the hellenistic era.

But economic pressure was only part of the crisis. The hellenization of the ancient world raised other cultural and religious questions for Palestinian Jews loyal to the post-exilic understanding of Torah and Temple. For Alexander's death and the subsequent division of the empire did not stop the spread of hellenistic culture. Two of Alexander's generals founded dynasties that were to have a direct and long-lasting impact on Jewish life. In the parcelling up of territory following Alexander's death, Ptolemy Lagi was given control over Egypt and Cyrenaica; in about 320, Palestine was added to the Ptolemaic empire. Members of this dynasty controlled affairs in Palestine for roughly one hundred years (ca. 300-200 B.C.E.). Another of Alexander's generals, Seleucus I Nicator, had been given Babylonia as his portion of the empire. Shrewd political and military maneuvering brought further territory into the Seleucid empire (Armenia, Cappadocia, northern Syria, Asia Minor). During the reign of Antiochus III the Great (ca. 223-187 B.C.E.) Palestine was annexed from the Ptolemies and transferred to Seleucid control.

It is well known that subjugated peoples, stimulated by ambivalent emotions of love and hatred, will often imitate their oppressors. This psycho-social rule of thumb seems to be borne out by events in Palestine under Ptolemaic and Seleucid rule (roughly, the period between 300 and 150

[31]See Seán Freyne, *The World of the New Testament,* (New Testament Message, Volume 2; Wilmington, Delaware: Michael Glazier, Inc., 1980), pp. 8-9.

B.C.E.). It should be remembered, first, that the population of Palestine had never been totally Jewish. Nor did all Jewish refugees return to Palestine after the exile. Some stayed on in other lands, forming communities in the "diaspora." Both Palestinian and diaspora Jews were subjected to hellenistic influence, with the result that even in Palestine the Jewish community produced leaders who were thoroughly hellenized, whose cultural and religious views were shaped by Greek language and thought.

Persons who stood to benefit from the economic effects of Alexander's conquests were probably inclined to cooperate with the Ptolemaic and the Seleucid authorities. An instance of such cooperation is provided by the Tobiads, an old and distinguished non-priestly family whose members could trace their ancestry back to the era of Ezra and Nehemiah.[32] One Joseph, a member of the Tobiad clan, achieved considerable prominence at the court of Ptolemy Philadelphus (283-246 B.C.E.) in Alexandria. Active throughout Judaea and influential in Jerusalem, Joseph was eventually chosen to represent Jewish interests at the court of Ptolemy III Euergetes (246-221 B.C.E.). One could say, perhaps, that this Joseph represented a cosmopolitan "new breed" in Palestinian society under the Ptolemies: non-priestly, financially shrewd, committed to cooperating with non-Jewish rulers. And this new breed got results: Joseph's wide-ranging fiscal interests brought revenues pouring into Judaea, especially into urban centers like Jerusalem.[33]

I have emphasized the non-priestly origins of Joseph and the Tobiad family because this will help us understand one of the sources of social resentment in the Jerusalem of the hellenistic era. Priestly families were pillars of the Torah and Temple movement fostered by leaders of the post-exilic

[32]See M. Stern, "Aspects of Jewish Society: The Priesthood and Other Classes," in S. Safrai and M. Stern, *et al.,* eds., *The Jewish People in the First Century,* (2 vols.; Compendia Rerum Iudaicarum ad Novum Testamentum, Section 1, Volumes 1-2; Assen: Van Gorcus, 1974-1976), Vol. 2, 561-630.
[33]*ibid.*

community like Ezra and Nehemiah. With the "royal" high priest as head of the nation, these priestly families had become firmly entrenched in the top echelons of society, particularly during the period of Persian rule prior to the conquests of Alexander (roughly 540-330 B.C.E.). With the advent of hellenistic civilization, however, the old priestly aristocracy began to see some of its prestige erode. Non-priestly interlopers like Joseph and the Tobiads challenged the social supremacy of established priestly families.

Nor was that all. During the reign of the Seleucid Antiochus IV Epiphanes (175-163 B.C.E.) attempts to hellenize life in Jerusalem reached a new peak. The name of the city was changed to Antiochia and a gymnasium was established to rival (perhaps even replace) the temple as a center of social life. Traditional Jewish sensibilities were further insulted in 169 and 176, when Antiochus plundered the temple, banned the practice of Jewish religion and imposed the worship of Zeus. Antiochus's actions precipitated the revolt led by the Maccabee brothers (see 1 Mac 1-6). The rebellion succeeded, and the temple was rededicated in 164 B.C.E. It is important to note, however, that the Maccabean ideology (Torah and Temple versus hellenization) was not shared by all Jews in Palestine. Some members of the upper class society in Jerusalem—including both lay and priestly families—were either hellenist sympathizers or aggressive hellenists in their own right.[34] One gathers that members of even the high priest's family were sympathetic to the helle-nists' cause. This may explain why Jason, son of the high priest Simon "the Just", was himself appointed high priest by Antiochus IV in 175 B.C.E.[35] According to strict Maccabean ideology such an appointment was illegitimate, since the high priesthood was supposed to be lifelong, inherited by natural succession. Jason's tenure was short-lived; he was replaced in 172 by Menelaus, a devoted hellenist who was not a member of the Zadokite clan (an essential requirement

[34]See *ibid.*, pp. 585-590.
[35]See Jeremias, *Jerusalem in the Time of Jesus*, p. 184.

for legitimate high priesthood, given the Maccabean ideology).

The Maccabean ideology is the one that survives in the biblical literature, and it provides an extremely unfavorable account of hellenists and their works. But 1 and 2 Maccabees do not give us the whole story. The hellenists cannot simply be dismissed as wicked apostates bent on destroying their ancestral Jewish faith and its customs. From their point of view, hellenism meant economic opportunity, a chance to enhance the prosperity of Palestine. Separation from the larger world for religious motives—the view championed by Maccabean ideology— had deprived the Jewish community of the enormous fiscal possibilities created by the expansion of trade and commerce that followed Alexander's conquests.[36] It was time, the hellenists argued, for Palestinian Jews to get their fair share of the pie (see 1 Mac 1:11-13). This could be done only if the Jewish community were willing to modernize its patterns of life by accepting some of the "new ways" offered by hellenistic civilization. To borrow the phrase popularized at the II Vatican Council, the hellenists were calling for a social and religious "*aggiornamento.*"

But Jewish traditionalists would have none of this "updating." Their viewpoint can be discerned in works like the "Wisdom of Sirach." Its author, Jesus ben Sirach, is commonly identified as a sage who lived in Jerusalem and wrote sometime between 200 and 175 B.C.E. He may have belonged to a priestly family; in any case he was almost surely a member of the patrician upper crust, and he was keenly aware of his superior social status. We learn, for example, that ben Sirach's aristocratic sensibilities were somewhat offended by the lower classes of Jerusalem society: artisans, farmers, common laborers. Though he recognized their importance for a city's well-being ("without them no city could be lived in") and admired their skill and industry ("they maintain God's ancient handiwork"), he

---

[36]See Freyne, *The World of the New Testament,* p. 8.

denied they could ever become wise or hold influential positions (see Sir 38:24-34). Like virtually everyone else in the ancient world, Sirach took the institution of slavery for granted: "Fodder and whip and loads for an ass. . . . Food, correction and work for a slave" (Sir 33:25-27). Jesus ben Sirach's attitudes toward people of lower social standing reveal a mixture of contempt, compassion and caution. He drew parallels between slaves and asses, yet insisted that one should "never lord it over any human being" (Sir 33:30); he cautioned wealthy readers against associating with the poor, yet criticized the callousness of the rich (see Sir 13).

Ben Sirach's religious sympathies are also evident. Ecstatic praise and exotic imagery are woven into his poem about the high priest Simon ("the Just"), whose presidency of the temple liturgy on the Day of Atonement is likened to "a luxuriant olive tree thick with fruit. . . . a cypress standing against the clouds" (Sir 50:10). A champion of "old-time religion," ben Sirach appears to have been fiercely dedicated to the traditional cult and creed of his ancestral Jewish faith. He shows little sympathy for the new ways in religious doctrine or practice; his heroes are the early patriarchs, judges, kings and prophets—Moses and Aaron, Joshua and Caleb, David and Solomon, Elisha and Elijah, Isaiah and Jeremiah (see Sir 44-49). He also admires those loyal leaders who helped reconstitute Israel as a religious body after the exile: Nehemiah, Zerubbabel, Jeshua the high priest (see Sir 49:11-13).

Ben Sirach's list of worthy ancestors causes little surprise; the heroes' names are familiar and their role in Israel's history is well known. But if we place the Wisdom of Sirach in its proper chronological context (ca. 200-175 B.C.E.) we begin to see that its author's apparently innocent list of ancestral heroes is really an implicit polemic against things that were going on in the Palestine and Jerusalem of his day. Read in this light, Sirach is an emphatic testament to the traditionalists' religious ideology in an era when political and cultural upheaval threatened to produce change.

There can be little doubt that the temple, its cult and

priesthood, played a role in the conflict between hellenists and traditionalists like Jesus ben Sirach. The high priesthood provided an especially sensitive focus for this conflict. During the forty years between 200 and 160 B.C.E., at least five different men were high priest, some of them appointed through Seleucid intervention.[37] This disturbance in the Zadokite "succession" of "Aaronic" high priests would have rankled traditionalists like ben Sirach. It even caused one of the Zadokite claimants, Onias III, to set up a rival temple at Leontopolis in Egypt.[38] This sanctuary, with its Oniad line of priests, survived until 70 C.E.

After an interregnum of seven years, between 159 and 152, the Maccabean line of high priests appeared. Eight of them functioned between 152 and 37 B.C.E., and they included John Hyrcanus I (134-104), the one responsible for demolishing the Samaritan sanctuary on Mt. Gerizim.[39] The Maccabees claimed to be a priestly family, but according to Jewish *hasidim* ("pious ones", possibly forerunners of the Pharisees) they were deficient since they were not of the Zadokite line.[40] This is an important point because it shows that not all Jews who shared the Maccabean ideology and joined the guerrilla resistance against the Seleucids were satisfied with what resulted. What resulted was, of course, the independent "Hasmonean" state, so called because a forebear of Mattathias (father of Judas Maccabaeus and his brothers) bore the name Asamonaios.[41] The Hasmoneans seem to have linked civil leadership with the high priesthood. This linkage first appears in the person of Jonathan, who after spending several years as ruler of the Jews assumed the high priesthood in 152. Later, with Alexander Jannaeus (103-76), the Hasmoneans appropriated the title of king.[42]

---

[37]See the list in Jeremias, *Jerusalem in the Time of Jesus,* p. 377.
[38]See *ibid.,* pp. 185-186.
[39]See *ibid.,* p. 377.
[40]See *ibid.,* p. 189.
[41]See John Bright, *A History of Israel,* (Third edition updated and revised; Philadelphia: Westminster Press, 1981), p. 425, note.
[42]See Jeremias, *Jerusalem in the Time of Jesus.* p. 188, note 131.

Disillusionment with the Hasmonean king/high priests took different forms. The Pharisees, who had begun to emerge as an identifiable movement in the second century B.C.E., regarded the Hasmonean claims to priesthood as tenuous, at best.[43] They opposed both John Hyrcanus and Alexander Jannaeus, citing as their motive the questionable status of John's mother.[44] But this motive was merely a mask concealing much deeper doubts about the legitimacy of "high priests" who could not even claim full membership in a priestly course, much less the Zadokite genealogy which, Pharisees insisted, was essential for legitimate succession to the high priesthood. Other groups also resisted Hasmonean pretentions to priestly status. The Qumran sectarians represented by the Dead Sea scrolls seem to have viewed their differences with the Hasmonean kings/priests as irreconcilable.[45] Their number included, quite possibly, Zadokite priests who had lost influence in Hasmonean Jerusalem. Excluded from the temple cult, they withdrew in the waning years of the second century B.C.E. to the Judaean wilderness.[46]

The hellenistic crisis thus produced dramatic changes in the Israelite priesthood. When it began, about 333 B.C.E., the Zadokites were firmly in control of the priesthood of the Second Temple; but within roughly 150 years, their grip on the high priesthood was lost. Seleucid intervention, followed by Hasmonean politics, played havoc with the postexilic compromise that had supported a "priesthood of Aaron" headed up Zadokites who traced their origins to Phineas and Eleazar. In a characteristically ironic turn, the Levites' fate—a priesthood reduced in status—now claimed the Zadokites as well.

PRIESTHOOD IN ROMAN PALESTINE

The Hasmonean dynasty was effectively ended by the

[43]See *ibid.*, p. 189; cf. Bright, *A History of Israel*, p. 461.
[44]See Jeremias, *Jerusalem in the Time of Jesus*, p. 189.
[45]See Bright, *A History of Israel*, p. 462.
[46]See *ibid.*

Roman occupation of Palestine under Pompey in 63 B.C.E. Although the line continued under Hyrcanus II (63-40) and Antigonus (40-37), it was finally exterminated by Herod the Great.[47] A shrewd politician, Herod perceived that the continuing presence of Hasmoneans in the high priesthood would threaten his rule. He thus arranged for the high priest Aristobulus, a seventeen year old, to be drowned after the feast of Tabernacles in 35 B.C.E. Herod also made certain that no further Hasmonean claimants remained alive.

Once more kingship and priesthood were separated. The royal Herodian dynasty functioned as client kings responsible, ultimately, to imperial Roman authority. Herod the Great, whose long reign stretched from 37 to 4 B.C.E., was an Idumaean and thus only a "half-breed" Jew from a racially purist point of view. Still, his impact on Israel's religious life was profound. Among other projects, he undertook the restoration and expansion of the temple—a work still not fully completed in the lifetime of Jesus of Nazareth. Herod also exercised firm control over the high priesthood: first, by appointing relatively obscure persons from priestly—but not necessarily Zadokite—families; and secondly, by doing away with lifelong tenure in the office. During the Roman-Herodian era from 37 B.C.E. to 70 C.E. there were no less than twenty-eight high priests, some of whom were in office for less than a year.[48]

It should not be assumed, however, that the priesthood had become nothing more than a political puppet under the thumb of Herodian rulers. If anything, the Jerusalem priesthood saw its position enhanced during the Roman-Herodian era. For one thing, the Herodians lived in the coastal city of Caesarea; this provided the priests with an opportunity to stress the specifically *religious* character of Jerusalem.[49] As a holy city with a temple, moreover, Jerusalem could claim certain legal privileges such as tax exemp-

---

[47]See Jeremias, *Jerusalem in the Time of Jesus*, p. 190.

[48]See *ibid.*, pp. 377-378.

[49]See Gerd Theissen, *Sociology of Early Palestinian Christianity*, translated by John Bowden, (Philadelphia: Fortress Press, 1978), pp. 54-55.

tions.[50] This brought economic advantages to a city where a majority of the population was dependent on the temple for a living. Herod's program of restoring the temple provided employment for a large number of craftsmen and artisans. In addition, the daily sacrifices created a "cultic industry" which required ample supplies of flour and wine, oil, livestock (rams, sheep, cattle, doves), salt, wood and incense.[51] And since the temple was an important pilgrimage center, additional revenues were forthcoming, especially on major festivals like Passover, Pentecost and Tabernacles. Even diaspora Jews who did not regularly come to Jerusalem on pilgrimage seem to have been faithful in paying the annual half-shekel temple tax.[52] All these sources of revenue and expenditure—tax exemptions, building projects, the "cultic industry", pilgrimages, charitable works and annual temple taxes—fell under the supervision of temple treasurers who were priests.[53] From an economic viewpoint alone, this would have enhanced the power and prestige of the Jerusalem priesthood.

Who were these priests of the Roman-Herodian period? We have seen that Herod's policy of dealing with temple personnel was rather innovative: his very first appointee to the high priesthood, Ananel (37-36; again, from 34 B.C.E.), was a Zadokite—but from the Babylonian diaspora rather than from Jerusalem.[54] Subsequent appointees included Jesus, son of Phiabi, and Simeon, son of Boethus; both of them were from the Egyptian diaspora. Through clever appointments like these Herod was able to establish a "new priestly elite" drawn from the diaspora and from the border areas of Palestine.[55] This strategy perhaps reflected Herod's

---

[50] *Ibid.*

[51] See S. Safrai, "The Temple," in S. Safrai and M. Stern *et al.,* eds., *The Jewish People in the First Century,* Vol. 2, pp. 881-884.

[52] See *ibid.,* pp. 880-881.

[53] See *ibid.,* pp. 879-880; cf. Jeremias, *Jerusalem in the Time of Jesus,* pp. 166-174.

[54] See Jeremias, *Jerusalem in the Time of Jesus,* p. 193.

[55] See Stern, "Aspects of Jewish Society," in S. Safrai and M. Stern *et al.,* eds., *The Jewish People in the First Century,* Vol. 2, pp. 612-615.

own origins, since he came from a prominent Edomite family which had been converted under the Hasmonean John Hyrcanus I.[56] Herod's grandfather Antipas had been made governor of Idumaea by the Hasmoneans, and his father Antipater had achieved success in the political life of Palestine toward the end of the Hasmonean state. Since Herod's own family background included proselytes and persons of non-Palestinian origin, he need not feel indebted to the old priestly aristocracy of the Jerusalem establishment. The way was open for creation of a new priestly elite, one unencumbered by loyalties to either the Old Zadokite families or the Hasmonean aristocracy.

New priestly families thus emerged during the years between 37 B.C.E. and 70 C.E. Four of them—the families of Boethus, Hannas (Annas), Phiabi and Kamith—produced twenty-two of the twenty-eight high priests during that period.[57] Significantly, none of these families was of Jerusalem origin. They came from Alexandria and elsewhere in the Egyptian diaspora (Boethus, Phiabi), from the Babylonian diaspora (Hannas), or from parts unknown (Kamith). Prominent lay families, many of them also from the diaspora, joined these priestly clans to form a social hierarchy different from that of the earlier Hasmonean era. Among these lay families were the house of Bathyra (of Babylonian origin) and the house of Hillel, which had also migrated from Babylonia to Palestine.[58] Not all these families were enamored of Herod and his policies. The house of Hillel, for example, produced leaders of the Pharisaic movement, and although Herod seems to have supported Pharisees,[59] he did not necessarily share their interpretation of Torah and *halakah* (the body of oral laws refined and interpreted by scribes and teachers who were not priests).

The religio-political sympathies of the Herodian priestly aristocracy probably lay with the Sadducees. This group

---

[56]See *ibid.*, pp. 604-608.
[57]See Jeremias, *Jerusalem in the Time of Jesus*, pp. 193-195.
[58]See Stern, "Aspects of Jewish Society," pp. 600-604.
[59]See Theissen, *Sociology of Early Palestinian Christianity*, p. 71.

may have originated during the Seleucid period.[60] Their attitude is often described as "conservative", since they gave allegiance only to the *Torah* (not to *halakah*), rejected "modern" doctrines like personal resurrection, and insisted on the exact performance of the temple ritual. Their doctrinal fundamentalism distinguished them from the Pharisees, who were willing to accept new developments in doctrine and to admit the authoritative role of *halakah* in Jewish life. The Sadducees wished to maintain the political and religious *status quo,* since they had nothing to gain, economically or socially, from a change in the policies of the Herodian client kings.

Both the priestly and the lay nobility were represented in the Sanhedrin, the religious council responsible for Jewish affairs. The Sanhedrin had replaced the pre-Hasmonean *gerousia* during the era that followed the Maccabean revolt, and its power in Jerusalem was enormous. During the Roman-Herodian period its composition was both lay and priestly, Sadducean and Pharisaic. Priestly representatives, Sadducees or Sadducean sympathizers, included the chief executive officers of the temple: the high priest (together with the retired high priest), the "captain of the temple", the temple overseer(s) and the temple treasurer(s).[61] These officers (the "chief priests" mentioned in the New Testament) formed an independent legal and administrative body responsible for matters touching the temple and the priesthood.[62] They also controlled the activities of the temple police, Levites who served as gatekeepers, guards, patrollers and night watchmen.[63] And, perhaps more importantly, they controlled a large block of seats in the Sanhedrin. This priestly aristocracy thus combined social, political, religious and fiscal power in Jerusalem.

There were, of course, thousands of Jewish priests who had no part in the aristocratic oligarchy which controlled

[60]See Bright, *A History of Israel,* p. 460.
[61]See Jeremias, *Jerusalem in the Time of Jesus,* pp. 177-179.
[62]See *ibid.,* p. 179.
[63]See *ibid.,* pp. 209-210.

the Jerusalem temple. Often poor, they lived in the Judaean and Galilean countryside and made their living as craftsmen or farmers. Since the priesthood at this period was organized into 24 weekly "courses", these country clergymen would have gone to Jerusalem to serve in the temple about twice a year. John the Baptist's father Zechariah provides a convenient illustration: he belonged to the priestly course or "division" of Abijah and is pictured in Luke's gospel as going down to Jerusalem to fulfill his duties (Lk 1:5-23). An interesting detail is provided in Lk 1:9-12: Zechariah was selected by lot to offer incense, and he experiences a vision while performing this task. Luke's description matches what we know of priestly practice in the Roman-Herodian era. Each day, shortly before dawn, the priests of the weekly course gathered in the temple's "Chamber of Hewn Stone" to cast lots for the distribution of the sacrificial duties. These included the daily whole-offering (two lambs, one in the morning and another in the evening) and the daily incense-offering. The privilege of offering incense at the golden altar within the temple's sanctuary (immediately in front of the Holy of Holies) was considered a supreme honor. It was the high point in a series of impressive rites which deserve some comment here. A brief outline of the daily sacrifices will show where and when the incense-offering took place:[64]

• The priests selected by lot for the sacrifices sanctified themselves through a ritual bathing of hands and feet.

• Meanwhile, the temple's sanctuary was prepared: the golden candelabrum was trimmed; ashes from the previous day's offering of incense were removed from the golden altar; the sanctuary gates were opened.

• The sacrificial lamb for the morning ritual was slaughtered and dismembered.

• Gathering again in the Chamber of Hewn Stone, the priests offered prayer and recited the Decalogue and the Shema.

[64]See Safrai, "The Temple," in S. Safrai and M. Stern *et al.*, eds., *The Jewish People in the Frist Century,* Vol. 2, pp. 887-890.

• A special lot was then cast for the priest who would offer the incense. Only those priests who had never exercized this privilege were eligible. Lots were also cast for the duty of bringing the parts of the dismembered lamb to the altar. (Recall that in the Second Temple period priests had reserved to themselves all tasks that involved contact with the altar.)

• The incense was then solemnly offered by the priest-officiant, who was accompanied by a deputy. Meanwhile, the other priests entered the sanctuary and prostrated themselves. The Levites sang, while the people gathered for prayer in the temple courts. After the incense had been offered, the priest-officiant departed the sanctuary and stood on the steps of the temple porch to bless the assembled people.

• Following these rites, the remainder of the morning sacrifice was offered. The lamb's parts were sacrificed as a meal-offering; a cake (oil and flour) was burned as the high priest's offering; and wine was poured out as a libation. These were performed at the altar of holocausts (not at the golden altar within the sanctuary). Immediately before the wine was offered, the priests blew the trumpets and the Levites were signalled to sing the psalm assigned for that day. The psalm was divided into two or three portions; at the beginning of each section the people prostrated. When the singing ended, the morning sacrifices were complete. From then until about three in the afternoon, when the "evening" sacrifice was offered, the priests chosen to perform ritual tasks devoted themselves to the "free-will offerings" (e.g., peace-offerings, thank-offerings) and to the "obligatory offerings" (e.g., for purification of lepers or of women after childbirth). Meanwhile, the other priests of the weekly course prayed and read the Torah.

One can see from this description that the temple liturgies of this era were elaborate and would have required a sizeable body of priest-officiants. Joachim Jeremias has estimated that about three hundred priests would have been needed each week— and this number does not include the Levites who functioned as singers, musicians, custodians and police officers.[65] Although in theory the priests were supported by tithes from flocks, herds and grain, it is doubtful whether the country clergy could have survived on these; they functioned, after all, only a couple of times a year. The priestly aristocracy of Jerusalem itself—the "chief priests" and temple executives—would have enjoyed a far greater economic advantage; their duties were daily and they had immediate access to the temple's storerooms and treasury. These aristocrats were the principal beneficiaries of the tithing system and, if they were landowners, they also benefitted from tax-revenues.

We are justified, then, in concluding that during the Roman-Herodian era resentment between priestly aristocrats and country clergymen intensified. This conflict between "city" and "country" has been noted before in our discussion of tensions between priests of the royal establishment in Jerusalem and those of the old tribal sanctuaries. When the opposition between Roman authorities and Palestinian Jews reached a crisis in the 60's C.E., therefore, it is likely that priests were to be found on both sides of the conflict. The aristocrats, Sadducean in sympathy if not always in fact, were probably reluctant to join the "freedom fighters" who inspired the First Revolt in 66 C.E. This revolt was, it appears, directly related to oppressive taxation with concomitant indebtedness, and the taxes in question were both secular (owed to the Romans) and religious (tithes owed to temple and priests). The priestly aristocracy in Jerusalem stood to lose a great deal in this situation; country priests, on the other hand, had little to lose by joining the resistance movement.

This does not mean that the entire priestly aristocracy sympathized with the Romans; indeed, the opposite seems to have been true. Among the leaders of the freedom fighters in the First Revolt were Ananus, a retired high priest, and one of his sons.[66] Nor did the guerrillas themselves oppose the

[65]See Jeremias, *Jerusalem in the Time of Jesus,* pp. 203-206.
[66]See *ibid.,* p. 198.

temple and the priesthood. One of their first acts after gaining temporary control in Jerusalem in 67 C.E. was to select a high priest (Pinchas) through the ancient custom of casting lots. But this was a short-lived achievement. The Romans put down the rebellion in 70 C.E., razed the Temple, and the Israelite priesthood came to a brutal end.

SAGES AND SYNAGOGUES

Neither temple nor priesthood survived the catastrophe of 70 C.E., but one religious institution did—the synagogue. Its origins are obscure, and a number of theories have been proposed to explain its emergence in post-exilic Israel.[67] Here, it is sufficient to note that synagogue origins are best explained by conditions that obtained in both Palestine and the diaspora after Cyrus's edict (ca. 537) permitted Jews to return home from Babylon. We need to recall, first, that some Jews did not return to Palestine and, secondly, that some had never been deported in the first place. The returnees ("men of the exile", the "holy race") looked askance at the "people of the land" (a derogatory term for those who never suffered deportation).[68] It is the returnees' ideology that we find preserved in the Bible, especially in the books of Ezra and Nehemiah. This view emphasized separation of the Israelite community from contact with "outsiders", recovery of ancient tradition and its commitment to writing (Torah), and scholarly study as a means of interpreting tradition.

Within this atmosphere the synagogue seems to have developed. For the returnees it provided a "meeting place" for the study and prayerful discussion of the recovered traditions; for those who chose to remain in the diaspora it supplied a forum where the ancestral Jewish faith could be preserved and transmitted. The synagogue was thus both a "house of study" (*beth ha-midrash*) and a "place of assembly"

---

[67]See, for a discussion of these theories, S. Safrai, "The Synagogue," in S. Safrai and M. Stern *et al.*, eds., *The Jewish People in the First Century*, Vol. 2, pp. 908-944.

[68]See Freyne, *The World of the New Testament*, pp. 88-89.

(*beth ha-keneset*). It is highly unlikely that the synagogue was regarded as a replacement for the temple and its worship; even diaspora Jews continued to contribute annually to the temple's support. Nor was the synagogue simply an expedient alternative to participation in the temple liturgy. If this were the case one would have difficulty explaining the presence of synagogues in Jerusalem itself and accounting for the constant flow of pilgrims who came to the temple, especially at the festivals of Passover, Pentecost and Tabernacles.

Originally, then, the synagogue was not a "building" but a *way of gathering,* a form of assembling to study, pray and exchange ideas about God's revelation to Israel. It is better understood as a popular "movement" rather than as a place. Lay leadership, not priestly function, characterized the synagogue, and among these leaders were both scribes and sages. The term "scribe", in its earlier sense, was neither specifically religious nor specifically Jewish. Most ancient urban cultures possessed a body of scribes who performed routine administrative tasks, handled diplomatic correspondence and kept archival records.[69] In this sense, scribes would have formed part of the court of monarchs like David and Solomon. Later, in the restored post-exilic community, "scribe" acquired a more technical meaning; thus Ezra is a scribe (Ezra 7:12) in the sense that he functions as a commissioner of the government in affairs that are specifically religious and Jewish.[70] Ezra is also a priest (Ezra 7:12)—a signal that in his day (perhaps 400 B.C.E.), and probably later as well, the two functions were considered compatible.[71] Later still, "scribes" like Jesus ben Sirach belonged to a class of persons who studied Torah and gathered disciples to whom they transmitted their learning (Sir 38:24-34).[72]

Possibly, scribes like ben Sirach represented a group that came to be known as "sages" or "wisdom teachers". Promo-

---

[69]See Bright, *A History of Israel,* p. 219.
[70]See *ibid.,* p. 386.
[71]For a discussion of later Israelite priests who were also scribes, see Jeremias, *Jerusalem in the Time of Jesus,* pp. 233-234.
[72]See Bright, *A History of Israel,* p. 437.

tion of Torah and its effect on all areas of life was not the only qualification for a sage; he also had to be a person of high moral stature.[73] Nor was social standing important: a sage might emerge from upper, lower or middle class. And although many of them may have come to Jerusalem, their native home could have been anywhere in Palestine or the Diaspora.

Scribes and sages represented an egalitarian impulse within Israelite society. Their prestige derived not from their genealogy but from their learning, personality and moral qualities. Since they could come from any social class, high or low, priestly or non-priestly, they tended to relativize the class distinctions prized by nobles and aristocrats. They constituted, in short, a moral and intellectual elite rather than one dependent upon inheritance or socio-economic advantage.[74] Sometimes, an entire family became renowned for its sages, as did that of Hillel, whose members were prominent in the Pharisaic movement.

By the beginning of the first century C.E., sages—most of them Pharisaic—constituted a bloc in the Sanhedrin. The seventy members of this body were thus drawn from the priestly aristocracy, lay "elders" (the aristocracy of the rich), and scribes/sages (the aristocracy of the educated). This is an important point because it reveals that new groups could enter the Sanhedrin only by becoming educated—as scribes and sages were—in the law. The "chief priests" and elders protected their own position in the Sanhedrin through dynastic and economic privilege.[75] One can see, too, that the Sanhedrin of this period formed a cross-section of social groups that may have been at odds with one another: Sadducees (priestly aristocrats) and Pharisees, the privileged upper crust (priests and elders) and the more egalitarian "wisdom teachers" (scribes and sages).

There was no way a non-priestly sage could break into the

[73]See Stern, "Aspects of Jewish Society," pp. 619-620.
[74]See *ibid.,* p. 620; cf. Jeremias, *Jerusalem in the Time of Jesus,* pp. 633-635.
[75]See Theissen, *Sociology of Early Palestinian Christianity,* p. 70.

prestigious body that administered the temple. But the synagogue was a different matter; no priest was required for any of its activities. There, worship, prayer, preaching, reading and study of Torah could proceed without any clerical intervention. This does not mean that the synagogue was an utterly unstructured institution. The well-known story of Jesus in the synagogue at Nazareth (Lk 4:16-30) refers to an "attendant" who assists the reader by handing him the biblical scroll and returning it to its place after its use. Acts 13:15 refers to "leaders of the synagogue", and it is often assumed that these formed a recognizable "college of elders" responsible for overseeing synagogal activities. One should not jump to the conclusion, however, that such "attendants" and "leaders" constituted a quasi-permanent and official body of ministerial officers. Only in the Judaism reconstituted under Pharisaic leadership after the fall of the temple (70 C.E.) do we find indisputable evidence of more structured forms of leadership in the synagogue.

Before leaving this brief discussion of sages and synagogues, one final point should be made. A synagogue could exist wherever there were Jews; it was thus a widespread institution throughout Palestine and the diaspora. This means, among other things, that there were synagogues where Greek was the dominant language and the Greek scriptures, in the Septuagint translation, were familiar. The hellenization of Jewish life may well have been aided by the synagogue system itself; some of its sages may even have been educated in Greek philosophy and rhetoric.[76] Such Greek-speaking synagogues of hellenized Jews existed even in Jerusalem—as one can gather from the account of Stephen and his companions in Acts 6.

---

[76]See Abraham Malherbe, *Social Aspects of Early Christianity,* (Baton Rouge: Louisiana State University Press, 1977), p. 35.

Conclusion

The Israelite priesthood was a religious institution that emerged slowly, developed locally during the period of settlement in Palestine after the exodus, became part of the royal establishment during the monarchy, and achieved considerable power in the era of the Second Temple. Initially, the priests were little more than oracular consultants and sanctuary servants, but when the tribal confederacy developed after the exodus, the "sons of Levi" emerged as a class of "professional priests" who made their living at sanctuaries like Gilgal, Bethel, Shiloh, Beer-sheba, Shechem and Mizpah. With the move toward centralization of cult and government at Jerusalem under the monarchy, royal priests became temple personnel dedicated to sacrificial functions. Compromises before and after the exile resulted in the supremacy of a "Zadokite" line of priests who traced their lineage back to Aaron. The post-exilic Second Temple was thus administered by Zadokites, with Levites serving as clergy of inferior status. But the crisis of hellenism brought an end to Zadokite supremacy: in both the Hasmonean and Roman-Herodian periods, not even the high priest had to be Zadokite.

From this complex history several important facts surface. The Israelite priesthood was not a vocation, a "charism", a "call from the community", or a "pastoral ministry": it was a religious function strictly related to one's genealogy. And although a ceremony of "ordination" did arise during the Second Temple period,[77] it was still heredity and exercise of function that "made" one a priest. By the first century C.E. the Jerusalem priests constituted a wealthy aristocracy of prominent families, Sadducean in sympathy and thus "conservative" in matters of doctrine, cult and politics. The high priesthood, a post-exilic development, was also an inherited function, controlled by a few families, though by the Roman-Herodian period its incum-

---

[77]See Jeremias, *Jerusalem in the Time of Jesus*, pp. 214-216.

bents had lost the right of life-long tenure. Country priests continued to exist, as they had from the days of the old tribal confederacy, but their influence was severely limited.

Temple and priesthood were unquestionably a major aspect of Jewish life in the first century C.E. The economic stability of Jerusalem depended on the temple with its regular pattern of worship, its revenues, tithes and tax-exemptions, and its many pilgrims. And as we shall see in the following chapter, most of the "renewal movements" that developed in Palestine during the first century defined themselves in either positive or negative relation to the temple. The catastrophe that befell Jerusalem in 70 C.E. was thus a devastating jolt to all who identified themselves with the Jewish community, including those sectarians who claimed to follow the "way" of Jesus of Nazareth.

Recommended Reading

Bright, John. *A History of Israel.* Third edition updated and revised. Philadelphia: Westminster Press, 1981. A fine, lucid survey of Israel's history in all its formative aspects: religious, social and political.

Cody, Aelred. *A History of Old Testament Priesthood.* Analecta Biblica 35. Rome: Pontifical Biblical Institute, 1969. The best work on the subject available in English; covers the development of the Israelite priesthood from its remote origins until the period of the Hellenistic crisis.

de Vaux, Roland. *Ancient Israel.* Two volumes. Translated by John McHugh. New York: McGraw-Hill Book Company, 1965 (paperback edition). A classic study of Israel's social and religious institutions, including the development of the temple, its cult and its priesthood.

Jeremias, Joachim. *Jerusalem in the Time of Jesus.* Translated by F.H. and C.H. Cave from the third German edition (1962), with author's revisions to 1967. Philadelphia: Fortress Press, 1975 (paperback edition). A detailed study of life in Jerusalem in the first century, C.E. Especially valuable for understanding the structure of officialdom in the temple at Jesus' time.

Safari, S. and Stern, M. (eds.). *The Jewish People in the First Century.* Two volumes. Compendia Rerum Iudaicarum ad Novum Testamentum, Section 1, Volumes 1-2. Assen: Van Gorus, 1974 - 1976. A collection of essays on all the important social, political and religious movements in first-century Palestine. Of special value are the essays on temple, priesthood and synagogue.

CHAPTER TWO
THE EARLIEST PATTERNS
OF CHRISTIAN MINISTRY

Introduction

After John's arrest, Jesus appeared in Galilee proclaiming the good news of God: "This is the time of fulfillment.
The reign of God is at hand! Reform your lives and believe
in the gospel!" (Mk 1:14-15,NAB).

In these two verses Mark provides us with a succinct
summary of Jesus' origins and his career as a wandering
preacher. Three clues in the text help locate Jesus in the
world of first-century Palestine: the reference to John's
ministry; the remark that Jesus appeared in Galilee; and the
emphasis on Jesus' urgent announcement of God's "reign"
or rule. All these clues are important for understanding the
kind of movement and ministry that was associated with
Jesus. As we shall see in this chapter, first-century Palestine
was rife with preachers and parties who sought to renew
Israel's religious life. Some of these renewal movements are
well-known to modern readers of the Bible — e.g., the
Pharisees; others are familiar mainly to scholars or professional exegetes — e.g., the Essenes of Qumran. Unless we
spend some time inspecting these movements, we will not be
able to understand why the Jesus movement emerged and
how it was both similar to and different from other renewal

movements of the period. Our first task will thus be to situate Jesus within the social, economic and political framework of first century Palestine.

During his own lifetime Jesus proclaimed God's reign, i.e., God's decisive ("eschatological") deed of offering salvation to all who are willing to hear good news. But after his death, Jesus' disciples proclaim something rather different: God's decisive deed is *Jesus himself*—dead, but raised up and soon to return to complete his work. The "Christian movement" thus makes Jesus, rather than the reign of God, the content of its proclamation. These earliest Christian believers did not immediately constitute a new "religion"; they were instead a sectarian group within Judaism. Our second task in this chapter will be to understand how this Christian movement appeared after Jesus' death, how it faced and resolved some of its early internal conflicts, and how it dealt with its relation to the Jewish community. We will also need to ask what kinds of people were attracted to the Christian movement, and why.

Finally, our attention will focus on the patterns of ministry that began emerging in the first Christian generation (between roughly 35 and 70 C.E.). Four topics will receive particular scrutiny: the wandering charismatic preachers in Palestine; the Jerusalem church and its influence; the mysterious "Twelve"; and ministry in the churches of the Gentile mission, especially those connected with Paul.

I
The Jesus Movement

RENEWAL MOVEMENTS IN FIRST CENTURY PALESTINE

First century Palestine was a society in transition. The sources of change were several: economic, cultural, political, religious. In the previous chapter we noted some of the ways these factors affected religious institutions like the temple and priesthood in Jerusalem. We saw, for example, that the economic stability of Jerusalem was closely linked to the temple and its cultic industries. Conflict between city-dwellers and inhabitants of the countryside was also discussed. And we observed, too, that even within a single social class—e.g., the aristocracy—there were divisions between the old established families and the "new elite" created by Herod.

The "Pax Romana" of Emperor Augustus created new opportunities and problems for Palestinian Jews. Under relatively peaceful conditions, trade and commerce expanded throughout the Mediterranean world. Judaea benefitted from this, although the new prosperity was concentrated more in the coastal cities and in the Transjordanian region.[1] A new "middle class" of farmers, merchants and craftsmen began to emerge. The economy was based on agriculture (its mainstay), cattle raising, fishing and crafts which included what we might today identify as "Construction-workers". Cereals such as wheat and barley, grapes and olives were the agricultural staples—and there were important balsam groves as well. Though the land was *worked* by farmers and their families, it was often *owned* by Jewish or non-Jewish landowners; the balsam groves, for example, were directly in the hands of the Romans.

Palestine was not an economic paradise. Famine and overpopulation led to an intense struggle over control and distribution of land and goods.[2] There were also conflicts between economic classes: the old aristocracy looked suspiciously upon the rising "middle class"; native Palestinians competed with Roman occupiers for a share in the land. As always, taxes were an issue, and virtually everyone from aristocrat to common laborer felt they were too oppressive.

---

[1] See M. Stern, "Aspects of Jewish Society: The Priesthood and Other Classes," in S. Safrai and M. Stern *et al.*, eds., *The Jewish People in the First Century*, (2 vols.; Compendia Rerum Iudaicarum ad Novum Testamentum, Section 1, Volumes 1-2; Assen: Van Gorcus, 1974-1976), Vol. 2, p. 574.

[2] See Gerd Theissen, *Sociology of Early Palestinian Christianity*, translated by John Bowden, (Philadelphia: Fortress Press, 1978), pp. 40-45.

Devout Jews suffered from a system of double taxation: religious (tithes and temple-tax) and secular (payment to the Romans). Farm tenants who worked but did not own the land were often compelled to hand over their produce to cancel debts caused by heavy taxation.[3]

Conditions like these can easily lead to social disintegration and to intensified conflict between haves and have-nots, natives and foreigners (of whatever stripe), those who hope to gain from change and those, both very rich and very poor, who expect nothing. Signs of such disintegration were evident in first century Palestine. Some people responded to the impasse created by debts and taxation by emigrating; others took up careers as beggars or bandits.[4] Public safety, especially on the roads between Jerusalem and other parts of the country, became a major problem.

Within this atmosphere of social and economic restlessness a number of religious "renewal movements" emerged in first century Palestine. Some of them, like the Pharisees and Essenes, had already begun to form in the previous century, perhaps even earlier. Others, like the movements connected with John the Baptist and Jesus of Nazareth, appeared in the first decades of the first century. Still others, like the Zealots, became intensely active toward the middle of the century, especially around the time of the first Jewish rebellion against the Romans.

These movements had a number of features in common. All of them may be described as "theocratic": i.e., God, the only ruler, was at the center of their vision of Israel's destiny. For some (the Zealots), this meant that active political resistance and subversion of the Romans was essential for ushering in God's reign among a chosen people; for others (the Essenes), it meant that an apocalyptic "war" would sift the sons of light from the sons of darkness. The renewal movements also shared convictions, positive or negative,

[3]See Stern, "Aspects of Jewish Society," p. 577.
[4]See Theissen, *Sociology of Early Palestinian Christianity,* p. 35; cf. Stern, "Aspects of Jewish Society," p. 577.

about the temple. The Essenes regarded its cult and priest-hood as illegitimate and so withdrew to the wilderness; the Pharisees felt that "temple purity" should be available to all Jews in their relation to God. Radical ethics were another feature of the renewal movements. The Pharisees, for example, intensified the requirements for godly living by insisting that *halakah* (custom transmitted by oral law) stood with *Torah* as an authoriative source of ethical norms; the Zealots maintained the legitimacy of violent insurrection as a means to achieving political goals; and the Essenes entertained bloody visions of the apocalyptic slaughter of Israel's enemies.

There were important differences, too. Most of the renewal movements felt it was important to pursue their aims from *within* Jewish society; the Essenes, by contrast, withdrew from it. The Zealot party's radical left wing, the "Sicarii" ("dagger-men"), functioned in a manner not vastly different from modern terrorists and hired assassins, while the Jesus movement appears to have been more pacifist in outlook. By the first century the Pharisees had already made an impact on the Jewish establishment of Jerusalem: they probably held some seats on the Sanhedrin and their interpretation of the laws regulating the temple liturgy were respected, even by the Sadducean priesthood. The other movements either gained adherents more slowly or, like the Essenes, had "opted out" of the establishment altogether.

There were, of course, other groups in Palestine which did not share the ideology of the renewal movements. Perhaps the most important of these were the Sadducees. Their origins are murky, though scholars generally agree that "Sadducee" is derived from "Zadok", an indication that they may have been organized within the priestly circles of the hellenized Jewish aristocracy.[5] Their social and economic position in the first century was so intimately linked with the temple and its cult that one can understand why they would

---

[5]*See Seán Freyne, The World of the New Testament,* (New Testament Message, Volume 2; Wilmington, Delaware: Michael Glazier, Inc., 1980), pp. 99-105.

have resisted any change in the *status quo*. Their biblical fundamentalism placed them at the opposite end of the spectrum from the Pharisees, who adopted a far more liberal attitude toward what we might call "the development of doctrine." The Sadducees were interested only in the law codes of the Pentateuch, and again one can understand why: these texts (in their post-exilic redaction) provided a perfect charter for Sadducean claims to superiority in matters of priestly cult and temple administration. In short, the Sadducees had nothing to gain and a great deal to lose through any "renewal" that might challenge or alter the role of the temple in Jewish life.

Because these renewal movements form a significant part of the milieu from which Jesus and his disciples emerged, it will be useful to spend some time inspecting them more closely. Besides, some of these movements—e.g., the Pharisees—were probably viewed as more important by Jesus' contemporaries than was the wandering prophet from Galilee, whose brief career ended in apparent failure.

THE PHARISEES

The popular Christian imagination usually views the Pharisees as the wicked antagonists of the New Testament's stories about Jesus. They are portrayed as arrogant, treacherous and fundamentally hypocritical. John the Baptist attacks them and the Sadducees as a "brood of vipers" (Mt 3:7), while Jesus likens them to "white-washed tombs" (Mt 23:27). But caution is required in dealing with such textual broadsides. The Pharisees contemporary with Matthew's community were not the same ones who lived during Jesus' lifetime. Moreover, Matthew's gospel appears to have been written for a Jewish Christian community locked in a struggle with other Jews over the question: who is more faithful to the Torah—those who accept Jesus as the fulfillment of righteousness promised by the law, or those who reject him? Matthew proposes that Jesus did not reject the Torah, but offered a "fuller righteousness" (see the "Sermon on the Mount", Mt 5-7); in short, he is convinced that those who believe and follow Jesus are more faithful Jews than those who don't (e.g., the Pharisees of the period that followed the fall of Jerusalem in 70 C.E.).

The New Testament's portrayal of the Pharisees is thus shaped by conditions that obtained after 70 C.E. It is interesting, incidentally, that Paul's letters, written during the 50's, do *not* contain a polemic against the Pharisees; Paul's principal opponents were others who, like him, believed in Jesus! We must admit, then, that the gospels' accounts of Pharisaism are colored by concerns of second- and third-generation Christians. They reflect the life of churches who are beginning to realize they are no longer welcome in the synagogue— or who have even been excluded altogether from it.

The Pharisees of Jesus' own time were perhaps the most influential renewal group in Palestine. Unlike the Sadducees, they were neither doctrinal and biblical fundamentalists nor priestly aristocrats anxious to maintain the *status quo*. Indeed, they may well have been the more "liberal" party of that time. Open to the development of law and doctrine, they believed that "temple purity" was not an exclusive preserve of priests but should be extended to *all* Jews in everyday life. This implied that Israel's unique relation with God was not confined to the temple and its cult but could be experienced by the faithful Jew immersed in the hurly-burly of quotidian affairs. Without denying the centrality of the temple, the Pharisees wanted to extend its holiness to the practical sphere of work, rest, human relationships, business and commerce, the family, and contact with those outside the Jewish community. Though the Pharisaic movement may have begun among priests dissatisfied with the compromises made by the Hasmoneans in the second century B.C.E., it was a predominantly *lay* group in the first century. Pharisaism was especially popular among members of the emergent middle class, those artisans and merchants of Palestine and the diaspora who had benefitted from the Pax Romana of Augustus. One should remember that Paul himself, an artisan (tent-maker)

LUTHERANS
+ e.g. CALVINITS

born in a hellenized city of the diaspora (Tarsus), had been a Pharisee (Phil 3:5).

What the Pharisees offered Jews was an attractive ideal that exceeded Sadducean attention to the Pentateuch and temple religion. They had a message particularly appealing to an urban middle class which no longer relied on agriculture for a livelihood. The ancient temple festivals—Passover, Pentecost, Tabernacles—had originated, after all, among people who tended flocks and tilled fields, and who were thus concerned about the fertility of both. For many inhabitants of hellenized cities of the first century, however, such rituals were not especially gripping; for them, Greek philosophies, with their visions of an ordered universe regulated by Fate, may have offered more interesting possibilities.[6] The Pharisaic program with its more flexible attitude toward Torah and temple, made room for these hellenistic influences.

Pharisees were thus responding to the "signs of the times" in a world strongly charged with Greek thinking about the universe, its destiny and a human being's place in it. As Seán Freyne has noted, Pharisaism transposed the "temple charter" of the Pentateuch into a sort of "cosmic charter" that provided each person with a satisfying role in a universe regulated by order.[7] The many laws and customs which a Pharisaic Jew was expected to observe were not perceived, therefore, as an insuperable burden, but as a way to "find one's place" in a physical world which possessed a wholeness and integrity that manifested the holiness of God the Creator.[8]

This helps explain why Pharisees disdained the "people of the land", those Jews descended, as we saw in Chapter One, from families who had never suffered deportation at the time of the exile. From a Pharisaic viewpoint, the "people of the land" were rednecks who had a habit of capitulating whenever they were confronted by a crisis.[9] They were inclined

[6]See *ibid.,* pp. 23-28.
[7]See *ibid.,* pp. 110-118.
[8]See *ibid.,* pp. 116-117.
[9]See Leander Keck, *The New Testament Experience of Faith,* (St. Louis: Bethany Press, 1976), p. 26.

simply to absorb an alien culture's values—e.g., those of hellenism—rather than to sift and test them, as the Pharisees proposed, against the traditions of Jewish belief and practice. The people of the land, many of them living in Galilee, lacked both sophistication and fidelity; in the eyes of the Pharisees, they were secularists too stupid and too careless to understand what was at stake in the religious crisis of the first century.

The Pharisees were unenthusiastic about the Romans, but were willing to tolerate them so long as they did not interfere with the practice of Jewish religion. There is no evidence that the Pharisees, as a group, supported the insurrectionist activities of the Zealots, nor is there evidence that they counselled withdrawal from society like the Essenes. Neither political terrorism nor "monastic" retirement from social life would have fit in with the Pharisees' religious views. They sought to create a program that would preserve the distinctiveness of Jewish identity and, at the same time, respond to the cultural challenge posed by hellenism, especially as it touched middle class urban society.

THE ESSENES

Among the renewal movements contemporary with Jesus, only the Essenes produced a literature that sheds light on Judaism as it existed in the earliest decades of the first century.[10] The Dead Sea Scrolls from Qumran are thus invaluable clues to the extraordinarily diversified religious situation of this period. Like the Pharisees', the Essenes' origins are earlier; they may have withdrawn during the Maccabean/Hasmonean era when the Zadokite priesthood lost its supremacy in Jerusalem. It has been suggested that their founder was the "Teacher of Righteousness", a figure whose exact historical identity has not been recovered.[11] In

---

[10]We have an abundant Pharisaic literature from the reconstituted Jewish community after 70 C.E., but none from the early years of the first century.

[11]See Seán Freyne, *Galilee from Alexander the Great to Hadrian.*

the literature of the movement this "Teacher" is represented as a saint betrayed by a "Scoffer" or "father of lies" and persecuted by a "wicked priest".[12] The identity of the Teacher's opponents is also unknown. It may be that the "Scoffer" and the "wicked priest" are alternative designations for the same historical person. Geza Vermes has suggested that Jonathan, the Maccabean hero who became high priest in 152 B.C.E., fits the bill.[13] Jonathan lacked the credentials which those who fled to the Judean wilderness would have considered essential for the high priesthood; he was not a Zadokite, nor was he very interested in religious matters related to the temple. If this hypothesis is correct, the Teacher of Righteousness may have been a highstanding Zadokite priest who "filled in" during the interregnum in the high priesthood between 159-152 B.C.E., and who subsequently refused to serve under the "illegitimate" Jonathan.[14]

Whatever the exact historical circumstances may have been, the Qumran sectarians clearly perceived themselves as a "holy remnant" whose purity of life and fidelity to the Covenant outshone those "sons of darkness" who now controlled the Jerusalem temple and its worship. Their literature is rife with the desperate language of apocalypticism: The Teacher of Righteousness vs. the Wicked Priest; the sons of light vs. the sons of darkness; the holy congregation of the desert camps vs. the "company of Satan." The Essenes expected an eschatological war that would vindicate their beliefs, usher in a New Age, and crush their foes:

> This shall be a time of salvation for the people of God, an age of dominion for all the members of His company, and of everlasting destruction for all the company of Satan. . . . for the sons of darkness there shall be no escape. The seasons of righteousness shall

---

[12]See the Damascus Rule, 1; Commentary on Habbakuk, 1; translations in Geza Vermes, *The Dead Sea Scrolls in English,* (Baltimore: Penguin Books, 1962), pp. 97, 235.

[13]See *ibid.,* p. 63.

[14]See Freyne, *The World of the New Testament,* pp. 106-107.

shine over all the ends of the earth; they shall go on shining until all the seasons of darkness are consumed and, at the season appointed by God, His exalted greatness shall shine eternally to the peace, blessing, glory, joy, and long life of all the sons of light.[15]

Like the Pharisees, the Essenes understood themselves in relation to the temple; but whereas the former sought to extend the advantages of temple purity to all Jews in everyday life, the latter tried to create an "alternative temple-community" characterized by utter purity in a place (the desert camps) distant from the defiled precincts of Jerusalem. This creation of an "alternative world" is common among apocalyptic groups, especially after they have been excluded from an historical community.[16] Such a world permits the excluded group to regain, through apocalyptic speculation, power and control that have actually been lost. In effect, the Essenes compensated for their losses in the Jerusalem temple and priesthood by withdrawing to create a rival "temple" (the pure community at Qumran) in the desert wilderness. Ironically, this Essene "temple" suffered the same disaster that befell its rival in Jerusalem; the inhabitants of Qumran appear to have abandoned their settlement sometime after the failure of the First Revolt (66-70 C.E.).

THE ZEALOTS

If the Essenes patiently awaited an apocalyptic new age, the Zealots felt that waiting was a pipe dream. The new age demanded radical action, not patience; God's purposes for Israel could best be served by aggressive guerrilla fighting. These militant nationalists formed a kind of underground network of freedom-fighters in the years immediately prior

[15]The War Rule, 1; translation from Vermes, *The Dead Sea Scrolls in English*, p. 124.
[16]See Freyne, *The World of the New Testament*, pp. 116-117.

to the outbreak of the First Revolt in 66 C.E.[17] Convinced of the absolute sovereignty of God and of the need for Israel's political and religious independence, the Zealots may have emerged as a left wing within Pharisaism.[18] Like the Pharisees, they regarded the usurpation of the high priesthood by non-Zadokite priests as distasteful. And indeed, upon seizing control in Jerusalem in 67 C.E., they promoted as high priest a legitimate Zadokite who had been living in the countryside as a stonemason.[19]

But there is also a parallel between the Zealot freedom-fighters and the Qumran sectarians. Both groups were suspicious of the hellenized cities of the first century Palestine.[20] There is good reason to believe that the Zealots' chief support came from the countryside rather than from urban areas. More specifically, the earliest Zealot leaders seem to have come from Galilee. Acts 5:37 mentions "Judas the Galilean" who arose "in the days of the census" and attracted a band of followers. The allusion is probably to events that took place around the year 6 C.E., when a revolt broke out against the tax policies of the Roman-Herodian government. (We have already noted that oppressive taxation was one of the sources of social discontent in Palestine during the first century.) When the great rebellion began in 66 C.E., descendants of Judas (Judah) the Galilean were among its leaders. Menachem, who seized power in Jerusalem at the outset of this rebellion, was one of Judah's sons; Eleazar, a relative of Menachem and descendant of Judah, led the Jews' final stand against the Romans at Masada in 73 C.E.[21] These leaders represented the concerns of country people who were especially hard hit by taxation and indebtedness.

The Zealot movement, like many revolutionary groups

[17]See Keck, *The New Testament Experience of Faith*, p. 27.

[18]See Freyne, *The World of the New Testament*, pp. 118-122.

[19]See Joachim Jeremias, *Jerusalem in the Time of Jesus*, translated by F.H. and C.H. Cave from the third German edition (1962), with author's revisions to 1967, (Philadelphia: Fortress Press, 1975 paperback edition), pp. 192-193.

[20]See Theissen, *Sociology of Early Palestinian Christianity*, pp. 49, 50-51.

[21]See Jeremias, *Jerusalem in the Time of Jesus*, p. 277.

before and after, was split by factions. In the early stages of
the revolt of 66 C.E., leadership seems to have been in the
hands of the "moderates" who included Sadducees and
former high priests (e.g., Ananus) among their number. But
after Galilee was lost to the Romans, leadership passed to the
more extreme factions within the movement. The Sicarii, led
by the Menachem mentioned in the preceding paragraph,
took more aggressive measures against the ruling classes:
e.g., they burned the memoranda of debts kept in the temple
treasury. Other leaders, like Simeon ben Giora and his
followers, called for the emancipation of slaves and fought
relentlessly against the aristocratic rich. Some of the wealthy
themselves became radicalized and joined the more extreme
Zealot factions, e.g., Johanan ben Levi of Gischala, who had
been a prosperous exporter of oil and a leader in Galilee.[22]
There was also serious in-fighting among these resistance
groups. An example is provided by the activities of Matthias,
a member of the high priestly family of Boethus which had
achieved such prominence under King Herod. Matthias
helped promote the rise of Simeon ben Giora as leader of the
rebels in Jerusalem in order to undercut Johanan ben Levi of
Gischala. For his efforts, Matthias appears to have been
executed by order of Simeon ben Giora![23]

Even if the Zealots had not been split by factions and
in-fighting, it is doubtful whether they could have overcome
the military superiority of the Romans. After Jerusalem fell
in 70 C.E., a small band of freedom fighters held out on the
heights of Masada until 73 C.E., when they chose suicide over
surrender to the Roman legions. But the resistance movement did not die out completely; it surfaced once more in the
early second century C.E., when a Second Revolt was led by
bar Kochba (132-135). This rebellion brought even greater
catastrophe; Jerusalem was destroyed and replaced by a new
city (Aelia Capitolina), where Jews were forbidden to live
under penalty of death.[24]

[22]See Stern, "Aspects of Jewish Society," pp. 578-579.
[23]See *ibid.,* pp. 605-606.
[24]See Keck, *The New Testament Experience of Faith,* p. 26.

THE BAPTIST MOVEMENT

Among the renewal groups in first century Palestine were some which might be described as "prophetic and apocalyptic penitential" movements.[25] These combined the old and the new. On the one hand, they preached the need for conversion in a style reminiscent of the prophets of pre-exilic Israel; on the other, they were influenced by more recent apocalyptic speculation about the "End", a theme common in the intertestamental literature and in biblical works like the book of Daniel.

In his message and personal conduct John the Baptist appears to have emerged from such a penitential movement, with this difference: his style of preaching was more in line with the ancient Israelite prophets than with apocalypticists who considered themselves merely "interpreters" of the ancient prophets.[26] Although he probably was not associated with Qumran, John shows some affinities with Essene ideology: he is, for example, a desert figure who has disassociated himself from the temple and priesthood in Jerusalem. Ritual baths of both a purificatory and an initiatory sort were practiced at Qumran, and John is pictured in the New Testament as one who proclaims a "baptism of repentance".[27]

John's preaching, however, puts him at a distance from renewal movements such as the Essenes. His message was a frontal assault on three common Jewish expectations of his time:

1. The apocalyptic expectation that God's (and thus Israel's) foes would be destroyed in an "eschatological war", a theme that permeates the literature of the Dead Sea Scrolls;

2. The eschatological hope that Israel would ultimately triumph and achieve dominion over the world (another apocalyptic theme);

---

[25]See Edward Schillebeeckx, *Jesus.* An Experiment in Christology, translated by Hubert Hoskins, (New York: Seabury Press, 1979), pp. 116-126.

[26]See *ibid.*, pp. 119, 130.

[27]See Vermes, *The Dead Sea Scrolls in English,* p. 45; cf. Mk. 1:4.

3. The notion that reliance on the covenant with Abraham would guarantee salvation.

In the New Testament, John is seen as a violent debunker of all these expectations: God can raise children for Abraham from the stones (3); the axe is laid to the root of the trees (2); God's wrath is already on its way and will sift Israel (1) (see Mt 3:1-12). Allowance must be made, of course, for the synoptic writers' theological agendas in this portrait of John; still, there is good reason to believe that the main outlines of John's preaching are accurately reflected there.[28]

John thus appears as one who not only disassociated himself from Jerusalem and the temple (like the Essenes) but also from the common apocalyptic argot of his day (unlike the Essenes). Like the older Israelite prophets, he is intent on righteousness achieved through personal reform and repentance. John's vision of the future is grim: God's judgment is imminent—and it will be wrathful. One can escape God's coming condemnation of the unrighteous only by accepting the "baptism of repentance". In that sense, John's baptism is eschatologically definitive: it permanently affects one's relation to God in view of the imminent judgment that will burst upon the world in fire and wrath. John does not seem to have preached the coming of God's reign ("kingdom"); what is coming, according to him, is a drastic divine judgment which no one can escape.

The New Testament indicates that John's preaching had appeal and that he gathered disciples (Mt 11:2). Scholars like Raymond Brown have suggested that John's disciples survived the death of their leader; some of them may later have joined the Jesus movement and, later still, have become members of Christian churches (e.g., the Johannine community.)[29] One may even detect a rivalry between adherents of John the Baptist and followers of Jesus, another clue that a baptist renewal movement succeeded in gaining loyal disciples who continued their founder's work and message (see

---

[28]See Schillebeeckx, *Jesus,* pp. 127-28.
[29]See Raymond Brown, *The Community of the Beloved Disciple,* (New York: Paulish Press, 1979), pp. 26-31.

Acts 18:25; 19:1-7). John is revered among the Mandaeans, a still extant gnostic sect that originated in the Jordan region during the first or second century. This is still another clue that his personality and preaching influenced others for a considerable time after his death.

THE JESUS MOVEMENT

When Jesus of Nazareth began his ministry, therefore, Palestine was rife with renewal movements and powerful religious personalities. These latter included not only John the Baptist but also messianic figures like Menachem ben Hezekiah, leader of the revolt in 66 C.E.[30] One is tempted to theorize about Jesus' possible involvement with one or another of these movements, but hard evidence for a connection between him and groups like the Essenes or Zealots is lacking. More plausible is Edward Schillebeeckx's suggestion that Jesus found the Baptist's message personally convincing, accepted the baptism of repentance, but had a growing awareness of a prophetic mission different from John's.[31] This does not mean that Jesus was originally among the circle of John's disciples until a rift between the two leaders sent them on separate paths; it does mean, however, that Jesus chose not to pursue two major aspects of John's program—the ministry of baptizing and the message of impending wrathful judgment.

The various portraits of Jesus painted by the synoptic writers are obviously colored by the catechetical, polemic, liturgical and theological interests of later Christian generations. One must be extremely cautious, then in attempting to reconstruct the historical features of Jesus' own character and ministry. New Testament exegetes today do agree, however, about certain aspects of Jesus' career. He was, first, a wandering preacher/prophet whose central message was the

[30]See Jeremias, *Jerusalem in the Time of Jesus*, p. 277.
[31]See Schillebeeckx, *Jesus*, pp. 138-139.

"reign of God." In this we can detect resonances of the radically theocratic viewpoint common to many renewal movements in first century Palestine: God is the only ruler. But Jesus' understanding of God's rule differed appreciably from certain apocalyptic (Essene) and political (Zealot) ideologies. God's "rule" is neither a place, nor an object, nor the result of eschatological warfare ushered in by political woes and bleeding moons. As Jesus preached it, God's rule is a deed: the activity of God bursting into human life in unsuspected ways among apparently undeserving people. Through parables, subversive stories aimed at jolting the hearer into the sudden perception of God's activity as ruler, Jesus offered both a new vision of God and a new possibility for salvation. The God of Jesus is One beneficently intent on humanity, One whose own cause is nothing more or less than the *human* cause.[32] The future God has in store for the human world is blessedness, not condemnation and punishment.

What was distinctive about Jesus' ministry, then, was not his use of the symbol "rule (kingdom) of God"—it was a popular notion in Judaism—but his understanding of it and his way of preaching it in parable. Implied by this symbol was an eschatology that differed from both the Essenes, with their apocalyptic hopes for victory by the sons of light, and from John, with his vision of eschatological doom. The "future", for Jesus, is *potential*, not judgment. God manifests his rule, his being-God in the human world, in the most ordinary events. But these events reveal truths about God and us that unsettle, confound or even provoke anger. Thus, God's rule (his being-God in the world) is like leaven (messy, sour, fermenting) or like a mustard plant (hardly as impressive as a cedar of Lebanon) or like a woman who cleans her whole house to recover a small amount of money (persistent, but with little to show for it). These colorful comparisons are a bit homely when one contrasts them with fervent eschatological predictions like the one cited earlier from the Qumran War Rule. They are also humorous, an adjective one would

[32]See *ibid.,* pp. 140-154.

probably not use to characterize the message of John the Baptist.

Still, there are aspects of Jesus' career that resemble the renewal movements described earlier. Like John and the Essenes, Jesus comes across as one who disassociates himself from the temple, and there are strong reasons for believing that Jesus' trial and execution were linked with his reputation as an opponent of the temple's cult and priesthood. His Galilean origins may also shed light on this point; throughout the first century, as we have seen, Galilee regularly produced leaders who were put off by the wealthy conservatives who controlled the temple and administered its financial interests. Jesus also seems to have shared a suspicion of hellenized cities; he avoids Jerusalem until late in his career and favors the countryside or small villages as places for his preaching.[33] Later, of course, Christian missionaries made hellenized non-Palestinian urban centers their home, but Jesus himself shows little interest in taking his message to people outside Israel.

In some respects it is difficult to speak of a "movement" linked with Jesus. Becoming his disciple did not, apparently, involve joining a community, if by that word one means a distinctive sociological group with its own internal structure and cohesion.[34] Unlike John, Jesus practices no special ritual like baptism that would act as a badge distinguishing those who belong from those who don't. The very openness of the circle around Jesus marks it out sharply from more tightly-knit renewal groups like the Pharisees and the Essenes.[35] Nor does Jesus commission his followers to continue his role as prophet and teacher; the apostolic "commissioning scenes" in the synoptics and John reflect the situation of Christians after the events of Easter. Among Jesus' followers the only real "ministry" is *his*.[36] Even the "Twelve"—a term bristling

---

[33]See Theissen, *Sociology of Early Palestinian Christianity,* pp. 50-51.

[34]See James D.G. Dunn, *Unity and Diversity in the New Testament,* (Philadelphia: Westminster Press, 1977), p. 105.

[35]See *ibid.*

[36]See *Ibid.,* p. 106.

with difficulties, as we shall see later—appear to be a symbol of the "eschatological people of God"; they are certainly not, in Jesus' lifetime, a hierarchy whose special power and authority distinguish them from other disciples.[37]

The Jesus "movement" is thus a rather loosely organized circle of disciples similar, perhaps, to a rabbi and his "school" of pupils. We may legitimately wonder who might have been attracted to such a movement. Gerd Theissen has proposed that Jesus'ministry would have appealed primarily to persons whose socio-economic condition was changing, either "upward" or "downward", because of developments in Palestine.[38] These would have included members of the new upper class (nouveau riche), as well as representatives of the marginal middle class whose fortunes were subject to rapid change (e.g., farmers, fishermen, craftsmen). Like most of the other renewal groups, the Jesus movement probably made little impact, initially, on the poorest people, who had nothing to gain or lose.

Before leaving our brief discussion of the Jesus movement, a final point needs examination: as a call for renewal, what made this movement different? Earlier we observed that all the renewal groups showed signs of an "ethical radicalism", of the search for a fuller way to observe the Torah. All of them supported an "intensification of norms" that would lead to a more faithful interpretation of God's revelation and will for Israel, even as they differed about the mode by which these norms could best be fulfilled.[39] This common search for a "fuller observance" of the law was engendered, at least in part, by the profound crisis of identity experienced by Jews in first century Palestine. This crisis had its roots in a series of events that had befallen post-exilic Judaism: the pervasive influence of hellenism, disillusionment with the independent Hasmonean state, the Roman occupation of Palestine after 63 B.C.E. Conflicts arose at every level of human life:

---

[37]See *ibid.*, pp. 105-106.
[38]See Theissen, *Sociology of Early Palestinian Christianity, pp. 45-46.*
[39]*See ibid.*

economic, ecological, political, cultural.[40] Given such an atmosphere, it is fairly easy to see why a first century Jew would have been concerned about questions like these: What really makes me "Jewish"? Can I be a fully participating citizen of a hellenized world and still remain a devout Jew? How can I be faithful to the customs and traditions of my ancestors—Abraham, Isaac, Jacob, Moses and Aaron, the prophets? Can I discover what God's will is for the people of Israel?

All the renewal movements offered responses to these questions. The Essenes offered the "fuller observance" of a community that lived, as all Israel had once lived, in the desert. The Pharisees broadened the base of Jewish ethics by including *halakah* as an authoritative guide to devout living. Radical theocracy through political resistance was proposed by the Zealots, and John offered a baptism of repentance. The Jesus movement was unique, however, in that it pointed to the *radical impossibility of fulfilling such heightened norms*, even those of its own devising.[41] Not even pious, just and religious people can, in fact, fulfill all the norms all the time. Whether "radical" or "moderate", "liberal" or "conservative", all people are sinners and thus face the judgment of God who is the only ruler. But, Jesus insisted, God's judgment is compassionate forgiveness of sins and his "rule" means an inexhaustible source of blessing for humankind. In the Jesus movement, the "eschatological anxiety" produced by the imminent expectation of God's judgment was relaxed. The very impossibility of fulfilling all the religious norms all the time becomes, then, a powerful signal of God's grace.[42] "Ethical radicalism" is transformed into a radical proclamation of God's compassion that shines on both "the just and the unjust". Such a view makes any and all self-righteous judgments on "transgressors" impossible, since *everyone* is a transgressor, *all* are sinful.

[40]See *ibid.*, p. 95.
[41]See *ibid.*, p. 105.
[42]See *ibid.*

The Jesus movement seems to have understood that the crisis of Jewish identity could never be resolved through the heightening of norms for fuller observance of the Torah, for this leads, inevitably, to one group's trying to outbid and upstage the other. The solution can be found only through "a new relationship to all norms: putting trust and freedom from anxiety before demands of any kind."[43] This new relationship also provides a way of coping with the aggression against self and others which usually accompanies anxiety. In a word, the radical proclamation of God's grace (all are sinners and thus need compassion) became a model for self-acceptance as well.

The Jesus movement thus offered a way to cope with the anxiety and concomitant aggression produced by Israel's crisis of identity and by the competitiveness among the diverse renewal movements. It was, one might say, the "peace movement" among the conflicting groups in first century Palestine. This may help explain the ideology of "defenselessness" preserved in various sayings of the synoptic tradition: "Turn the other cheek"; "If someone asks for your coat, give him your cloak as well"; "Do good to those who persecute you". Such reactions to external aggressors would force them at least to "stop and reflect"—and this pause in hostilities could provide space for that "new relationship to all norms" that places trust and freedom ahead of anxiety.[44]

Jesus' own fate modelled this technique of dealing with anxiety and aggression. Quite simply, his mission failed. This failure did not happen merely at Jesus' trial and execution. As Edward Schillebeeckx has observed, the breaking point must be located earlier, "within the ministry of the historical Jesus".[45] Resistance against his manner of life and his message may have been aroused already in the period of his Galilean ministry. One gets this impression from reading Mark. The earlier chapters of the gospel are a success story; "great crowds" follow Jesus in Galilee and all are impressed

[43]See *ibid.,* p. 107.
[44]See *ibid.*
[45]See Schillebeeckx, *Jesus,* p. 294.

by his teaching (Mk 4:1; 5:20). But clouds begin gathering in Mark 7; the crowds diminish and conflict intensifies.[46] It may well have been rejection and failure in Galilee that led Jesus to decide on going to Jerusalem, where more decisive opposition was certain to be encountered. This act of "defenselessness" can be considered characteristic of the movement when faced with external hostility. It was an act calculated to break the cycle of aggression and counter-aggression and thus to open up the possibility of a non-violent, non-competitive relationship between "victim" and "oppressor". Jesus' failure, symbolized ultimately by the cross, became in fact a central theme of the later movement's preaching, as did the phrase "love your enemies".

THE TRUE ISRAEL

None of the renewal movements, including the one associated with Jesus, sought to create a "new religion". The principal question for all of them was "who is the true Israel?", i.e., "who best represents the authentic expression of Israel's ancestral faith?" Linked with this fundamental concern for identity were other issues: Whose interpretation of the Scriptures reflects God's will for Israel most accurately? How should a Jew respond to hellenism, to the Romans, to "outsiders"? How are Jews, both in Palestine and in the diaspora, related to the temple? What does the future hold for God's people?

Diverse answers to these questions generated conflict among the renewal movements—and sometimes, one suspects, *within* a single movement. An example of such internal conflict has already been noticed between moderates and radicals in the Zealot party. Similar dissension, as we shall see, troubled those men and women who saw in Jesus an example of that "fuller righteousness" promised to God's faithful ones. In death, Jesus himself became an object of

[46]See *ibid.*, p. 295.

conflicting interpretation. His dying became a final "prophetic sign", something left for *others* to interpret.[47]

II
The Christian Movement

CHRISTIAN SECTARIANS

Jewish persons who came to believe Jesus and his message did not constitute a new "religion"; they were rather sectarians within Judaism. As a sect, these "Christians" (a name given them in the hellenized, non-Palestinian city of Antioch) were a small group that claimed its understanding of Torah, the Scriptures, and God's purpose for Israel was the uniquely authentic one.[48] Sociologically, this is characteristic of sectarian movements: they do not challenge the entire system of the "parent" religion, but emphasize a point which, they claim, represents the truest form of that religion.[49] Christians claimed that the life and death of Jesus were an ultimate ("eschatological") disclosure of God's intentions for Israel. At his death, moreover, Jesus' work was unfinished: he would "come again" to complete his mission and bring the fulness of salvation to those who awaited him in hope. If Jesus had proclaimed the coming of God's rule, with its unfathomable blessings for Israel, Christians now proclaimed the ("second") coming of Jesus.

The death of Jesus had been, however, a nasty shock. How could one claim that a man whose mission failed, whose animus against the temple—God's dwelling—was well known, who was tried and executed as a criminal, represented God's intentions for Israel? One of the first tasks facing the Christian sectarians was to make sense of Jesus' death by showing a) that it was not contrary to the Scriptures, and b)

---

[47]See *ibid.,* p. 318-319.
[48]See Keck, *The New Testament Experience of Faith,* p. 13.
[49]See *ibid.*

that it fit God's plan for offering salvation to and through the Jews. This was hardly an easy assignment, especially since the Hebrew Scriptures said a man hanged on a tree is "accursed by God" (Deut 21:23). How, moreover, could one man's death usher in the New Age of God's blessings?

These questions were answered, eventually, in light of an experience which we now call "Easter". Actually, Easter is not "an" experience but, as we shall see, an ensemble of events that included the conversion of Jesus' disciples, God's act of vindicating Jesus by raising him from death, and an extraordinary release of spiritual power which awakened in the disciples an urgent sense of mission and witness. The Easter story is, above all, a story of conversion. The New Testament never attempts to describe the act by which God raised Jesus; it merely insists that this happened and offers the disciples' conversion as proof. To put it another way, the disciples do not believe because they inspect an empty tomb; rather, *they believe* and thus "know" and "understand" (="see") that the tomb is empty, that death had no ultimate power over Jesus, that Jesus has entered fully into life with God.[50]

The New Testament thus speaks of Easter through two kinds of story: those that involve "seeing the Lord" (resurrection appearance narratives) and those that involve events at Jesus' tomb. The former are probably earlier; Paul, for instance, alludes to appearance of the Risen One, but not to the tradition of the empty tomb (see 1 Cor 15:3-7). In any case, the disciples come to understand ("see") that the Jesus who truly died is truly alive and with God. This paradoxical conviction leads to conversion, to the knowledge that although they failed to understand him during his earthly career, their obtuseness and hard-heartedness have been forgiven. Conversion thus corresponds to the experience of forgiveness—and this experience comes about as the result of Jesus' gracious initiation: it is *He* who reveals himself, alive, to them.

Here we can see the Jesus movement's technique of dealing

[50]See Schillebeeckx, *Jesus*, pp. 320ff.

see
p 9v

with anxiety and aggression at work. The damning knowledge that even his disciples and close friends failed to understand and fled Jesus at his critical hour led to the
self-aggression of accusation, guilt and sorrow; but now,
aggression is transformed into self-acceptance. Failure
becomes forgiveness, initiated by Jesus; confusion becomes
conversion, proof that God has acted decisively and raised
Jesus from death. The disciples' conversion is at the heart of
Easter; it is what leads them to the conviction that "He is
Risen".

This conviction shaped the disciples' interpretation of
Jesus' death and its significance. The earliest interpretations,
of course, varied. Some converted believers regarded Jesus'
death as the martyrdom of God's final ("eschatological",
definitive) prophet; like all authentic interpreters of Torah,
Jesus had suffered because of his fidelity to God's revelation
to Israel.[51] Others grappled with the Torah's own seeming
condemnation of criminals who hang on a tree (Deut 21:23).
Perhaps Jesus was that righteous servant celebrated in the
poetry of Isaiah 53; if so, then Jesus' death might very well be
seen as a fulfillment of God's plan to bring salvation through
an innocent one who suffers. Still another interpretation
emphasized Jesus' death as one that brought atonement,
reconciliation between a loving God and a hostile people.[52]

Common to all these interpretations was the conviction
that God remained faithful: to Israel, to the covenant, to the
promises made to the "fathers". In the life and death of Jesus
God had acted to offer Israel a full and final "way" to
righteousness and salvation. This was good news, and it
presaged, according to the Christians, an end to the competitiveness, anxiety and doubt that afflicted the many renewal
movements in Palestine. The solution to Israel's crisis of
identity was to be found in this man Jesus, rejected, tried and
humiliated, executed as a criminal and now raised by God's
power. Jesus would come again soon, bringing God's final

---

[51]See *ibid.,* pp. 274-282.
[52]See *ibid.,* pp. 282-294.

assessment (judgment) of the world, its people and its history. One's destiny at this judgment thus depended upon how one reacted to Jesus and his prophetic message. Jesus *is* the "crisis" (Greek for "judgment" or decision), the fulcrum balancing Israel's destiny as a people of God's special choice and election.

CONFLICTS IN THE SECT

For the earliest disciples of the movement the choice was not between "being a Jew" and "being a Christian" but between accepting or rejecting Jesus. Synagogue and temple were still appropriate places of study and worship; God had not reneged on his promises, indeed he had brought them to an unexpected fulfillment. But these very convictions raised a question: Were God's actions in Jesus intended for everyone, including gentiles, or were they aimed exclusively at Jews? Israel was, after all, a "light to the nations" and first century apocalypticists speculated that God's blessed visitation of Israel would result in an eschatological extension of mercy to all peoples, with Jerusalem as the center of a worldwide theocracy in a New Age.

Even among Jews who did not believe in Jesus there was no universal agreement about the fate of the gentiles. It is thus not surprising that those Jews who experienced the conversion of Easter were similarly divided over the question. Within the first generation of believers, however, this matter came to a head. One can discern at least three different points of view in the New Testament literature, and each of them is associated with a prominent figure. First, there was James, the "brother of the Lord". We do not know exactly how and when James emerged as a leader of the Christian sectarians in Jerusalem, but it was probably not until at least a decade or so after Jesus' death (probably after 44 C.E.).[53] There was also Stephen, a leader of hellenized Jews whose thinking and style

[53]See Dunn, *Unity and Diversity in the New Testament*, pp. 108-109.

of life were drastically different from the more conservative outlook of James. It is quite conceivable that hellenized Jews had come to Jerusalem from the diaspora in search of that "fuller righteousness" promised by the renewal movements; they may have been disillusioned, upon their arrival, by what they saw in the temple and its aristocratic administrators. It is possible they were attracted to the Jesus movement by what they perceived as its opposition to temple religion. There was also, a bit later, Paul, a Jew born in a hellenized city, a Pharisee, and a sometime persecuter of the Christian sectarians. We cannot be sure how much contact Paul might have had with Jerusalem in the period immediately after his conversion. He tells us that he didn't go there until three years after his conversion (Gal 1:18)—and then not again until fourteen years later (Gal 2:1). Other New Testament sources indicate a closer relationship between Paul and Jerusalem. This has led some scholars to accuse Paul of "alibi reasoning" designed to downplay Jerusalem's influence on his early career as believer and missionary.[54]

Whatever the precise historical circumstances may have been, the differences between these three figures—James, Stephen, and Paul—reflect more fundamental divisions among the sectarians who believed in Jesus. The "gentile question" was the tip of an iceberg; the underlying conflicts were deeper. There was the old issue of hellenism, a point on which Jews were divided before and after the appearance of the Jesus movement. The differences between James and Stephen thus had roots in earlier "liberal" and "conservative" attitudes toward the acceptance of hellenistic ideas into Jewish life. A common belief in Jesus did not automatically relax tensions between Aramaic-speaking (James) and Greek-speaking (Stephen) Jews. Each had their own synagogues in Jerusalem, and each had a different attitude toward the relation between Judaism and hellenistic culture. The eventual expulsion of hellenized Jewish Christians from

[54]See Bengt Holmberg, *Paul and Power*, (Philadelphia: Fortress Press, 1978), pp. 16-17.

Jerusalem after Stephen's death may have been supported as much by Aramaic-speaking Jewish Christians as it was by Jews who had no connection with the Jesus sect.

The episode involving the party of James and the party of Stephen was thus entangled, it would appear, in cultural conflict between opponents of hellenism and other Jews who actively sympathized with or supported it. Racial conflict was another source of tension among the Christian sectarians. The question of whether to take the gospel to the gentiles was not merely one of strategy; involved in it was the more general problem of contact between Jews and non-Jews. Jesus was obviously a Jew and had pursued his mission among the "lost children of Israel". Did this mean that one must first become a Jew, accepting circumcision and the obligations of Torah, before one could become a Christian? Paul thought not; a pagan who was not racially Jewish and had never become a Jewish proselyte had no need to embrace Judaism in order to join the Christian movement (see Gal 2-3). But such freedom for former pagans was not, one gathers, the universally agreed-upon opinion.

This issue eventually became so sensitive that it required a meeting of Christian leaders in Jerusalem. Two reports of the meeting are found in the New Testament: Paul's, in Gal 2:1-10, and Luke's, in Acts 15:4-29. Paul's is the earlier report and possibly the more accurate one, though Paul was not above slanting the account to serve his own purposes. He and other delegates from the missionary center at Antioch (Barnabas and Titus) are described as standing up to the Jerusalem "pillars", a sarcastic reference to James, Cephas and John (Gal 2:9). It was agreed, Paul insists, that the mission to the Gentiles should go forward without any stipulations (Gal 2:10). In a word, Paul claims the Jerusalem meeting granted unqualified approval of his mission and methods among pagan converts to the Christian sect.[55] But it is reasonably clear even from Paul's own report that many Jewish Christians did not interpret the meeting in the same way he did.

[55]See *ibid.*, p. 21.

[handwritten margin note top right: Paul's apology for gospel to gentile]

They felt that Paul's so-called "gospel of freedom" omitted a vital requirement—the need to circumcise Gentile converts—and these "Judaizers", as Paul sardonically calls them, went to Galatia to explain that Paul had misrepresented the decisions reached at Jerusalem (see Gal 3; 5:7-12). The account in Acts 15:4-29, if it has any historical accuracy, also suggests that Paul's radical interpretation of the meeting differed from what had actually been discussed and decided.

[handwritten margin note left: Acts also trancend Paul, we contradies win?]

This feud was not, then, a politely academic difference of opinion. It had practical repercussions. Could, for example, a circumcised Jew and an uncircumcised Gentile who were both Christian sectarians sit down together and share a common meal? This very question of inter-racial association was raised by an incident in Antioch, where Christian Jews and Gentiles both lived. Cephas had apparently come to Antioch as a guest of Paul, Barnabas and others (Gal 2:11). At first, Cephas accepted the revolutionary compromise of eating with the Gentile converts who had received Paul's gospel of freedom. But after Jewish leaders from Jerusalem appeared on the scene, Cephas appears to have lost confidence and disassociated himself from meals with Gentile Christians (Gal 2:12-13). This infuriated Paul, who accused Cephas of buckling under pressure from Jewish Christians who represented James and the community at Jerusalem (Gal 2:14).

Paul's report of all this may not be trustworthy in every detail, but it is surely reliable evidence that inter-racial conflict was still a serious problem for the Christian movement in the 50's C.E. Eventually Antioch became the first successful inter-racial church, but this success was neither thorough nor immediate in the movement's first generation.[56] We must observe, then, that both cultural and racial conflicts caused divisions in the Christian sect. Hellenism and inter-racial relations were issues not fully resolved until well after the fall of Jerusalem in 70 C.E. Paul's conviction that Gentiles are completely free from circumcision and

[handwritten margin note left: yes]

[handwritten margin note left: From here to 104 based on KECK]

[56]See Keck, *The New Testament Experience of Faith*, p. 55.

Torah later became "standard policy", and this certainly helped the Christian sect to expand significantly in areas outside Palestine. It also helped promote the idea that Christianity is an independent "religion" accessible to all, rather than a sectarian movement within Judaism. Still, it was not until later in the first century that Christianity began to emerge as an independent religion with its own distinctive system of doctrine, cult, custom and organization.

Within the first two decades of the movement's existence, then, we can discern at least three different types of Christian sectarianism. There were those Jews like James whose devotion to Temple and Torah did not slacken at all after their conversion to the way of Jesus.[57] Others, hellenized Jews of the Stephenite sort, had quite possibly lost interest in the temple even before their conversion; they already represented a different kind of Judaism and were used to living more or less as Greeks.[58] These hellenized Jews, with their outright opposition to the temple, could only have been offensive to traditionalists like James. Then there was Paul, a maverick who must also have bewildered James and the Jewish Christian community in Jerusalem. Flamboyant and daring in his "gospel of freedom", Paul surely appeared to some as a betrayer of his own racial and religious roots. In sum, there is not the slightest evidence that the Christian movement was a coherent body of believers who lived amicably and practiced a mild form of socialism. Luke's idealized portrait in Acts 2:42-47 conflicts sharply with what we know about the serious bickering and infighting that erupted among the earliest believers in Jesus.[59]

THE CRISIS OF 70 C.E.

The tragedy that befell Jerusalem in 70 C.E. was a crisis not only for Jews but for Jewish Christians as well, at least for those who followed James's pattern of devotion to Temple and Torah. The question of Israel's liberation from Roman

[57]See *ibid.*, pp. 33-34.
[58]See *ibid.*, p. 33.
[59]See *ibid.*, pp. 45-47.

rule was, after all, a more pervasive contemporary issue than
were the interests of a small sectarian movement like the
Christian one. Faith in Jesus did not automatically free Jews
from concern about their homeland and its destiny. When the
First Revolt broke out in 66 C.E., Jewish Christians in
Palestine would have had tough decisions to make: should
they join the freedom fighters in resisting the Romans?;
should they emigrate and take up residence among Jews in
the diaspora?; should they cooperate with the Roman
authorities and hope for a peaceful solution to the conflict?;
does faith in Jesus provide any insight into the situation?

These questions must have vexed Jewish Christians, but
the New Testament says virtually nothing about the revolt or
its consequences. Scholars are divided over whether this
silence was deliberate or accidental; in any case, we find a very
little in the New Testament that reflects the turbulent goings-
on in Palestine during the 60's C.E. We have already examined the conditions that fostered the rebellion in our
discussion of the Zealot movement. Here we may simply
draw attention to a few of the factors that precipitated a
full-scale revolution.

During the 40's C.E., Roman control over Galilee and
Judaea was intensified. Galilee was placed directly under a
procurator in 44 C.E.; the Emperor Claudius outraged Jews
by appointing Tiberius Alexander, an apostate, as procurator of Judaea in 46. T. Alexander's successor Cumanus
(48-52) was particularly inept in dealing with the Jewish
situation. During his incumbency, Roman soldiers sparked
near-riots; one of them made an obscene gesture at pilgrims
in Jerusalem for Passover; another burned a copy of the
Torah.[60] The extensive powers of these procurators also
rankled Jewish nationalists. Jurisdiction over the collection
of taxes, over capital cases, and over the appointment of the
High priest were among a procurator's responsibilities; this
meant that the last vestiges of political and religious auto-
nomy for Palestinian Jews were disappearing. By 66 the

[60]See *ibid.*, p. 48.

situation had deteriorated badly. Civil war erupted in Jerusalem, the priests stopped offering the daily sacrifices on the emperor's behalf, and insurgents seized control of the fortress at Masada near the Dead Sea.[61]

How did Christians respond to this revolution? To answer this, we must note that some very practical issues were at stake. First, what should be done about taxes? Since they were a sign of submission to Roman authority, withholding them would be tantamount to linking up with the freedom fighters. Secondly, what about the temple? It was not only a national center of Jewish life, but the abiding symbol of God's presence to Israel as well. What would its destruction or defilement mean?

Leander Keck has suggested that traces of the Jewish Christian response to these questions may be detected in Mark's gospel, the earliest of the four. Mark 12:13-17 contains the famous story about the coin bearing Caesar's inscription and Jesus' reaction to it: "Give to Caesar what is Caesar's, but give to God what is God's" (Mk 12:17). It matters little whether or not Jesus actually said these words. As Mark tells it, we have a story which offers Christians practical advice: don't get too involved in the tax-controversy; let Caesar have his money and let God have what is "his" (viz., human hearts).[62] In effect, the story outlines a middle way between open rebellion and complete compliance: one may pay the tax while withholding internal allegiance from the emperor. Similarly, Mark 13, a text filled with apocalyptic language, may represent a Christian response to the temple. Here the advice appears to be: get out of town; the temple and the city are doomed; have nothing to do with the insurrection.[63] In all likelihood Mark's gospel was itself written shortly after the cataclysm of 70. If so, it may be seeking to justify what has already transpired: the choice, by at least some Jewish Christians, to flee Jerusalem and search for homes elsewhere.

[61]See *ibid.*, p. 49.
[62]See *ibid.*, p. 50.
[63]See *ibid.*, pp. 51-52.

Keck's reconstructions are certainly plausible, but their testimony is, as he notes, indirect. Our first-hand knowledge of what happened to Jewish Christians in Jerusalem during the rebellion is meager. Later reports indicate some of them fled to Pella, a city in the Decapolis region east of the Jordan. Jewish Christianity survived here and there, but its existence in Jerusalem was virtually obliterated by the events of 70 and by the subsequent revolt of 132-135 C.E. When the Jerusalem church was refounded in the second century, its composition was, ironically, Gentile.

Increasingly after 70 C.E., the Christian movement became identified with gentile cities and hellenized culture. Antioch, Corinth, Ephesus, Rome—all became centers where "house-churches" existed and all could claim that the Christian message had reached them sometime during the "first generation" (before 70). While diaspora Jews were surely among those who converted to the Christian way in these cities, they rather quickly became a minority in a Gentile "church".

WHAT KIND OF MOVEMENT?

The Jesus movement was, we have said, one of several renewal movements in first century Palestine. Gerd Theissen prefers to assign the phrase "Jesus movement" to the sect as it developed in Palestine and Syria between roughly 30 and 70 C.E.; after that, the "Christian movement" arises.[64] I have altered this distinction by identifying the Christian movement as the sect that emerged in the years after Jesus' death and the events of Easter, from roughly the mid-30's to the end of the first century, when the break between Judaism and Christianity had become inevitable and irreparable. In this latter sense, the "Christian movement" was a complex form of Jewish sectarianism which gradually developed into an independent religion. Here we need to specify more clearly

---

[64]See Theissen, *Sociology of Early Palestinian Christianity*, p. 1.

just what kind of movement the Christians constituted.

John G. Gager, in his book *Kingdom and Community* (1975), has presented an attractive argument for viewing early Christianity as a millenarian movement.[65] Working from research gathered by I.C. Jarvie, Kenelm Burridge and others, Gager lists four characteristic features of such movements: "the promise of heaven on earth—soon; the overthrow or reversal of the present social order; a terrific release of emotional energy; and a brief life span of the movement itself."[66] If the movement is to survive, elements of this primitive millenarian ideology must either be modified or eliminated. We can observe this happening among Christians of the first few decades. The earliest believers, we have seen, expected an imminent "parousia": Jesus, dead but raised by God's power, will come again soon to complete his work. But time was cruel to this expectation; the decades moved on, the early leaders and witnesses died—and still no sign of Jesus' coming. By the time Luke wrote, in the 80's or 90's, for example, Christians had revised their chronology. The church will be around awhile—and its very existence and expansion proclaim God's continuing fidelity to believers in Jesus. "Christianity survived," Gager writes, "but *not* as a millenarian cult".[67]

Although there are differences between the two, Gager's proposal meshes well with Gerd Theissen's study of early Palestinian Christianity.[68] Theissen has emphasized the social and economic conditions that nurtured the origins and initial success of the renewal movement associated with Jesus. Economic change was a particularly significant condition, and this fits in with Gager's assessment of millenarianism as a movement linked with the "disinherited".[69] The disinherited are those people in a society who are "relatively

[65]See John Gager, *Kingdom and Community. The Social World of Early Christianity*, (Prentice-Hall Studies in Religion Series; Englewood Cliffs, New Jersey: Prentice-Hall, Inc., 1975), pp. 20-65.

[66]See *ibid.*, p. 21.

[67]*Ibid.*

[68]See note 2, above for citation of Theissen's work.

[69]See Gager, *Kingdom and Community*, pp. 22-28.

deprived"—not necessarily the destitute, but those excluded from the principal channels of social power.[70] Attracted to millenarian movements are those who feel they have been unjustly shunned by the powerful (i.e., by those who control money, social standing, or the "media of redemption" — e.g. the priestly aristocracy of the Jerusalem temple). In such a movement, the charismatic prophet plays a key role; "he combines criticism of the old with a vision of the new".[71]

Understanding early Christianity as a millenarian movement offers two advantages: it helps clarify the kind of "prophet Jesus was, and it shows how early Christians were related to apocalyptic Judaism, with its concern for the "New Age" ("heaven on earth") and for the eschatological vindication of Israel (reversal or overthrow of the present social order). As a millenarian prophet Jesus offered a new vision of "redemptive media": the "rule of God" is not bound to the temple and its priestly aristocracy; it bursts in upon human life anywhere, anytime, provided people sincerely repent and admit they are sinners.[72] This would have been welcome news to the relatively deprived of Palestine, for it meant that their relation to God did not need the temple's mediation. And if this is true, then the New Age has dawned in Jesus' prophetic ministry, now vindicated by God's raising him from death. One can begin to understand why the earliest believers looked toward Jesus' coming with such apocalyptic fervor: it would bring the full daylight of an Age in which their own deprivation and powerlessness would be transformed. At Jesus' coming, the old order will vanish, the saints will reign, and God's blessings will flow in every direction.

The earliest Christians were more interested in the immediate future (the parousia) than in the immediate past (Jesus' death and resurrection). They were relatively unconcerned, too, about long-range provisions for leadership and ministry.[73] This latter is another typical feature of millenarianism,

---

[70]See *ibid.*, pp. 25-28.
[71]See *ibid.*, p. 29.
[72]See *ibid.*, pp. 30-31.
[73]See *ibid.*, p. 33.

along with opposition to hierarchical relationships that distinguish between rulers and subjects.[74] At this point, however, we come to the threshold of another topic: leadership and mutual service among Christians.

III
Ministry Among Christians

To accept John Gager's contention that millenarian movements are relatively unconcerned about structures of leadership and service is not to deny that authoritative teachers and guides emerged among Christians. It is clear that such persons did arise: Paul is one of them, James another, and Stephen, leader of hellenized Jewish Christians, a third. There were others too: men like Cephas, Barnabas, John; and women like Prisca (or Priscilla, Rom 16:3; Acts 18:18), Phoebe (Rom 16:1), Junias (Rom 16:7). I am purposely using general terms like "leadership" and "service" here because, as we shall see, it is difficult to speak of permanent "offices" or "ordained" personnel in the early New Testament period. There were, nevertheless, persons in the earliest Christian communities who possessed "power" and "authority", provided we understand these terms functionally. Bengt Holmberg has shown that patterns of power existed in the primitive churches, though these were often informal and implicit.[75] Defining "power" as a person's ability to "induce or influence another . . . . to carry out his directives", Holmberg notes that a community may manifest rather explicit patterns of superiority and subordination without structuring these into formal offices or organizations.[76] Less explicit patterns are also possible: there are those whose "authoritative words" command respect or obedience, and others whose appeals for

[74]*Ibid.*
[75]See Holmberg, *Paul and Power*, pp. 9-14.
[76]See *ibid.*, pp. 9-10.

money or support are generally heeded. These latter are examples of "power" as well.[77]

In assessing leadership and ministry in the New Testament period, then, we must take care not to assume that officers and organized ministries exist where, in fact, there are none. We cannot assume, for example, that the "overseers" whom Paul greets in Philippians 1:1 are "bishops" (*episkopoi*) of the sort we encounter in the early second-century letters of Ignatius of Antioch. Nor can we identify the "helpers" (*diakonoi*) mentioned in the same passage as "deacons" like those whose ordination is described in the third-century *Apostolic Tradition* of Hippolytus. Nor, finally, can we assume that Jesus himself selected certain disciples, ordained them to the apostleship (or priesthood/episcopacy), and commissioned them to continue these offices.

One of the astonishing things about the New Testament, indeed, is its utter avoidance of priestly language to describe ministry among Christians. Nowhere are Christian leaders or ministers called "priest", nor are such persons compared to the Israelite priesthood which we studied in Chapter One. The Letter to the Hebrews speaks of Jesus as "high priest" (Heb 4:14) precisely in order to show that among Christians priestly mediation is no longer needed: Jesus has done it all, has put an end to priesthood by offering his own blood as an all-sufficient sacrifice. We cannot legitimately speak of a "priesthood" in the new Testament sources, except in the sense that the whole Christian people constitute a "royal priesthood" (1 Pet 2:9), called to declare God's wonderful deeds.

There is, then, an enormous discontinuity between the Israelite priesthood, as it had evolved by the first century C.E., and the Christian leaders, workers and ministers whom we encounter on the pages of the New Testament. This discontinuity must be borne in mind whenever we discuss the influence of Jewish institutions on Christian life in the early period. For some early Christians, like James and his party,

---

[77]See *ibid.*, pp. 11-12.

the temple and its priesthood continued to be taken for granted as the authentic way to worship the God of Israel and of Jesus. For others, like the hellenized Jews of Stephen's party, the temple and priesthood were either irrelevant or superseded. As we have already noted, attitudes toward temple religion varied considerably among the earliest adherents of the Jesus movement.

Caution is required, then, in discussing "Christian ministry" in the New Testament. There is no single "theology" or structure of leadership in the early communities. Paul's understanding of "apostleship" differs from what we find in Luke/Acts; the Pastoral Letters (1, 2 Tim, Titus) differ from what we find in Paul; and the Johannine community seems to have rejected the notion of authoritative "teachers" altogether. And although a "priesthood of Jesus" is recognized by the Letter to the Hebrews, it is vastly different from the cultic functionaries we meet at the end of the Second Temple period in Jerusalem. In the early New Testament literature we are better advised to speak of "deeds of service" rather than "ministerial offices"; of "persons performing acts of leadership" rather than organized structures. This is not to deny that power and authority, as analyzed by Holmberg, existed among early Christians; it is merely to note that these had not yet fully crystallized around offices and office- ⋆ holders.

WANDERING CHARISMATICS IN PALESTINE

The Jesus movement was begun by a Jew, for Jews, and among Jews, and Jesus himself spent most of his career in and around the small towns of Galilee. Shortly after Jesus' death, however, *Jerusalem* appears to be the center of the movement—at least this is what Luke would have us believe. According to Acts, the Eleven took charge of things there immediately after Jesus' ascension: they elected a replacement for Judas, experienced Pentecost, and began preaching (Acts 1:12—2:47). Luke thus points to Jerusalem as

DEVELOPMENT
⋆ But this is exactly the way an organization develops over time! or is this an artistic device
see p 115 also

mother of the Christian movement, the center from which all subsequent activity, including missionary work, proceeded. As the mother community, Luke implies, Jerusalem enjoyed a certain authority over all other centers—like Antioch, e.g., where Paul and Barnabas were active. Jerusalem's leaders— the "twelve" and later James, the brother of the Lord (Acts 15)—are likewise seen by Luke as possessing a power of direction over others, a point hotly contested by Paul's earlier appraisal of the situation (see Gal 2:1-10).

Luke's version of Jerusalem's authoritative role in the early Christian movement is not wholly fanciful, despite Paul's argument that his apostleship needed no legitimation from the "pillars" of that city. Jerusalem does seem to have enjoyed a privileged status as "the source and centre, not only of the Palestine Jewish Christian church but of *all* churches."[78] Still, there are problems with Luke's version of things. What happened to the Twelve, for instance? They seem to fade from the scene rather quickly, though Peter's activities are described in some detail. By Acts 15, the Christians in Jerusalem are led by James, the "brother of the Lord", who was not one of the Twelve. Luke's intentions are rather obvious: it all began in Jerusalem; the original leaders were the Twelve, companions of Jesus in his ministry and witnesses to his resurrection; James is a later leader, assisted by "apostles and elders" (Acts 15). In this way Luke legitimates Jerusalem's status as "mother of all the churches," even though by the time he wrote Jerusalem had been devastated by the Romans and its Christian community was virtually extinct.

One can accept Luke's conviction about the early importance of Jerusalem without admitting that his report is accurate in every detail. Particularly intriguing, in addition to the "disappearance" of the Twelve in Luke's account, is the question of Galilee. It was certainly the principal scene of Jesus' activities, and in Matthew, Mark and John, it is important as a place where the Risen One manifests himself to the disciples (Mt 28:16-20; Mk 16:7; Jn 21). But Luke omits these appearances in Galilee (Lk 24); for him, all the Easter

[78]See *ibid.*, p. 56.

events are clustered in and around Jerusalem. Luke's handling of the appearance stories thus matches his report in
Acts: everything begins in Jerusalem, where the Risen One
reveals himself (Lk 24:13-43), commissions the apostles
(24:44-47), and instructs them to remain in the city until they
are "clothed with power" at Pentecost (24:49). Acts then
picks up the story, with the apostles still in Jerusalem taking
care of business and receiving the Spirit (Acts 1-2). Galilee is
simply the place where Jesus had been earlier in his ministry,
but it has no importance for Luke in the situation after
Easter.

Neither Luke nor the other evangelists, of course, provide
us with the earliest example of the tradition that the risen
Jesus appeared to his followers; that is found in 1 Cor 15:3-7.
What is common to all these, however, is that they function as
"church-founding" stories which link Jesus with the community after Easter and with "apostles" who are "commissioned" to preach and witness.[79] Paul thus defends his own
work as apostle by connecting it with an appearance of the
Risen Jesus (1 Cor 15:8-11; Gal 1:16). Luke legitimates the
centrality of Jerusalem by locating all the appearances there;
he also implicitly downgrades Paul's experience, which he
records in Acts 9:3-6, since Paul was not among the "originals"
to whom Jesus appeared in Jerusalem. And Mark alludes
only to the link between the Risen Jesus and Galilee, perhaps
in order to legitimate the mission to the Gentiles. Several New
Testament writers thus use the same tradition—Easter
appearances—to support different connections between
Jesus, Christians and apostolic mission.

For our purposes, the importance of all this lies in its
diversified portrayal of early Christianity. Luke seems deliberately to have suppressed the Galilean appearances because
they did not fit his program.[80] If that is so, there may well have
been Christians in other parts of Palestine who did not

[79]See Reginald Fuller, *The Formation of the Resurrection Narratives*, (New
York: Macmillan, 1971), pp. 35-49.
[80]See Willi Marxsen, *The Resurrection of Jesus of Nazareth*, translated by
Margaret Kohl, (Philadelphia: Fortress Press, 1970, paperback edition), pp. 48-54.

consider themselves especially indebted to a "mother-church" or to an authoritative "college of apostles" at Jerusalem. The Easter stories which speak of Jesus' appearing in Galilee (e.g., Mt 28:16ff.) may thus point to traditions of church-founding that are independent of the Jerusalem-centered ideology emphasized by Luke.

All this becomes more plausible when we consider the sociology of early Palestinian Christianity. As Gerd Theissen has observed, the "movement" that Jesus called into being was not a well-organized body of co-workers hierarchically deputized to preach, but rather a loosely-knit band of wandering charismatics.[81] There is no reason to assume that these charismatics were all from Jerusalem or that they first encountered Jesus or "Jesus-sympathizers" there. As itinerant preachers they may have contributed decisively to the synoptic tradition of Jesus' "sayings" and may in fact have been "the first early Christian authorities".[82] Gerd Theissen believes the wandering charismatics were responsible for transmitting the earlier ethical norms for discipleship reflected in the synoptics. (Theissen, 1978; 10-14). These include "homelessness" (cf. Mk 1:16, 10:28ff; Mt 8:20), "lack of family" (cf. Lk 14:26), "lack of possessions" (cf. Mk 10:25), and "lack of protection" (Mt. 5:38f.). All four of these conditions for discipleship reflect the sociological situation of vagabonds in first century Palestine and Syria, for these wandering preachers would have been outsiders living on the margins of society. For them, the ordinary social patterns of security—property, domicile, kinship, self-defense against aggression—appear to have been meaningless, given the urgency of that "rule of God" announced by Jesus. This may help explain why the synoptics "remember" Jesus as having said things like:

"The Son of Man has nowhere to lay his head" (Mt 8:20);
"Leave the dead to bury the dead!" (Mt 8:22);
"It is easier for a camel to pass through a needle's eye,

[81]See Theissen, *Sociology of Early Palestinian Christianity*, p. 8.
[82]See *ibid.*, p. 10.

than for a rich man to enter the kingdom of God" (Mk 10:25);
"Offer no resistance to injury" (Mt 5:39).

These wandering preachers were not missionary "church founders" in the way that Paul was, nor were they community leaders of the more settled sort whom we meet in documents like 1 and 2 Timothy. Their power came from authoritative words spoken in Jesus' name under the impulse of the Spirit; in this they resembled the Christian prophets whom Paul recognizes, for example, in 1 Cor 12:28. In churches of the Pauline mission such prophets seem to have formed a distinctive group within the larger body of believers, but more about this will be said later in the chapter. For now, it is enough to note that these early itinerants were an unorganized body of preachers living a harsh and free existence "without homes and without protection, travelling through the country with no possessions and no occupation."[83]

For a livelihood and for attention to their message, these roving charismatics probably relied on "local sympathizers"—families or family members who may later have formed the nuclei of local "communities" of Christian sectarians.[84] Some of these sympathizers may have been attracted to the Jesus movement at an early stage: e.g., Martha, Mary and Lazarus; Simon the leper; groups of women who seem to have been among the earliest and closest of Jesus' disciples. As time went on the "ethical radicalism" of the wandering charismatics—homelessness, lack of family, lack of possessions, lack of protection—was tempered by the more settled conditions that obtained among the sympathizers. The local Palestinian communities were thus less radical than the charismatic missionaries.[85] They were willing to accept traditional norms that regulated religious behavior: e.g., rules about fasting and prayer; the continuing legitimacy of the temple and its priesthood; the scribes' authoritative

[83]See *ibid.*, p. 13.
[84]See *ibid.*, p. 17.
[85]See *ibid.*, p. 18.

teaching; the positive value of marriage and family.[86] It was among these more settled groups of sympathizers, too, that procedures for admitting or rejecting members—e.g., through the practice of baptism—would have been formulated.[87]

THE JERUSALEM CHURCH

Although it seems likely that local clusters of Christian sympathizers sprang up in several different regions of Palestine, the only community that gained much prominence was Jerusalem.[88] Determining precisely who were "ministers" in the early Jerusalem church is, however, no simple task. Luke's view, as we have already noticed, was that the "Twelve" (apostles) were from the beginning the ultimate authorities in Jerusalem, overseeing its life and mission.[89] Later, the "Twelve" were given "helpers" (the so-called "deacons" of Acts 6) who took charge of tasks like the distribution of food to needy persons (the widows). Still later, "elders" (greek, *presbyteroi*) assisted the apostles in their ministry (Acts 11:30). Luke thus traces a portrait of ministers in Jerusalem which fits the "classic" model: apostles (succeeded later by "overseers" or "bishops"); deacons (the "Seven" of Acts 6); and elders.[90]

Even if one grants, with Bengt Holmberg, that the Jerusalem church and its leadership were central in the evolution of early Christianity, there are still historical riddles to be untangled. Luke's neat report about the community in Jerusalem faces at least three problems.[91] First, it is not at all clear that the earliest "apostles" are to be automatically identified with the "Twelve". One gathers from the primitive tradition

[86]See *ibid.*, pp. 18-19.
[87]See *ibid.*, p. 21.
[88]See *ibid.*, p. 17.
[89]See Dunn, *Unity and Diversity in the New Testament*, p. 106.
[90]See *ibid.*, p. 107.
[91]See *ibid.*, pp. 107-108.

cited by Paul in 1 Cor 15:3-7, that "apostle" was a broad category which included men and women whom Luke would have excluded from his list. Secondly, the "Seven" mentioned in Acts 6 were hardly "deacons" in the later ecclesiastical sense of that term; they were Greek-speaking, hellenized Jews who had probably come into sharp conflict with the Aramaic-speaking Jewish community in Jerusalem over such questions as the continued legitimacy of the temple and its worship. As Leander Keck has observed, Stephen is presented as an evangelist and missionary in his own right, rather than as a mere "table-waiter"; he probably acted as leader of a type of Christianity that was emerging among hellenized Jews.[92] Finally, though "elders" may later have enjoyed prominence in the Jerusalem church, it is not clear— even in Acts—exactly when and how their leadership emerged.[93]

Luke's version of the Jerusalem church thus raises as many questions as it resolves. James D.G. Dunn has proposed that at its earliest stage, ministry among believers in Jerusalem was probably "more spontaneous and charismatic in nature" than Luke's contrived portrait suggests.[94] Even in Acts, the "elders" do not appear immediately—a hint that their status was recognized only later. The sudden disappearance of the "Twelve" has already been noted; only two or three of them gain any later notoriety (Peter, James, John).[95] Dunn argues that it probably took a decade or better before leadership and authority in Jerusalem "stabilized around the figure of James, the brother of the Lord and not an apostle."[96] This James may have been the one responsible for promoting the collegiate structure of authoritative "elders" in Jerusalem.

If Dunn's proposals are accurate, one may discern an evolution of leadership in Jerusalem in three stages: 1) a primitive charismatic stage in which the power of authorita-

[92]See Keck, *The New Testament Experience of Faith*, p. 33.
[93]See Dunn, *Unity and Diversity in the New Testament*, pp. 107-108.
[94]See *ibid.*, p. 108.
[95]See *ibid.*, pp. 108-109.
[96]See *ibid.*, p. 109.

tive teaching is diffused among many men and women who
speak prophetically in the name of Jesus; 2) a second stage
(after about 44 C.E.), in which James, the brother of the
Lord, emerges as the chief spokesperson among Aramaic-
speaking Jewish Christians in Jerusalem; and 3) a third
stage in which "elders" exercise a power of deliberation and
decision-making together with James and the "apostles"
(see Acts 15). That this evolution of ministry and leadership
was not smooth is indicated by the "power-struggle" that
developed between the party of James (Aramaic-speaking)
and the party of Stephen (Greek-speaking). Eventually, the
Stephenites lost ground, fled Jerusalem, and took the Christian message to Samaria (Acts 8:4-25), to hellenized Jews
living outside Palestine (Acts 11:19), and to Greek pagans in
Antioch (Acts 11:20).[97]
    The struggle between Aramaic-and Greek-speaking Jew-
ish Christians suggests that these early "missionaries" to
Samaria and Antioch were not "sponsored" by Jerusalem
but were escaping from what had become an intolerable
situation for them there. This would conflict with Luke's
vision that *all* Christian missionary activity begins in Jerusalem under the sponsorship of the apostles who guide and
direct the infant church. It also implies that Jerusalem's
authority, however prominent, was not universally recognized in the early decades of the Christian movement.

THE TWELVE : APOSTOLIC SUCCESSION

    The role of the Jerusalem church is related to another
sticky question in the evolution of ministry among Christians: the meaning and significance of the "Twelve." Among
Roman Catholics, the Lukan version of the Twelve has
served as the basis for an understanding of both apostolic
ministry and episcopal office. Called and commissioned by
Jesus, "ordained" by him at the Last Supper, the Twelve are

[97]See Keck, *The New Testament Experience of Faith*, p. 32.

perceived as a divinely established college of apostles whose successors are the bishops. Even the documents of the II Vatican Council assume that this view is the correct one: "The order of bishops is the successor to the college of the apostles in their role as teachers and pastors, and in it the apostolic college is perpetuated."[98] That the apostles referred to here are the "Twelve" is clear from the Council's scriptural allusions: Mk 3:13-19; Mt 10:1-42; Lk 6:13.[99] The Council assumes, in short, that the "college of apostles" and the "twelve" companions called by Jesus are substantially the same thing.

New Testament exegetes note, however, that in the earliest traditions about the Twelve no such assumption is made (see, e.g., 1 Cor 15:5 and 7, where a distinction between "The Twelve" and "apostles" is implied). Originally, the term "apostle" described a function rather than an office, nor was that function limited to the Twelve.[100] In Acts 14:4, for instance, Paul and Barnabas are "apostles"—an indication that even Luke's understandng of apostleship was not entirely consistent. Moreover, by the time most of the New Testament literature was written, the Twelve already appear to belong to the past; they are seen as contemporary with Jesus' historical career and with the very early stages of the Christian movement.[101] Their function, as companions of Jesus' ministry, is generally symbolic and eschatological: they point to that "rule of God" in which Jesus' disciples will exercise power and authority. It is also implied, in Acts, that the Twelve had an historical ministry directed toward

---

[98]Dogmatic Constitution on the Church, (*Lumen Gentium*), no. 22; English translation in Austin Flannery, ed., *Vatican Council II*. The Conciliar and Post-Conciliar Documents, (Collegeville, Minnesota: The Liturgical Press, 1975), p. 375.

[99]Dogmatic Constitution on the Church, no. 19; English translation in Flannery, *Vatican Council II*, p. 370.

[100]See Elisabeth Schussler Fiorenza, "The Twelve," in Leonard and Arlene Swidler, eds., *Women Priests. A Catholic Commentary on the Vatican Declaration*, (New York: Paulist Press, 1977), p. 115.

[101]See *ibid.*, p. 120.

Israel.[102] Nowhere in the New Testament are the Twelve understood as having successors.[103]

To say this is not to deny the possibility that a New Testament writer like Luke saw some connection between later Christian ministry and the Twelve. Thomas P. Rausch, for example, has argued that in Luke's narrative of the Last Supper a deliberate effort has been made to link eucharist, church order and ministry, and the Twelve who are with Jesus at the meal and receive the command to "repeat" his actions. The structure of Lk 22:15-34 lends plausibility to Rausch's interpretations:

Institution account:	22:15-20
Betrayal (Judas):	22:21-23
Who is greatest?	22:24-32
Betrayal (Peter):	22:33-34

As Rausch notes, Luke has sandwiched a tradition about church order and ministry ("who is greatest?", Lk 22:24-32) between the references to Judas' betrayal and Peter's denial of Jesus.[104] The implication is that Christian ministers, like the Twelve, must do as Jesus did: lead by serving (cf. Lk 22:26-27). Nor is that all. Rausch notes that Jesus' command to "repeat" (Greek, *poiēte*) his eucharistic actions (Lk 22:19) is a form of the same word which the Septuagint used for the appointment of priests in Israel—and that this word appears in Mark's story of Jesus' calling the Twelve (Mk 3:14). One might conclude, then, that there is a linkage established between the vocation of the Twelve, their being commanded to repeat Jesus' eucharistic action, and the implied instruction that later ministers should continue doing what the Twelve did (Lk 22:24-32).

Such an interpretation, though plausible, is not conclu-

---

[102]*Ibid.*

[103]See *ibid.*, p. 119; cf. Raymond Brown, *Priest and Bishop,* (New York: Paulist press, 1970), pp. 51-59.

[104]See Thomas Rausch, "Ordination and the Ministry Willed by Jesus," in Leonard and Arlene Swidler, eds., *Women Priests*, pp. 124-125.

sive. For one thing, the Lukan linkage between the Twelve, the eucharist, and church ministers is not found in the other synoptics or in John (see Mt 26:20-35; Mk 14:17-31; Jn 13-17). Further, even in Luke's work the Twelve have no obvious or visible successors, and one may thus wonder how they passed along to later ministers the "command" to "repeat" Jesus' eucharistic words and deeds. One might argue hypothetically that some form of authoritative appointment ("ordination") linked the Twelve with later Christian leaders, but none of the New Testament writings picture the Twelve directly commissioning others to continue their work.[105]

The Lukan view of the Twelve does not, then, portray them as early "bishops" (heads of local churches), nor does it regard them as "sacramental practitioners" responsible for activities like baptism, eucharist, "ordination" or reconciliation.[106] Raymond Brown suggests that in Luke's portrait the Twelve emerge as a kind of "Council" which convenes Christians whenever decisions must be made that affect the destiny of the church as a whole.[107] This seems to be their role in passages like Acts 6 (the controversy over the Hellenists) and Acts 15 (the "Jerusalem Council"). There is possible a parallelism, Brown notes, between this Lukan "Council" of the Twelve (apostles) and the permanent "Community Council" which served as a higher authority within the general assembly "Session of the Many" of sectarians at Qumran.[108] Limited to twelve men and three priests, the Qumran Community Council was composed of members "who had undergone the training and initiation necessary to qualify them for the highest rank in the sect's hierarchy."[109] The requirements

---

[105]A possible exception occurs in Acts 6:1-6, though in this passage it is not clear who lays hands on the "Seven" (The Twelve—or the entire community?). See Brown, *Priest and Bishop,* p. 55. For another interpretation of the passage in Acts see Joseph Lienhard, "Acts 6:106: A Redactional View," *Catholic Biblical Quarterly* 37 (1975), 228-236.

[106]See Brown, *Priest and Bishop,* pp. 52-55.

[107]See *ibid.,* p. 58.

[108]See *ibid.,* pp. 58-59.

[109]See Vermes, *The Dead Sea Scrolls in English,* p. 27; cf. the Community Rule, VIII (Vermes, p. 85).

for membership on the Council were rather stringent: "When they have been confirmed for two years in perfection of way by the authority of the Community, they shall be set apart as holy within the Council of the men of the Community...."[110] Although parallelisms like this one cannot be pressed too far, Brown's suggestion is illuminating. Just as the members of the Qumran Council are "perfectly versed in all that is revealed of the Law",[111] so the Lukan Twelve are privileged witnesses of Jesus' ministry and resurrection (cf. Acts 1:21-22). Similarly, the man admitted to the Qumran Council is obliged to "offer his counsel and judgment to the Community"[112]—functions parallel to those of the apostles in Acts 6 and 15. Finally, it is interesting that in Acts 6:4, Luke represents the apostles as seeking helpers so that the former can "concentrate on prayer and the ministry of the word." The Qumran Community Rule indicates that those who belong to the higher Council are devoted to study and contemplation of the Scriptures.[113]

That the Christian sect of Jews in Jerusalem might have been influenced by the authoritative structures of other renewal movements like Qumran is certainly plausible.[114] As we have seen earlier in this chapter, all such movements were engaged in a common search for greater fidelity to their ancestral religion, for a fuller righteousness rooted in the Scriptures. Luke's portrait of the Twelve thus immortalizes the symbolic heroes of a movement which hoped to renew Israel from within; at the same time it may give us a fairly accurate report about how these Twelve functioned as a "council" of sages who had been companions of Jesus in his earthly career. This would not mean that the Twelve were a "hierarchy" commissioned by Jesus during his historical ministry. As James D.G. Dunn remarks, "there is no hint

---

[110]Community Rule, VIII; translation in Vermes, *The Dead Sea Scrolls in English*, p. 85.
[111]Community Rule, VI; translation in Vermes, p. 85.
[112]See Vermes, *The Dead Sea Scrolls in English*, p. 27.
[113]*Ibid.*
[114]See Brown, *Priest and Bishop*, p. 59.

whatsoever of them playing 'priest' to the other disciples' 'laity'."[115] Like other believers, the Twelve were first and foremost *disciples* of Jesus. Their stature—both as historical figures and as immortalized heroes—derived from their relation to Jesus as his "followers" rather than as his deputies or vicars.

THE PAULINE CHURCHES

The earliest literature of the New Testament is Paul's letters. Written between 50 and 60 C.E., they provide invaluable information about the Christian movement as it spread into the Gentile world.[116] Although we commonly think of Paul as the "first Christian missionary", this is not an entirely accurate perception. First, Paul was a *Jewish* missionary before he was a Christian one;[117] and secondly, there were other Christian preachers whose work pre-dated that of Paul. We have already encountered some of these latter: the wandering charismatics in Palestine; the hellenistic Jewish Christians linked with Stephen's party. Philip, one of the "Seven" (Acts 6:5), an "evangelist" whose daughters were prophets (Acts 21:8), may have been responsible for organizing the hellenistic refugees' mission to Samaria.[118] Other hellenists appear to have gone as far as Phoenicia, Cyprus and Antioch.[119]

Unquestionably, then, there had been Christians working in the gentile mission field prior to Paul's conversion, and it is quite likely that these pre-Pauline missionaries were hellenists who had fled Jerusalem following Stephen's execution.

[115]See Dunn, *Unity and Diversity in the New Testament,* p. 106.

[116]For a scholarly assessment of the Pauline letters, see Leander Keck, *Paul and His Letters,* (Proclamation Commentaries; Philadelphia: Fortress Press, 1979).

[117]See Norman Perrin, *The New Testament: An Introduction,* (New York: Harcourt, Brace, Jovanovich, 1974), pp. 90-93.

[118]See Acts 8:5, 12, 26-40; cf. Edward Schillebeeckx, *Ministry. Leadership in the Community of Jesus Christ,* translated by John Bowden, (New York: Crossroad Publishing Company, 1981), p. 144, note 5.

[119]See Acts 11:19; cf. Keck, *The New Testament Experience of Faith,* p. 55.

The church at Antioch, from which Paul's own career as a missionary was launched (Acts 13:1-3), was probably organized by such hellenists; this may explain why Christianity in that city was something more than a mere "transplant" from Jerusalem.[120] It was at Antioch that a deliberate decision emerged to sponsor an all-out mission to Gentiles, with Paul and Barnabas (themselves hellenized Jews from the diaspora) at the head of it.[121]

Paul did not, therefore, invent the notion that the message about Jesus could be carried to others besides the people of Israel, even though he is rightly considered the most prominent figure in the early Christian mission to the Gentiles. As an "apostle" Paul did not fit the Lukan model of the Twelve. Though he claimed to have been called by the risen Lord, he had not been a companion of Jesus in his historical ministry. Moreover Paul's (and the Antioch church's) decision to sponsor a Gentile mission could find no precedent in Jesus, who worked exclusively within a Jewish framework and appears to have had no interest in preaching to "outsiders."[122] As Raymond Brown observes, Paul was forced to legitimate his apostolic mission by arguing that since Jesus had been crucified as a "violator of the law", his death could benefit those (the Gentiles) who stood outside the law.[123] We see Paul pushing this innovative point forcefully in the letter to the Galatians. The cross, Paul implies, reveals that Jesus died as one outside the law; thus all other outsiders are invited to experience freedom as God's children.[124]

Our focus here, however, will not be on the innovative aspects of Paul's theology, but on the types of ministry that characterized the churches he founded. Three points will occupy our attention: the Pauline understanding of church; the meaning of "charism"; and the forms of mutual ministry that emerged in churches of the Gentile mission.

---

[120]See Keck, *The New Testament Experience of Faith*, p. 55.
[121]See *ibid.*, p. 57.
[122]See Brown, *Priest and Bishop*, p. 62.
[123]*Ibid.*
[124]See Galatians 3:13.

✻ yes, but the interior of Jesus' message + life had implications beyond sectarian.

1. Pauline understanding of church

Paul's preferred metaphor for the church is "the body of Christ", an image prominent in Rom 12 and 1 Cor 12. One must remember, however, that in these texts Paul is thinking not of a universal church but of "house churches", small communities that meet in the homes of Christians. Several such house churches may have existed in a large city, this may explain Paul's insistence on unity and his admonitions against factions or party-strife.[125] In Paul's churches, the basic unit was the household: members of the immediate family, slaves, freed persons, servants and laborers, perhaps business associates and tenants.[126] New converts joined the "church" by attaching themselves to a household. Paul seems to have known at least three such Christian households in Rome (see Rom 16:5, 14, 15), and cities like Corinth may also have had several.[127]

This system of house churches makes Paul's appeals for unity in the "body of Christ" more cogent. Loyalty to a household was an important virtue in the Greco-Roman world. It is understandable that when several households in a city gathered for a church-meeting, frictions could arise. Gaius (Rom 16:23), for example, appears to have been host for the whole community (all the house churches) of Corinth; he must then have been a rather well-to-do man with a large residence.[128] In such situations the sociological differences between poorer and wealthier households would have been more apparent—and perhaps this illuminates the conflict between rich and poor to which Paul alludes in his discussion of the Lord's Supper (1 Cor 11:17-34).[129]

The household system may also have provided a "training ground" for leadership in the local communities established by Paul. As Abraham Malherbe has observed, the house churches furnished a natural climate that favored the emer-

[125]See Abraham Malherbe, *Social Aspects of Early Christianity,* (Baton Rouge, Louisiana: Louisiana State University Press, 1977), p. 61.
[126]*Ibid.,* p. 69.
[127]*Ibid.,* p. 70.
[128]*Ibid.,* p. 73.
[129]*Ibid.,* pp. 77-82.

gence of the "host" as the most influential member of the Christian assembly.[130] If several such churches existed in a city, competition among these leaders might naturally have resulted. Significantly, Paul himself did not view the households as separate entities; his letters are written to *all* Christians in a locality—Rome, Corinth, Thessalonica. And since Paul expected his letters to be read in the churches, one may assume that regular church-meetings in the home and under the leadership of a single "host" were a common pattern.

This does not mean, however, that the person or couple (e.g., Aquila and Prisca at Ephesus) who hosted the church were always and necessarily considered its prime leaders. For Paul there are not two kinds of Christian: those who minister, and those who are ministered to.[131] All Christians, in his view, are "charismatics" who have gifts to offer and services to render. In the church all are interdependent for teaching and mutual help; no one in the "body of Christ"—not even the foot—can be excluded from ministry.[132]

To understand Paul's view of the whole body as "charismatic" and ministerial, one needs to clarify the Pauline notion of "charisma". In an illuminating essay, Ernst Käsemann notes that in Paul's thought charisma (often translated "gift" or "grace") means something very specific: the eschatological gift of God in Christ, the "eternal life" that claims and possesses believers *now*, in their very history and bodily existence.[133] A gift given to all, charisma is manifest in "spirit" (our present participation in eternal life) and in "power", through which the lordship of Christ acts to bring us into the "captivity" of his service.[134] Spirit and power are, in turn, expressed through various gifts (Greek, *charismata*) and services (Greek, *diakaioniai*) aimed at building up the

---

[130]*Ibid.*, p. 61.

[131]See Dunn, *Unity and Diversity in the New Testament,* p. 110.

[132]*Ibid.*, pp. 113-114.

[133]See Ernst Käsemann, "Ministry and Community in the New Testament," in *Essays on New Testament Themes,* translated by W.J. Montague, (Studies in Biblical Theology, Vol. 41; Naperville, Illinois: Alec R. Allenson, Inc., 1964), pp. 63ff.

[134]*Ibid.*, p. 68.

community of believers. According to the Pauline view the entire community is thus "charismatic"and ministrybelongs to *all* members rather than to a hierarchically constituted few.[135] It is important to recognize, however, that Paul thinks of charisma not as a permanent aptitude always "on tap", but as an event—a particular expression of grace, a particular act of service, a particular manifestation of the Spirit.[136] The unity of the body of Christ thus exists as an interplay among diverse gifts (*charismata*). In the words of James D.G. Dunn, "*Christian community exists only in the interplay of charismatic ministry,* in the concrete manifestations of grace, in the actual being and doing for others in word and deed."[137]

Ernst Käsemann has suggested that Paul's vision of charismatic community was shaped in response to a particular pastoral problem: the need to distinguish the church from those hellenistic mystery-cults which prided themselves on possession of flamboyant "spiritual powers" (Greek, *pneumatika*).[138] At Corinth, especially, Paul sensed the danger that possession of "*pneumatika*" might lead to a divisive fascination with the preternatural and the "marvelous"; he thus subordinates these *pneumatika* to the more general category of "gifts" (*charismata*).[139] The apostle's pastoral strategy was to counter the possibly elitist pretensions of the "pneumatics" by insisting that *all* Christians can and do perform acts of mutual service that consolidate the unity of the body. Further, Paul insists that the "*pneuma*" (usually translated "spirit") is not something we possess but a transcendent reality that possesses us: it is the power of the Risen One making itself visible in the very corporeality and historicity of the community. As Käsemann comments, "this Spirit (*pneuma*) invariably claims us for the Lord as we are in

---

[135]See Dunn, *Unity and Diversity in the New Testament,* pp. 109-111.
[136]*Ibid.,* p. 111.
[137]*Ibid.*
[138]See Käsemann, "Ministry and Community," p. 67.
[139]See *ibid.,* p. 66; cf. E. Earle Ellis, *Prophecy and hermeneutic,* (Wissenschaftliche Untersuchungen zum Neuen Testament, 18; Tübingen: J.C.B. Mohr (Paul Siebeck), 1978), pp. 24-25.

our corporeality. . . . In our bodies the Cosmocrator is taking possession of that world which hitherto has not acknowledged his lordship, and the Body of Christ is the real concretion before the Parousia of the universal sovereignty of Christ."[140]

Paul's ideas about "spirit" (*pneuma*) and "gifts" (*charismata*) in the Christian community are thus the direct opposite of any ethereal, "spiritualized", or invisible possession belonging to a few select initiates. The charismatic services rendered to all and by all Christians are public, visible deeds that touch all aspects of human life. Every human condition—including such things as being male or female, or being sexually committed as a virgin—are potentially "charismatic" insofar as they reveal our belonging to the sphere of Christ's lordship. Käsemann summarizes Paul's thinking in a memorable passage:

> Because and in so far as the body of Christ. . . is God's new world and creation; because and in so far as, Christ in and with his gifts calls each of his members to the *nova oboedientia,* quickens him and moves him to service and suffering; . . . . because and in so far as, in his gifts and in the ministries which they express and indeed create, he himself is present, proclaiming his title to the lordship of the world, consecrating the secular, ridding the earth of demons; therefore and to this extent can it be proclaimed in truth that he fills all things with the power of his resurrection. [141]

3. Forms of mutual ministry

But Paul's view of charismatic community is not a kind of egalitarian soup in which bits of mutual service randomly float to the surface. Paul is utterly convinced, for example, of his own unique role as an apostle and he does not hesitate to invoke or defend that role (see Galatians, 2 Corinthians). Further, Paul's apostolic ministry is supported by a large number of associates: workers and co-workers, "brothers", prophets and teachers. E. Earle Ellis notes that the terms just mentioned seem to be technical ones in Paul's writings.[142]

[140]See Käsemann, "Ministry and Community," p. 68.
[141]*Ibid.,* p. 74.
[142]See Ellis, *Prophecy and Hermeneutic,* pp. 3-22.

"Worker" (Greek, *ergatēs, synergos, kopiōntes*) appears to be Paul's term for one who has a special responsibility for the Christian mission. The workers, in turn, are assisted by "*diakonoi*", a special class whose ministry involves teaching and preaching and whose members are entitled to pay and support from the congregation.[143] Too, there is a special class of *diakonoi* who are "apostles"; each of these carries out a commission from the Risen Lord in relative independence and develops his or her own group of co-workers.[144] Finally, there are the "brothers" (Greek, *adelphoi*), a term sometimes used for Christians generally but probably with a more restricted meaning in Paul.[145] There is reason to believe that when Paul uses "the brothers" (with the article), he refers to a relatively limited group who have the Christian mission as their "primary occupation".[146] Their work appears to have included preaching, missionary activity, acting as "go-betweens" bearing letters from one church to another, serving as the apostle's travelling-companions.[147]

Two other ministerial terms in Paul deserve special comment: "co-workers" (Greek, *synergoi*) and "prophets". The co-workers (e.g., Rom 16:3, 9, 21) seem to be local converts who participate in the Christian mission and continue it after the apostle has moved on.[148] They may have been an appointed group, though this would not imply that they were authorities in a hierarchic sense.[149] For Paul, "charism" and "appointment" were not mutually exclusive categories, since all Christians must submit themselves to the Lord and to one another in the obedience of faith.[150] The co-workers were thus simultaneously "officials" in the community and cha-

[143]See *ibid.*, pp. 9-11.
[144]See *ibid.*, pp. 12-13.
[145]See *ibid.*, pp. 13-15.
[146]See *ibid.*, p. 15.
[147]See *iibid.*, pp. 15-18, 19-21. Ellis argues that "the brothers" may sometimes have been singled out as the special recipients of Paul's letters, and that it was their responsibility to see that the letters were read in the churches.
[148]See *ibid.*, p. 22.
[149]See *ibid.*, p. 7, note 24; p. 22.
[150]See Käsemann, "Ministry and Community," pp. 76-78.

rismatically endowed persons who were among the *pneuma-tikoi* (people with specialized spiritual gifts).[151] This last category, as we have seen, has a restricted meaning for Paul and is subordinate to the broader category of "gifts" (*charismata*). Distinguished from the general class of believers, the *pneumatikoi* are spiritual specialists who receive and mediate revelation from the Risen Lord, and who appear to have contributed to the formation of a Christian literature (e.g., 1 Cor 2:6-16, an "inspired"eschatological exposition of the "wisdom" theme).[152] The *pneumatikoi* may also have had a distinctive role in the church's worship, and their gifts may have been cultivated in smaller "prayer sessions" distinct from the plenary gatherings of the Christian assembly. E. Earle Ellis believes that a passage like 1 Cor 11:4-10 deals specifically with these prayer sessions of the pneumatics rather than with the regular meetings of the whole church for public worship—and this explains what might otherwise be taken as an anti-feminist attitude on Paul's part.[153]

The *pneumatikoi* are, in short, those persons in the Pauline churches who are especially empowered to speak "in the Spirit"—and whose gifts are so recognized by the larger community. Included among them are apostles, prophets and teachers (1 Cor 12:28), and thus Paul himself qualifies as a member of this group. Prophets are particularly notable because in both the Hebrew Bible and intertestamental literature the Spirit is linked with prophecy.[154] But prophecy is also connected, in apocalyptic Judaism and in Paul, with "spirits" (lower case, plural). This helps explain the advice in 1 Cor 14:12, where a more literal rendering of the Greek text might read: "Since you are zealous for the spirits, seek to abound in those that build up the church." The "spirits" here are those powers that lie behind the "spiritual gifts" (*pneumatika*).[155] In both apocalyptic Judaism and at Qumran,

---

[151]See Ellis, *Prophecy and Hermeneutic*, p. 23.
[152]See *ibid.*, pp. 25-26.
[153]See *ibid.*, p. 27, note 25.
[154]See *ibid.*, p. 28.
[155]See *ibid.*, p. 31.

"spirits" commonly refer to angels or angelic powers who assist the pneumatics in their teaching and prophecy. At Qumran, especially, the "holy spirits" are closely attached to "the wise", i.e., to teachers.[156] E. Earle Ellis thus seems justified in remarking that "as recipients and transmitters of mysteries, possessors of wisdom, discerners of spirits and interpreters, 'the wise' at Qumran bear a striking resemblance to the pneumatics in the Pauline community."[157] Here again, familiarity with the type of angelology common in apocalyptic Judaism helps make sense of Pauline recommendations that are otherwise rather incomprehensible: e.g., the insistence that women keep their heads covered "because of the angels" (1 Cor 11:10). If we recall that Paul seems to be referring in this passage to special prayer sessions of the pneumatics—and that the pneumatics are assisted in their prophecy by angelic powers—the reference becomes more intelligible. Paul's recommendation is not a general one directed to all Christian women on all occasions of public worship, but a very specific bit of advice for very particular circumstances.

There is no reason to believe, moreover, that Paul excluded women from roles of leadership in the churches. In Rom 16:1, Phoebe is a "*diakonos*", while in 16:3 Prisca (Priscilla) and her husband Aquila are "*synergoi*" ("co-workers"), as Paul and Apollos are in 1 Cor 3:9. Similarly, Maria in Romans 16:6 has "worked hard for you" (Greek, *ekopiasen* = "worked"). If E. Earle Ellis is correct in his contention that Paul attaches technical ministerial significance to all these terms (*diakonos, synergos, kopiaō* and their cognates), then we must admit that Paul explicitly included women among the prominent leaders of local churches. There are good reasons, too, for believing that in Rom 16:7, a woman, Junias, is named as one "outstanding among the apostles".[158]

---

[156]See *ibid.*, pp. 33-34.

[157]See *ibid.*, p. 35.

[158]For further discussion of this passage and the history of its interpretation, see Bernadette Brooten, "Junia.... Outstanding among the Apostles (Romans 16:7)," in Leonard and Arlene Swidler, eds., *Women Priests*, pp. 141-144.

Whether one accepts Luke's narrower or Paul's broader understanding of apostleship, it is clear that women fulfill all the appropriate criteria: witnessing the life, ministry and resurrection of Jesus (Luke); engaging in missionary work (Paul).[159]

Before leaving our discussion of ministry in the Pauline churches, a final question must be raised: did Paul know of "overseers" (Greek, *episkopoi*; later translated "bishops"), "elders"(Greek,*presbyteroi*) or "deacons"(Greek,*diakonoi*) in the Christian community? In Acts 14:23, Luke pictures Paul and Barnabas installing presbyters in the churches they visited; in Phil 1:1, moreover, Paul greets the "bishops and deacons" of that community. On the other hand, Paul never uses the word "elder (s)", and the appearance of "bishops and deacons" in Philippians is unique in the authentic Pauline letters.[160] Once again we have a conflict between Luke's portrait of a missionary apostle who organized local churches around elders (Acts 14:23) or "bishops" (cf. Acts 20:28) and Paul's relative silence about residential leaders of this type.

Some have attempted to resolve this conflict by noting a regional distinction between churches in Palestine, whose local leaders are "elders" (presbyteroi) and those in Gentile territory, whose resident authorities are "overseers"(*episkopoi*). This distinction, it is thought, explains why Paul does not mention elders but refers to overseers ("bishops") in Phil 1:1. But as Raymond Brown has noted, such a regional distinction has only flimsy support.[161] While it may be true that Christian elders are derived from Palestinian customs of leadership in the Sanhedrin and/or the synagogue,[162] it is difficult to prove that overseers are simply the Gentile coun-

---

[159]See Elisabeth Schüssler Fiorenza, "The Apostleship of Women in Early Christianity," in Leonard and Arlene Swidler, eds., *Women Priests*, pp. 135-140.

[160]Together with most modern exegetes, Catholic and Protestant, I exclude the "Pastoral letters" (I and II Timothy, Titus) from among the works actually written by Paul. See Brown, *Priest and Bishop*, p. 70; Perrin, *The New Testament: An Introduction*, pp. 264-275.

[161]See Brown, *Priest and Bishop*, pp. 66-67.

[162]See Ellis, *Prophecy and Hermeneutic*, pp. 142-143.

terparts of Jewish Christian "presbyters". In fact, an analogue to the Christian overseer is to be found in the Qumran sectarians' "Supervisor of the Many" (*mebaqqar, pāquid*). The Hebrew *pāquid* is an exact equivalent of the Greek *episkopos*.[163] Further, there is a parallelism of both function and symbolic status between the Qumran suprvisor and the Christian overseer.[164] At Qumran, the *mebaqqar* was responsible for the community's property, for instructing candidates in doctrine, and for serving as the symbolic shepherd of the sectarians—duties which later Christian sources assign to overseers (e.g., Titus 1:7-10) or elders (e.g., Acts 20:28, 1 Pet 5:2-4).

These parallels force us to question whether "overseers" (*episkopoi*) were restricted to communities of the later Gentile mission. It is possible that both Jewish and Gentile Christians adapted Qumran's system of supervisory leadership at a rather early period.[165] If they did, then Luke's assertion that Paul and Barnabas installed "presbyters" (Acts 14:23) may not be far afield, especially since the distinction between elder and overseer appears to have been minimal in the earliest decades of the Christian movement.[166] Such conjecture does not, however, resolve all the problems. Paul's greeting to the church at Philippi alludes to "bishops (overseers) and deacons" in the plural, not to a solitary supervisor who leads everyone else in the church. A. Lemaire observes that the phrase in Phil 1:1 may simply be a global reference to all in the community who have responsibility for leadership and service, without any specialized meaning.[167] Even if one argues with E. Earle Ellis, that *diakonos* is a technical term for someone who serves by teaching and is thus entitled to support from the congregation, the Philippians greeting may still be nothing more than a general allusion

[163]See Brown, *Priest and Bishop,* p. 68.
[164]See *ibid.,* pp. 68-69.
[165]*Ibid.*
[166]See Schillebeeckx, *Ministry,* p. 15.
[167]See André Lemaire, *Les Ministeres aux Origines de l'Église,* (Paris: Editions du Cerf, 1971), pp. 96-103.

to all who are authoritative preachers. In that case, it might be preferable to translate Phil 1:1 along these lines: "Paul and Timothy, servants of Christ Jesus, to all the holy ones in Christ Jesus who are at Philippi—and especially to those who teach and preach . . . ."

The Philippian "bishops and deacons" may thus be functionally equivalent to those persons in other Pauline letters who are "co-workers", teachers and prophets, "the brothers". As authoritative guides, they constitute a recognizable body within the larger congregation and may even have been appointed to their task. And if this is so, then one need not make much of Paul's silence about such "bishops and deacons" in other churches (e.g., Corinth, Rome). The absence of these terms would not mean that other Pauline churches lacked authoritative local leaders, nor would it necessarily mean that the Philippian congregation functioned ministerially in a way that differed radically from the Corinthian church. Later, of course, the "elder/overseer" or "presbyter /bishop" emerged, even at Corinth, as a local leader whose pastoral responsibility seems to take up where the Pauline missionary apostle's left off, but this development will receive attention in the following chapter.[168]

We may conclude, then, that while Paul may have chosen helpers who continued working locally in the churches he founded after his departure, there is no exclusive ministerial pattern — e.g., "Philippian" or "Corinthian" — which we can identify as peculiarly Pauline. For that reason one must be very cautious about assuming, for example, that Corinth represents "free-floating charismatic ministry" while Philippi, with its "bishops and deacons," represents "incipient Catholicism" (hierarchically structured ministry). At the bottom line, Paul himself is unquestionably the ultimate supervisor and overseer of the communities he founded, and he exercises authority quite unapologetically when he feels that doctrine or discipline are threatened (e.g., 1 and 2 Corinthians, Galatians). Paul's service as an apostle is wide-

---

[168]See Brown, *Priest and Bishop,* p. 35.

ranging; it embraces ordinary labor like tent-making, fund-raising, prayer and suffering, travel, teaching and correction.[169] Other missionary apostles, both men and women, perform tasks that are similar to Paul's, sometimes to his chagrin (2 Cor 11:1-15) and sometimes to his admiration (Rom 16:7). Though he has become its chief representative, Paul was obviously not the sole apostle of the Gentile mission.

Conclusion

During the first generation of the Christian movement no single pattern of leadership emerges as the one "willed by Jesus" or as the one which is normative for all churches. Whether Aramaic-speaking or Greek-speaking Palestinian Jews, whether hellenized Jews of the diaspora or pagan converts, the first Christians constituted a sectarian movement within Judaism rather than an independent religion with its own cult and creed. To say this is not to deny that within the first generation certain persons and churches emerged as authoritative representatives of the message about Jesus. We have seen, for example, that despite Paul's tendency to downplay its influence, Jerusalem does seem to have enjoyed a special status in the diffusion of primitive Christianity. We have seen, too, that conflict between the party of James and the party of Stephen helped spur a missionary movement sponsored by hellenized Jews to places like Samaria and Antioch. This latter community was clearly something more than a mere transplant of Jerusalem Christianity; it became the first genuinely "inter-racial" church and consciously chose to sponsor an all-out mission to the Gentiles with Paul and Barnabas among its early leaders. Even before the cataclysm of 70 C.E., therefore, the Christian movement had spread rather widely in the ancient Mediterranean world. As Norman Perrin once wrote:

---

[169]See *ibid.*, pp. 29-34.

New Testament Christianity spread very rapidly from Palestine into the Hellenistic world and from Jerusalem to Rome. Jesus proclaimed the Kingdom of God in Aramaic and died in Jerusalem, according to Mark 15:34 ... Within twenty years Paul writes in Greek to the Christians in Thessalonica and can assume that they await expectantly the appearance from heaven of God's Son.... In twenty years we have moved from Aramaic to Greek, from Palestine to Europe, from the Jewish world to the Hellenistic, and from the proclamation by Jesus of the Kingdom of God as God's eschatological event to the proclamation of Jesus by the church as God's eschatological event.[170]

Leadership and ministry in the first generation of the Christian movement were extremely diversified. Some Christians, like the party of James, remained devoted to the temple, its worship and priesthood; they apparently saw no conflict between their own "apostles and elders" (Acts 15) and the traditional structures of priestly cult in the Second Temple. Others, like Stephen, the wandering Palestinian charismatics and perhaps Jesus himself, had either repudiated the temple or minimized its importance. In churches of the Gentile mission, apostles like Paul — assisted by "co-workers," "helpers" (*diakonoi*) and "the brothers" — developed patterns of mutual ministry that were in some cases simultaneously charismatic and appointive. Some gifts, such as prophecy and inspired teaching, were especially prized in the Pauline churches, and persons who possessed them may have constituted a distinct, recognized group of "*pneumatikoi*".

We may thus summarize the situation as it had developed by 70 C.E. as follows:

1. The "mother church" of Jewish Christians in Jerusalem was effectively eliminated by the events of 66-70 C.E.

2. Luke's "Twelve" were, by the second generation (ca.

---

[170]Perrin, *The New Testament: An Introduction*, pp. 41-42.

70-100 C.E.), a hallowed memory. Whatever their precise identity and historical function may have been, they had no successors. ✕

3. Missionary apostles of the Pauline sort were certainly active within twenty years of Jesus' death. These included both men and women, and each apostle appears freely to have developed his or her own group of associates in the missionary ministry. If Paul's case is typical, the apostle was unquestionably the "supreme authority" in matters of doctrine and discipline for the churches he or she founded. There is some evidence that Paul established leaders ("elders"?, "overseers"?) in local churches to continue pastoral supervision of the Christian mission after the apostle's departure.

4. Among first-generation Christians generally, ministry seems to have been viewed as a functional event common to many rather than as a hierarchical possession restricted to few. There is no evidence that these earliest Christians attempted to establish a "priesthood" of their own parallel to that of the Jewish Second Temple.

5. In both Palestinian and Gentile communities, prophecy appears to have been a prized manifestation of the Spirit and of the "New Age" inaugurated by God's act of raising Jesus from the dead. Some of these inspired teachers may have been responsible for the formation of a Christian literature (e.g., a passage like 1 Cor 2:6-16 or the "sayings" tradition reflected later in the synoptics); they may also have played a prominent role in liturgical assemblies. Like the missionary apostles, the prophets included both men and women.

The fall of Jerusalem in 70 C.E. had a decisive impact on the future development of the Christian movement. In the second (ca. 70-100) and third (ca. 100-140) generations, Christianity gradually lost its sectarian character and acquired the characteristics of an independent religion. The separation of "church" from "synagogue" obviously had repercussions on the evolution of Christian ministry and on the emergence of a Christian priesthood. These and related developments will be studied in the chapter that follows.

✕ *This eliminates apostolic succession.*

Recommended Reading

Brown, Raymond. *Priest and Bishop*. New York: Paulist Press, 1970. A succinct study of ministry in the New Testament, with special attention to those leaders who eventually came to be known as "bishops" and "presbyters".

Dunn, James D.G. *Unity and Diversity in the New Testament*. Philadelphia: Westminster Press, 1977. A valuable introduction to the pluralism that existed in earliest Christianity. Readers will especially want to consult the chapters on ministry and worship.

Freyne, Seán. *The World of the New Testament*. New Testament Message, Volume 2. Wilmington: Michael Glazier, Inc., 1980. An extremely valuable portrait of the world (Greco-Roman, Jewish) into which Christianity was born. Provides important information about the "religious renewal movements" of the first century in Palestine.

Keck, Leander. *The New Testament Experience of Faith*. St. Louis: Bethany Press, 1976. A study of the early evolution of Christianity as reflected in the literature of the New Testament and in the important geographical centers where Christians were found (e.g., Jerusalem, Antioch, Ephesus, Rome, Corinth, etc.).

Swidler, Leonard and Arlene (eds.). *Women Priests*. A Catholic Commentary on the Vatican Declaration. New York: Paulist Press, 1977. Challenging collection of essays by biblical scholars and theologians on the 1977 Vatican Declaration about women and priesthood.

Theissen, Gerd. *Sociology of Early Palestinian Christianity*. Translated by John Bowden. Philadelphia: Fortress Press, 1978. Analyzes the growth of both the "Jesus Movement" and the "Christian Movement" through the use of sociological categories.

CHAPTER THREE
MINISTRY IN THE LATER
NEW TESTAMENT PERIOD

Introduction

The disaster that befell Jews and Jewish Christians in Jerusalem during the First Revolt (66-70 C.E.) did not destroy the sectarian movement that had arisen in response to Jesus' preaching and to his later proclamation by believers as "Lord" and "Christ". As we noted at the conclusion of the second chapter, the Christian movement had spread rapidly in the first twenty years of its existence, and as it spread it changed to accommodate itself to new adherents and pastoral situations. The first "inter-racial" community at Antioch was a bold experiment that departed from the style of Christianity associated with James and the "pillars" of the Jerusalem church, and Paul's mission to the Gentiles was another radical step in the slow transformation of a sect into a "religion". By the end of the first generation, ca. 70 C.E., Christian churches were scattered across the Roman Empire. This diffusion was possible in part because of social mobility in the empire. Travel was relatively easy because of Rome's programs of road-building and political administration, and it was reasonably safe because of the security provided by the Roman army.[1] Paul was conscious of the missionary advan-

---

[1]See Abraham Malherbe, *Social Aspects of Early Christianity*, (Baton Rouge: Louisiana State University Press, 1977), p. 62.

tage provided by the Roman system of provinces; he established communities in cities or towns that were "centers of Roman administration, of Greek civilization, of Jewish influence, or of some commercial importance."[2]

This structure of the empire thus provided Christianity with a ready-made network of urban centers linked by roads or trade routes. This does not mean that the earliest Christian communities were an exclusively urban phenomenon. Jesus himself appears to have avoided hellenized cities, and there is reason to believe that his first sympathizers had closer links with rural life than with urban culture.[3] But this situation had already begun to change during Paul's missionary career, and after the fall of Jerusalem Christianity became, increasingly, a movement closely attached to hellenized urban centers.

By the second (ca. 70-100) and third (ca. 100-140) generations, therefore, the Christian movement was well on its way toward becoming more settled and less obviously "Jewish" or "sectarian". Paul's strategic victory of principle — Gentiles may become Christians without first becoming Jews —could obviously result in churches that were predominantly or exclusively non-Jewish. The loss of Jerusalem as the movement's center further eroded the specifically Jewish identity of Christian faith and origins. Factors other than social, economic and political ones were also at work in the early evolution of Christianity. We noted in the second chapter that the first believers were intensely preoccupied about Jesus' *return* to complete his work and usher in the final, decisive ("eschatological") era of God's rule in the world. Early Jewish Christians, like many of their co-religionists, were devoted to a specific kind of eschatological longing known as apocalyptic; we must inspect apocalypticism a bit more closely in order to appreciate some of the shifts of attitude that occurred as Christianity moved into the second and third generations.

[2]*Ibid.*

[3]See Gerd Theissen, *Sociology of Early Palestinian Christianity*, translated by John Bowden, (Philadelphia: Fortress Press, 1978), pp. 47-58.

FEATURES OF
APOCALYPTIC

According to Norman Perrin, the prime characteristics of apocalyptic were "a sense of despair about history that bred the belief that it was rushing to a foreordained tragic climax; a hope in God that fostered the conviction that he would act in that climactic moment to change things utterly and forever; and a conviction that it would be possible to recognize the signs of the coming of the climactic moment."[4] Both late Jewish and early Christian literature offer examples of such apocalyptic speculation (see Dan 7:13-14, Mk 13:7-8, 24-27). Many New Testament scholars are convinced that Christian prophets contributed significantly to those apocalyptic sayings which stress the expectation of Jesus as the "Son of Man" (cf. Dan 7:13) who will come from heaven suddenly, unexpectedly and surely (cf. Lk 12:8-9).[5] Paul too, as we have seen, shared many of the ideas common in Jewish apocalyptic of the first century. And even in late literature of the New Testament, like the Book of Revelation, apocalypticism survived.[6]

Despite this persistence of apocalyptic, however, it is clear that as Christianity moved into the second generation the expectation of Jesus' imminent coming had to be reinterpreted. The event had not occurred, the earliest witnesses were dying off, and it looked more and more as if Christians would have to endure the long haul of history. The literature produced in this second generation — e.g., Matthew's gospel and Luke's two-volume work—reflects communities that have begun to settle in and to devote themselves to work and witness in the world.[7] Increasingly, as we shall see, attention had to be given to such practical matters as the maintenance of pastoral leadership in local communities, the internal regulation of the church's members and their behavior, the

---

[4]See Norman Perrin, *The New Testament: An Introduction*, (New York: Harcourt, Brace, Jovanovich, 1974), p. 66.

[5]*Ibid.*, pp. 75-77.

[6]See Leander Keck, *The New Testament Experience of Faith*, (St. Louis: Bethany Press, 1976), pp. 125-132; cf. Perrin, *The New Testament: An Introduction*, pp. 80-83.

[7]See Perrin, *The New Testament: An Introduction*, pp. 58-59.

historical transmission of authentic faith in Jesus, and the continuing question of the church's relation to the synagogue.

THE PROBLEM

Christians of the second generation thus faced a double crisis: the loss of the "mother church" in Jerusalem and the delay of Jesus' return. Some writers of the period struggled to provide a theological interpretation of this situation; Luke-Acts, for instance, "sees Jerusalem as the place that rejected Jesus and so has been itself rejected."[8]

I

Second and Third Generation Christianity

CRISIS IN LEADERSHIP

In the introduction to this chapter it was noted that second-generation Christians faced a twofold crisis resulting from the fall of Jerusalem and the delay of Jesus' return. A third element was also at work: the death of pioneering church-founders like Paul left communities wondering how they might continue to guarantee the authenticity of their faith and traditions. Roman Catholics have often assumed that this could not have been a serious problem since the original apostles surely commissioned "successors" — the bishops — to continue their work. But "apostolic succession" in this literal sense is by no means evident in the writings of the New Testament. For one thing the role of an apostle was unique. Paul's missionary apostleship had been confirmed by a vision and a call from the Risen One, and although it is clear that Paul authorized others as co-workers and local leaders, we are never told that he commissioned or "ordained" bishops as his successors. Similarly, Luke's Twelve, who witnessed the life, ministry and resurrection of Jesus, could not by definition have had any successors in the literal sense. Second-generation Christians faced a transition

[8]*Ibid.*, p. 59.

from churches founded and led by apostles to churches deprived of such leadership.[9]

Christian congregations were thus required to deal with new problems in the latter part of the first century. Who had the right and the responsibility to teach authoritatively in the name of Jesus? How could one be sure that this right was linked to Jesus and to those apostles who were his primary witnesses? How could one distinguish between authentic tradition and teaching which departed from it? These and related questions forced congregations to reflect more directly on the structure and meaning of ministry.

Some solutions to these problems could be found among ministers who already existed in the churches. Like the apostles, for example, prophets claimed to speak directly in the name of the Risen One; they were promulgators of that "eschatological law" ushered in through Jesus' life, death and resurrection and could thus preface their revelations by formulas such as "the LORD says. . . . "(see Acts 15:16-18).[10] But reliance on prophetic utterances was not considered acceptable in all Christian congregations. Prophets could point only to their own personal authority as faithful messengers of God, and this was regarded by some as a very slim basis for authoritative teaching. We thus find numerous warnings against false prophets in the later literature of the New Testament, especially in documents like the gospel of Matthew (see Mt 7:15-23; 24:11, 24).[11] Written probably for a community of hellenized Jewish Christians, Matthew is particularly concerned about the link between those who believe in Jesus and those Jews who still belong to the "synagogue across the street".[12] His admonitions against

[9]See Edward Schillebeeckx, *Ministry*. Leadership in the Community of Jesus Christ, translated by John Bowden, (New York: Crossroad Publishing Company, 1981), pp. 11-12.

[10]See E. Earle Ellis, *Prophecy and Hermeneutic*, (Wissenschaftliche Untersuchungen zum Neuen Testament, 18; Tübingen: J.B.C. Mohr (Paul Siebeck), 1978), pp. 130-142.

[11]See Schillebeeckx, *Ministry*, p. 21.

[12]See Perrin, *The New Testament: An Introduction*, pp. 169-171.

false prophets are withering; they are "wolves on the prowl" disguised in "sheep's clothing" (Mt 7:15). Given the chance they will mislead others by false predictions about Jesus' return (Mt 24:11, 24). Unflattering references like these make it reasonably clear that the prophet's authority was being seriously challenged by at least some Christian congregations of the second generation.

Another second-generation document, the letter to the Ephesians, hints that prophets, like apostles, are now part of the church's remembered *past.* In Eph 2:19-20, the church is a temple "founded on apostles and prophets"with Jesus Christ as the "capstone". This text seems to reveal the situation of Christians after 70 C.E.: the Jewish temple has been destroyed, and a new sanctuary which is Christ's body has taken its place (cf. Eph 2:21-22). Further, in Eph 4:11-12, the church's ministries are listed as "apostles, prophets, evangelists, pastors and teachers". This list appears to combine an older ministerial vocabulary familiar to Paul (cf. the "apostles, prophets and teachers" of 1 Cor 12:28) with a newer one ("evangelists and pastors"). That these latter terms are not recent seems clear since they appear elsewhere in the New Testament only in documents from the period after 70 C.E. ("pastors": the gospels, Heb 13:20; 1 Pet 2:25; "evangelists": 2 Tim 4:5; Acts 21:8). In his *Ecclesiastical History*, moreover, Eusebius of Caesarea associates these evangelists and pastors with the post-apostolic generation of Christians (E.H. III 37:2-4).[13]

It is difficult to know precisely what ministerial functions "pastors and evangelists" were expected to perform. In 2 Tim 4:5, Timothy, who had been Paul's co-worker, is referred to as an evangelist, while Acts 21:8 applies the same word to Philip, one of the hellenistic "Seven" who, as we saw in the second chapter, was probably an important missionary. It is possible, therefore, that the term is a second-generation expression for persons who were not technically apostles in

[13]See André Lemaire, *Les Ministéres aux Origines de l'Église* (Paris: Editions du Cerf, 1971), pp. 105-107.

the Lukan or Pauline sense, but who have engaged in the "apostolic" work of evangelizing.[14] It may also be that "evangelist" had become a technical term for the chief leader of a missionary center such as Caesarea, Ephesus or Antioch.[15] In contrast to the evangelist, who seems to be responsible for directing the missionary outreach of the church, the pastor was probably a local residential leader charged with shepherding the church in its internal life and conduct. 1 Pet 5:1-4, for example, describes the work of elders (Greek, "*presbyteroi*") along these lines: "To the elders among you I... make this appeal. God's flock is in your midst; give it a shepherd's care... Be examples to the flock, not lording it over those assigned to you."

The appearance of words like "evangelist" and "pastor" does not mean, however, that a universally accepted vocabulary for ministers had developed among Christians of the second and third generations, nor does it imply that persons like the prophets had simply vanished from congregations. The *Didache*, a short manual of doctrine and discipline written somewhere between 70 and 150 C.E., refers explicitly to the ministry of prophets and provides principles for distinguishing true from false prophecy (*Didache* XI:7-12; XIII). And one can gather from a document like the *Shepherd of Hermas* that prophets still flourished in the Roman church as late as the mid-second century. There are, moreover, other generic words in the New Testament that appear to designate local church leaders: e.g., "*hēgoumenos/ prohēgoumenos*" (cf. Heb 13:7); and "*proistamenos*" (literally, "one who presides"), used as early as Paul's letters (1 Thess 5:12; Rom 12:8).

There is no single solution in the New Testament, then to the crisis of leadership that resulted from events such as the fall of Jerusalem, the delay of Jesus' return and the death of those pioneering apostles who witnessed the resurrection and/or founded churches. In the pages that follow we shall

[14]*Ibid.*, p. 187.
[15]*Ibid.*, p. 138.

examine in more detail some of the incipient ministerial structures that began emerging as Christians of the second and third generations continued the task of proclaiming Jesus as God's eschatological deed in and for the world.

THE TEACHER-SCRIBE IN MATTHEW

We have already seen that Matthew's gospel appears to contain a polemic against predatory prophets who prowl like wolves and misguide believers. A further example of Matthew's doubts about Christian prophets appears when we compare the following parallel texts:

> That is why the wisdom of God has said, 'I will send them *prophets and apostles*, and some of these they will persecute and kill....(Lk 11:49).
>
> For this reason I shall send you *prophets and wise men and scribes*. Some you will kill and crucify, others you will flog in your synagogues...(Mt 23:34).

J. Dillon has argued that Matthew's reference to "*prophets and wise men and scribes*" is an implicit attack on the rather free-wheeling attitude of Christian prophets toward the tradition of Jesus' sayings.[16] Whereas primitive Christian prophetism was innovative and formative, Matthew is custodial and conservative: he struggles to insure that Jesus' words are not further embellished or distorted by prophetic interpretation.[17] This may be one reason why Matthew — and the other synoptics as well — tend to "freeze" Jesus' sayings by locating them within the narrative framework of a "biography", by relating them to particular times and places in Jesus' public career.[18] Matthew thus seems to be an opponent of prophetic innovation, and he appeals to the Jewish tradi-

---

[16]See J. Dillon, "Ministry as Stewardship in the Tradition of the New Testament," in *CTSA Proceedings* (Volume 24; St. Joseph's Seminary, Yonkers, New York: 1969), pp. 29-40.

[17]*Ibid.*, p. 38.

[18]*Ibid.*, p. 41.

tion of the "teacher-scribe" whose primary job is to hand on what has been received rather than to create new traditions. Several texts hint at Matthew's anti-prophetic attitude; e.g.:

> When that day comes, many will plead with me, 'Lord, Lord, have we not prophesied in your name? Have we not exorcised demons by its power?'. . . . Then I will declare to them solemnly, 'I never knew you. Out of my sight, you evildoers!' (Mt 7:22-23).

In this passage the persons who are condemned and cast out on "that (eschatological) day" are precisely those who have "prophesied" in Jesus' name. In contrast, Mt 8:19 speaks of a "scribe" who is eager to become Jesus' disciple, with its hardships and homelessness. Further, Matthew's alteration of "prophets and apostles" (cf. Lk 11:49) to "prophets and wise men and scribes" (Mt 23:34) implies that wise teachers are now the guarantors of the Jesus-tradition which was formerly witnessed by the pioneering apostles. Finally, Matthew's missionary mandate at the end of the gospel (Mt 28:18-20) omits any references to charismatic "signs and wonders" that might accompany the preaching of the gospel (cf., in contrast, the longer ending in Mk 16:9-20, with its remarks about exorcisms, speaking in new languages, and snake-handling!).

One may conclude, then that Matthew is intent upon formulating a method for preserving Jesus' message that will prevent its distortion. Central to this method is the teacher-scribe, whose task is to sustain the community of "little ones" (cf. Mt 10:42) in a life of discipleship and fidelity to Jesus' words. Central too is the gospel text, a written record that purports to give a faithful account of Jesus' earthly message so that it may not be further "expanded, clarified, interpreted, or innovated upon".[19] In Matthew, the *past* — the gospel's carefully controlled portrait of Jesus' career — has become normative for the church's present and future. From this established tradition the wise teacher-scribe knows how

---

[19]*Ibid.*, p. 44.

to draw out treasures old and new: "Every scribe who is learned in the reign of God is like the head of a household who can bring from his storeroom both the new and the old"(Mt 13:52).

Precisely who were these teacher-scribes and what were their functions in Matthew's church? If one accepts a Jewish-Christian (albeit hellenized) background for Matthew's gospel, then there seems to be a parallel between the Christian teacher and the Jewish-scribe whose duty it was to preserve and transmit the Mosaic tradition.[20] "Scribe" may simply have been Matthew's term for the *true* prophet/ teacher, as opposed to those false wolves who periodically raid Christ's flock. In this sense the scribe may not represent a new ministry but simply the correct and authoritative form of an earlier Christian ministry, that of prophet or teacher. The first-generation prophet was a charismatic innovator; Matthew's second-generation scribe (= prophet/ teacher) is the custodian of an established Jesus-tradition.

THE JOHANNINE ALTERNATIVE

Although Matthew was convinced of the need for authoritative teachers in the community, he rejected the methods of "worldly rulers" who lord it over others: "You know how those who exercise authority among the Gentiles lord it over them: their great ones make their importance felt. It cannot be like that with you. Anyone among you who aspires to greatness must serve the rest" (Mt 20:25-26).[21] This is, of course, a radical departure from models of authority that rely on relations of superior/ inferior, master/ slave, or domination/ submission. More radical still, however, was what Edward Schillebeeckx has called "the Johannine alternative".[22] Johannine Christianity appears to have resisted

[20]*Ibid.*, pp. 41-42.
[21]See discussion in Schillebeeckx, *Ministry*, pp. 21-22.
[22]*Ibid.*, pp. 25-29.

investing any human minister with authority in teaching and discipline, since the risen Jesus will send the Paraclete to instruct believers in everything (see Jn 14:26). In order to understand this distinctive view of authority and teaching we need to inspect more closely the relation between John's gospel and his letters.

Many biblical exegetes agree that John's gospel was written in the late first century, possibly around the year 90 C.E.[23] The letters (1, 2, 3 John), however, were written later and reflect changes in the community's situation.[24] Some of these changes, as we shall see, touch upon questions of ministry and authoritative teaching. John's gospel itself is strangely silent about traditions related to early Christian "authorities" like the Twelve. Although John alludes to the Twelve (Jn 6:70), he does not provide a list of their names nor does he narrate the story of their call by Jesus as do the synoptics (see Mk 3:13-18; Mt 10:1-4; Lk 6:12-16). The central witness in John's gospel is "the beloved disciple", a mysterious figure who is obviously the community's hero but probably not "John the son of Zebedee", one of the Twelve.[25] Just as Jesus saw God, so the beloved disciple saw Jesus — and this disciple's followers now share the traditions he transmitted to them.[26] The Paraclete whom Jesus promised to send in his "farewell discourse" will continue guiding the community in the truth (Jn 16:14b-16). In John's gospel these two guarantees — the beloved disciple's witness and the Paraclete's presence — are considered sufficient to assure the integrity of the community's faith (see Jn 19:35; 21:24).

But by the time the Johannine letters were written, perhaps ca. 100 C.E., this halcyon situation has changed.[27] Disputes

---

[23]See Perrin, *The New Testament: An Introduction*, p. 230; cf. Raymond Brown, *The Community of the Beloved Disciple*, (New York: Paulist Press, 1979), p. 59.

[24]See Schillebeeckx, *Ministry*, pp. 25-26.

[25]See Brown, *The Community of the Beloved Disciple*, pp. 31-34.

[26]See Schillebeeckx, *Ministry*, p. 26.

[27]For the date of the Johannine Letters, see Brown, *The Community of the Beloved Disciple*, p. 97.

have apparently arisen within the community, and the conflict centers on the correct interpretation of the single tradition linked with the "beloved disciple".[28] The author of 1
John tries to expose his opponents as "false prophets" who
have deviated from the teachings transmitted by the beloved
disciple: "Beloved, do not trust every spirit, but put the spirits
to a test to see if they belong to God, because many false
prophets have appeared in the world.... There is One
greater in you than there is in the world. Those others belong
to the world; that is why theirs is the language of the world
and why the world listens to them." (1 Jn 4:1,4b-5). In
Johannine vocabulary "the world" has a specific meaning; it
refers not to the material creation but to the community's
hostile non-Jewish opponents.[29] By accusing them of
"belonging to the world", the author implies that his prophetic antagonists were never "part of us", i.e., that they had
never truly adhered to the teaching of the beloved disciple (cf.
1 Jn 2:19).

There are clues about what the beloved disciple taught
scattered throughout 1 John. First, believers have received
an "anointing" that allows all of them to interpret the (Johannine) tradition faithfully, without any need for human
instructors: "You have the anointing that comes from the
Holy One, so that all knowledge is yours.... the anointing
you received from him remains in your hearts. This means
you have no need for anyone to teach you" (1 Jn 2:20, 27).
Secondly, in a situation of conflict, the tradition of the
beloved disciple is to be interpreted through the witness of the
Spirit, which is linked both to Jesus' baptism ("water") and
his death ("blood"): "Jesus Christ it is who came through
water and blood — not in water only, but in water and in
blood. It is the Spirit who testifies to this, and the Spirit is
truth" (1 Jn 5:6-7). Thirdly, 1 John makes a point of linking the
Paraclete Jesus (1 Jn 2:1) with that "other Paraclete" whom

---

[28]See Schillebeeckx, *Ministry*, p. 26.

[29]See the discussion in Brown, *The Community of the Beloved Disciple*, pp.
63-66.

the Lord promised to send as an abiding teacher and guide for Johannine Christians (Jn 14:16). All this means that the only legitimate teacher is the Paraclete who anoints the hearts of the beloved disciple's authentic followers.

If this is true, however, what does one make of 2 and 3 John, where the author, probably the same one who wrote 1 John, identifies himself as an "elder" (Greek, *presbyteros*)?[30] By the end of the first century, as we shall see below, "elder" had probably begun to assume technical significance for authoritative status in the community. Does this mean that the Johannine community had changed its mind about the need for teachers and authority-figures? Had the community's crisis become so profound that it had no choice but to turn toward an authoritative "hierarchy" of elders? The answer to both these questions is probably no. It seems true that by the time 2 and 3 John were written internal dissension had become acute; there may even have been secessionists who left the Johannine group altogether (cf. 2 Jn 7). It is also true that in 3 John there is an open conflict between the author/elder and Diotrephes, who loves being "their" (the secessionists'?) leader (3 Jn 9). The quarreling has become so bitter, in fact, that Diotrephes has refused to welcome the delegates sent him by the author/elder (3 Jn 10).

Significantly, however, the only authority the elder of 3 John can muster in this situation is the authority of persuasion: "Do not imitate what is evil but what is good" (3 Jn 11). Unlike the apostle Paul who did not hesitate to correct and threaten (cf. Gal 1:6-10, 3:1-9), the Johannine elder can only plead for acceptance of his version of the beloved disciple's tradition. In the conflict between the elder and Diotrephes, Edward Schillebeeckx sees an opposition between two views of authority that had split the Johannine community.[31] Representing the "classic" Johannine viewpoint, the elder must rely on the believers' "anointing" and can only beg the dissidents to accept his teaching; Diotrephes, however, by

[30] *Ibid.*, p. 94; see also Lemaire, *Les Ministères*, p. 115.
[31] See Schillebeeckx, *Ministry*, p. 28.

refusing to welcome the elder's delegates, has "put himself first" (cf. 3 Jn 9) and has thus taken a step toward hierarchic authoritativeness. The elder complains, for example, that Diotrephes has expelled the delegates from his church — surely an authoritative action (see 3 Jn 10). Implicitly, the elder affirms that his own authority lies merely in his belonging to the "we" of a community whose life is directed solely by the Paraclete.[32]

There is evidence, however, that Johannine Christians later accepted, though with some reluctance, the tradition of "apostolic" authority associated with figures like Peter. From John's gospel one gets the impression that Christians of the "apostolic churches" — those who claimed historical attachment to Peter or other members of the Twelve — were among the many groups of "outsiders" despised by the beloved disciple's followers.[33] In John 21, however, a text added to the gospel perhaps at the time 1 John was written, Peter is commended as one who truly "loves Jesus" (see Jn 21:15-19). This commendation is explicitly linked to a pastoral responsibility, for Jesus says to Peter, "Feed my lambs ...Tend my sheep...Feed my sheep" (Jn 21:15, 16, 17). Such a story conflicts rather sharply with what one finds earlier in John's gospel, where Peter is portrayed as one who is puzzled by Jesus' deeds (Jn 13:23), denies the Lord (Jn 18:15ff.), and enters Jesus' tomb only *after* the "other disciple" has inspected it (Jn 20:3-6). The implication of these earlier texts is that the beloved ("other") disciple understood Jesus more thoroughly and more profoundly than Peter did.[34]

Still, in the gospel's appendix (Jn 21), there is a reluctant admission that Peter's authority is real and that it is rooted in his love for Jesus. There is also an embarrassed explanation of the beloved disciple's death, an event which distressed Johannine Christians who may have expected their hero to

[32]*Ibid.*, p. 27.

[33]See Brown, *The Community of the Beloved Disciple*, pp. 81-88.

[34]See Schillebeeckx, *Ministry*, pp. 28-29.

achieve some kind of immortality (see Jn 21:20-23). One may conjecture, then, that by the time the appendix was added to the gospel and the three letters were written, the classic Johannine view of authority — the Paraclete as sole teacher of disciples — was already losing ground. Johannine Christians were being forced to recognize other forms of leadership and status invested in human ministers. Those who accepted this state of affairs were probably absorbed into the "mainstream" of Christianity, while those who didn't may have slipped over into second-century Gnosticism.[35]

PRESBYTERS, BISHOPS, DEACONS:

Even though they resisted it, Johannine Christians obviously knew about structured ministry in other churches. Indeed, as we have seen, the author of the Johannine letters identifies himself as an "elder" (*presbyteros*), even if he does not attach much authoritative significance to the term. This surely means that by the end of the first century, a pattern of local leadership involving elders (or "presbyters") was widely known, even if not universally accepted.[36]

Many scholars today concur that elders, as a collegiate body of local leaders, are derived from Jewish synagogue practice.[37] If this is so, it is reasonable to assume that Jerusalem was the first church to adopt this model.[38] But it is not clear precisely how this presbyteral form of church order spread to other churches, including those of predominantly Gentile composition. Edward Schillebeeckx notes that there is a "uniform development in the direction of a presbyteral church order", and the later literature of the New Testament

[35] *Ibid.*

[36] *Ibid.*, p. 15.

[37] See Ellis, *Prophecy and Hermeneutic*, pp. 142-143; Lemaire, *Les Ministéres*, p. 125; Schillebeeckx, *Ministry*, p. 11; James D.G. Dunn, *Unity and Diversity in the New Testament*, (Philadelphia: Westminster Press, 1977), p. 115.

[38] See Schillebeeckx, *Ministry*, p. 11.

certainly seems to confirm this opinion.[39] Acts, for instance, presumes that there are presbyters at Ephesus (Acts 20:17), as well as in those cities evangelized by Paul and Barnabas on their first missionary journey (see Acts 14:23). Later still, in what some scholars call the "literature of emergent Catholicism" (written ca. 100-140), references to presbyters are rather frequent: 1 Tim 5:1, 17, 19 (Ephesus); Titus 1:5 (Crete); 1 Pet 5:1, 5; James 5:14.[40] Sometimes, qualifications considered appropriate for the presbyteral ministry are listed in these sources: e.g., a presbyter should be

> irreproachable, married only once, the father of children who are believers and are known not to be wild and insubordinate (Titus 1:6).

Similarly, 1 Timothy insists that "presbyters who do well as leaders deserve to be paid double, especially those whose work is preaching and teaching" (1 Tim 5:17). Procedures for handling charges brought against presbyters are also outlined: "Pay no attention to an accusation against a presbyter unless it is supported by two or three witnesses. The ones who do commit sin, however, are to be publicly reprimanded, so that the rest may fear to offend" (1 Tim 5:19-20).

One may assume from such explicit references that Christians of the second and third generations were familiar with the presbyteral pattern of local leadership. The "Pastoral Letters" (1 and 2 Tim., Titus), especially, testify to this development. These letters, Ernst Käsemann has argued, come from churches that were originally part of the Pauline mission-field and are now trying to rally around the traditions of "Paul's gospel".[41] Faced with opposition from Gnostics or other groups of "enthusiasts", the communities that produced the Pastorals looked toward recognized office-

[39]*Ibid.*, p. 20.

[40]See Perrin, *The New Testament: An Introduction*, pp. 253-275.

[41]See Ernst Käsemann, "Ministry and Community in the New Testament," in *Essays on New Testament Themes*, translated by W.J. Montague, (Studies in Biblical Theology, Vol. 41; Naperville, Illinois: Alec R. Allenson, Inc., 1964), p. 86.

bearers as guarantors of the Pauline tradition and as persons authorized to administer the "deposit of faith" (1 Tim 6:20).[42] In both their ecclesiological assumptions and their views of church order, however, the Pastorals depart from what we find in Paul's genuine letters. Paul sees the church as the body of Christ in which all members are charismatically endowed with gifts of mutual service; the Pastorals view it as the household of God exposed to external danger and needing protection. Such guidance is supplied by leaders whose qualifications are those of the head of a family, as one can see from the "lists of required qualities" in 1 Tim 3:2-7 (*episkopos*), Titus 1:6 (*presbyteros*), and 1 Tim 3:8-13 (*diakonos*).[43]

Does the mention of these three terms — *episkopos* ("bishop"), *presbyteros* and *diakonos* — indicate that three distinct "offices" or categories of leader are known in the Pastorals? Probably not, though scholars do not agree about the interpretation of church order in these letters. A common opinion, shared by Raymond Brown, Edward Schillebeeckx and Andre Lemaire, is that "presbyter" and "bishop" are virtually interchangeable terms at this point in the development of New Testament literature. In Titus 1:5, for example, the author ("Paul") reminds Titus that *presbyters* should be "appointed" (or "installed") in each town, but a couple of verses later the passage refers to a "bishop" (Titus 1:7ff.). The context indicates that the same type of local leader is being described by two different Greek words (*presbyteros, episkopos*). Some exegetes have thus concluded that in Titus (and the other Pastorals), these "appointed" local leaders ought to be called "presbyter-bishops" in order to show that at this stage a functional difference between the two terms had not yet appeared.[44] From his own study of the matter, Raymond Brown has further concluded that while the presbyter-bishops were not successors to the "Twelve", they may be

[42]*Ibid.*, p. 87.

[43]Further discussion in Käsemann, "Ministry and Community," pp. 85-88.

[44]See Raymond Brown, *Priest and Bishop*, (New York: Paulist Press, 1970), pp. 34-40, 65-73.

regarded as successors to the Pauline missionary apostles insofar as they exercised pastoral care among the communities those missionaries had founded.[45] Brown cautions, however, against assuming that this was a universal pattern followed by all churches, or that individual missionary-apostles necessarily appointed local presbyter-bishops in each church they founded.[46]

A different approach to the meaning of "presbyter" and "bishop" in the Pastorals and in non-biblical Christian literature of the second century has been proposed by Douglas Powell.[47] Powell argues that "presbyter" is a status-title, while "bishop" and "deacon" are functional titles related to ministries among the Christian people.[48] By this he means that "presbyter" was used to denote not a ministry or function or service in the community, but the status accorded to those persons who were "senior" in authority.[49] This seniority status, with its concomitant prestige and respect, belonged to those whose *conversion* and "rebirth" through faith in Jesus was long-standing and fruitful.[50] The "presbyterate", in short, was not a category of "office" or a "college" of ministers, but a designation for those whose lives demonstrated the fruitfulness of Christian maturity. Neither date of birth nor date of conversion made one a presbyter, since even a young person might manifest that mature and exemplary life characteristic of those who have given themselves fully to Christ, the first-fruits of all creation, the first-born from the dead.[51]

Powell argues further that the controlling image which stands behind the notion of "presbyterate" is not the "head-body-members" metaphor of 1 Cor 12, but the "first-

---

[45]*Ibid.*, pp. 72-73.

[46]*Ibid.*, p. 73.

[47]See Douglas Powell, "Ordo Presbyterii," *Journal of Theological Studies* 26 (New Series, 1975), 290-328.

[48]*Ibid.*, pp. 306-307, 321-322.

[49]The original meaning of "presbyter" in Greek is "a person of senior age."

[50]See Powell, "Ordo Presbyterii," pp. 305, 321.

[51]*Ibid.*, p. 321.

fruits/final harvest" image implied in 1 Cor 15:22-24.[52]
According to this latter image, Christ is the first-fruits
whose own rising from the dead promises that we — the rest
of the "lump" — will share his destiny, each in his own
"order", at the final harvest when the kingdom is delivered
to the Father (1 Cor 15:23-24). All Christians are part of the
lump that is rising, the crop that is growing to harvest, but
some believers — the presbyters — can claim special recognition and authority because of the quality of their conversion and the maturity of their faith. This claim is not a
matter of self-exaltation or of lording it over others. For just
as according to God's plan Christ is the "first-fruits of them
that sleep", so the presbyters are the first-fruits harvested in
the apostolic mission.[53]

This would help clarify the apparent overlapping of terms
in the Pastorals. The "presbyters" of 1 Tim 5:17, 19 and
Titus 1:5, for example, are neither an additional category of
ministers (like bishops and deacons), nor a governing council (college), nor an alternative designation for "bishop".
They are rather those first-fruits of the missionary apostles'
labors whose status is recognized and whose life is worthy of
imitation. The presbyters are thus the exemplar of the "nor-
mal" (though not the statistically "average") Christian life, a
life that grows to maturity in imitation of him who is the
first-fruits of that harvest which the Father will finally
gather to himself.[54] *Some* of these presbyters unquestionably do perform ministries in the church as "bishops" and
"deacons" — but that is because the status-title (presbyter)
has in the Pastorals begun to be "diversified by the application to it of two function-titles, bishop and deacon."[55] In
sum, presbyter is a generic title of status or condition, and
some of these presbyters may function ministerially as
bishops and deacons. We could thus speak of both

[52]*Ibid.*, pp. 296-297.
[53]*Ibid.*, p. 306.
[54]*Ibid.*, p. 321.
[55]*Ibid.*, pp. 306-307.

presbyter-bishops and presbyter-deacons in the Pastoral literature. Later, of course, presbyter itself becomes a function-title and deacons are excluded from the presbyterate — as appears to be the case in the early third-century *Apostolic Tradition* of Hippolytus (ca. 215).

CONCLUSION If Powell's analysis is correct, then we can conclude that in the Pastorals two "ministries" are alluded to: those of bishop and deacon. No detailed job-description is provided for either of them. The bishop's responsibility seems to have BISHOP! included three major areas: overseeing and regulating the community's life (which might result in correcting abuse and censuring offenders — Titus 1:9-11); administering its fiscal resources (thus the emphasis on good household management as a requirement — 1 Tim 3:3-4); and teaching sound doctrine (see Acts 20:28-29).[56] These services clearly point to a residential leader whose acquaintance with the local church is long-standing and intimate. And if the bishop is drawn from among the presbyters, as Powell's analysis suggests, one can understand why persons recently converted and baptized are considered inappropriate candidates for the job (see 1 Tim 3:6). By their very nature, presbyters could not be "recent converts".

DEACON! What, then, do the deacons described in the Pastorals do? We must first allow for the possibility that "deacon" is simply a further functional specification of the bishop's ministry. In Philippians 1:1, for example, there is no overwhelming indication that "bishops and deacons" are two distinct offices; as we noted in Chapter Two, the phrase may simply refer to all who exercise authoritative leadership in the church. Paul had described his own ministry as missionary-apostle with the word *"diakonia"* (2 Cor 3:6; 4:1), and in 1 Cor 16:15-18, the household of Stephanas —the "first converts in Achaia" — is to be obeyed and recognized because of their service (diakonia). In other words, Stephanas and his co-workers seem to "bishop" precisely because they "deacon".[57] It may be, then that the

---

[56]See Brown, *Priest and Bishop*, pp. 36-38.

[57]See Powell, "Ordo Presbyterii," p. 306.

ministerial function of episcopacy (literally, "overseeing") is expressed through the function of "deaconing" (serving others).

It is also possible, however, that in both Paul's letters and the Pastorals, *diakonos* has a slightly more technical meaning. As we have noted in Chapter Two, there is some reason to believe that "deacons" formed a special class of teacher/ preacher who assisted the Pauline "workers" and were thus entitled to support from the local congregation.[58] And if E. Earle Ellis is correct, some among these "deacons" formed yet another specialized class of minister, the "apostles".[59] This might explain why Paul could describe both himself and Apollos, missionary apostles, as *"diakoni"* (1 Cor 3:5). It might also shed light on the Pastorals' designation of Timothy as a *"diakonos"* (1 Tim 4:6); as Paul's co-worker and companion Timothy behaves as a *missionary* whose work is not restricted to that of a "presbyter-bishop".

Although the evidence is not conclusive, the "presbyter-deacon" of the Pastorals may have been a church leader recognizably different from the presbyter-bishop. But the precise difference is rather difficult to identify. Both deacons and bishops are expected to be good heads of households (1 Tim 3:4, 12), and this would seem to imply that both types of ministry are local and residential in nature. In the preceding paragraph, however, we noted that the Pauline "deacon" may sometimes have been a missionary, an apostle or an apostle's co-worker/companion. If this notion survived in the churches that produced the Pastorals, then perhaps the deacon was charged with *missionary* responsibilities that were not characteristic of the bishop's ministry. This is the opinion of André Lemaire, who notes that in the list of qualities required of the deacon (1 Tim 3:8-13), "hospitable" is omitted.[60] While the omission may have been purely accidental, it could make sense if the deacons were

---

[58]See Ellis, *Prophecy and Hermeneutic*, pp. 9-11.

[59]*Ibid.*, pp. 12-13.

[60]Lemaire, *Les Ministéres*, pp. 135-136.

engaged in a missionary (thus itinerant) ministry, since they would then ordinarily be the beneficiaries of hospitality rather than its providers. Lemaire notes further that this hypothesis would help explain why *diakonoi* are present at Ephesus but not at Crete (cf. 2 Tim 1:18; Titus 1:5). As a major missionary center for Asia Minor, Ephesus might well have needed itinerant co-workers like the "deacons", whereas their presence would not have been so necessary in each town of Crete.[61]

All this remains, of course, conjectural. We simply do not have indisputable proof of the deacons' identity in the Pastorals. Perhaps they were missionary figures who formed a distinctive class of worker similar to those who had collaborated with Paul several decades earlier. Again, perhaps the term "deacon" is nothing more than a functional description of one aspect of the bishops' ministry ("service"). The only thing we can say with certainty is that the Pastorals do not make any attempt to arrange "presbyter, bishop, and deacon" into a hierarchical pattern of "superior" and "inferior" leaders.

ORDINATION IN THE NEW TESTAMENT?

Closely related to the existence of "bishops" and "deacons" in the Pastoral Letters is the question of ordination. Traditionally, many Roman Catholics have believed that since holy orders is a sacrament and sacraments were instituted by Christ, some form of ordination must have existed during the period of Jesus' historical ministry or at least within the New Testament era. It is further assumed that this primitive form of ordination must have included the classic elements: laying on of hands and prayer (the "matter" and "form" of the sacrament, to use the vocabulary of a later age). Here we must ask whether these assumptions are valid

[61] *Ibid.*

in light of today's critical exegesis of the New Testament sources.

We may begin our probe into this question by asking whether first-century Jews were familiar with a rite of ordination for their priests or rabbis. In Chapter One we noted that the Israelite priesthood was principally a matter of genealogy rather than "vocation". One's birth determined one's priestly or non-priestly status, and thus it would have made little sense to speak of an ordination liturgy that conferred the office. Although later strata of the Hebrew Bible describe an "ordination" for Aaron and his sons (e.g., Ex 28-29), these ceremonies seem not to have existed prior to the Exile.[62] Even then, the "ordination" did not "make" one a priest but solemnly marked one's commencement of a service transmitted through heredity and membership in a priestly family.

Although some early Christians (e.g., the party of James) maintained a strong attachment to Temple and priesthood, none of the New Testament sources regard ministers within the Christian movement as "priests". After 70 C.E., furthermore, the destruction of the Temple eliminated the possibility of "ordinations" to a functioning Jewish priesthood. There remains, however, the question of ordination to the office of rabbi: Did such a custom exist in the first century C.E., and did it influence the practice of Christian communities?

Lawrence Hoffman has recently argued that in the reliable sources there is no proof for a Jewish ordination of rabbis at the beginning of the Christian era.[63] For one thing, Hoffman contends, the term "rabbi" became common only after 70 C.E., and there was no specific word used in Palestine to define one's "appointment" to the rabbinate.

---

[62]See Joachim Jeremias, *Jerusalem in the Time of Jesus*, translated by F.H. and C.H. Cave from the third German edition (1962), with author's revisions to 1967, (Philadelphia: Fortress Press, 1975 paperback edition), pp. 214-216.

[63]See Lawrence Hoffman, "L'Ordination juive a la veille du Christianisme," *La Maison Dieu* 138 (1979), pp. 7-47, especially 42-47.

Although a Hebrew word (*minuy*) for "appointment" existed prior to 70, its meaning was generic and covered a wide range of appointees in Jewish life; no special word or phrase characterized appointment as a rabbi. And although a liturgical ceremony linked with rabbinic appointment later developed, we know nothing about such a rite in the early period of the Christian movement. On the basis of the evidence available to us at present, Hoffman concludes, one cannot speak of a rabbinic "ordination" (Hebrew, *semikah*) practiced in Palestine during the first century.

If Hoffman's conclusions are correct, then we cannot appeal to rabbinic antecedents as a source for ordination in the New Testament. This would still not eliminate, however, the possibility that early Christians practiced some form of ritual appointment to authoritative office or role in the church. Perhaps the clearest hint of such a practice appears in 1 Tim 4:14, where the author writes: "Do not neglect the gift you have, which was given you by prophetic utterance when the council of elders laid their hands upon you." The passage occurs within the context of an exhortation to fulfill what we might call a "ministry of the Word": public reading of scripture, preaching, teaching (1 Tim 4:13). Furthermore, there is explicit reference to "laying on of hands" (Greek, *epitheseōs tōn cheirōn*) and to a "council of elders" (or presbytery; Greek, *presbyteriou*). All this sounds very much like an authoritative, official act, an "ordination".

Working from this and related texts in the Pastorals, Edward Kilmartin has proposed that the outlines of an ordination rite are discernible in the New Testament.[64] As he reconstructs it, the rite may have resembled the following:

1. The candidate is "elected" through an inspired utterance from the community's prophets (see 1 Tim 1:18, 4:14).

2. A recitation of basic elements contained in the gospel entrusted to the candidate then follows (a kind of *"traditio*

---

[64]See Edward Kilmartin, "Ministere et Ordination dans l'Eglise chretienne primitive," *La Maison Dieu* 138 (1979), pp. 49-92, especially 62-67.

symboli" or profession of faith) (see 2 Tim 2:2).

3. The candidate promises to guard the teaching faithfully (see 1 Tim 6:12).

4. Thereupon hands are imposed by the "elders" (presbyters) of the community (see 1 Tim 4:14). Prayer may have accompanied this action.

Kilmartin notes that the imposition of hands is intimately linked to a charism that supports the candidate in the ministry of the Word (see 1 Tim 4:11-13; 2 Tim 1:6). The rite does not bestow personal authority on the candidate but acts to mediate a charism that comes from God. This charism, Kilmartin observes, is one *for* office not one *of* office. Any authority which the candidate might come to possess stems from faithful fulfillment of the service imposed at "ordination". Relations between the ordained person and the community are specified in passages like 1 Tim 5:17-22, where practical matters like wages are discussed.

The attractiveness of this reconstruction cannot be denied. If accurate, it would provide a New Testament basis for a practice that became, by the third century, well-nigh universal: laying on of hands (with prayer) as the ritual mode of mediating the church's mandate for ministry. As Kilmartin admits, however, the origins of this "ordination liturgy" in the Pastorals are unclear. As a ritual gesture, the laying on of hands is quite ambiguous. In the sacraments as reformed by the II Vatican Council, for example, the gesture is linked with confirmation, reconciliation, the anointing of the sick, and ordination. The gesture's precise meaning depends upon its role in a larger ritual context.

The question becomes, then, whether or not the larger ritual context of the Pastorals implies an "ordination" conveyed by the laying on of hands. Since the Pastorals themselves are not concerned about supplying such information, we are forced to examine parallel situations in the New Testament where the same gesture (laying on of hands) appears in a similar context. One such situation is found in Acts 13:1-3. There, the church of Antioch, a great missionary center, is depicted as consciously choosing to sponsor a mission to the Gentiles. The decision is reached in a "liturgi-cal" context of prayer and fasting in which prophets and teachers play a visible role (see especially Acts 13:1-2). Paul (Saul) and Barnabas are chosen for the work and sent forth after "they" (who?) have "laid their hands upon them" (Acts 13:3). Delicious ambiguities abound in this short text. It is unclear, first, who does the laying on of hands: the prophets and teachers? the whole church at Antioch? No elders (presbyters) of the sort Luke links with the Jerusalem church (see Acts 15:6) are mentioned, nor is there any hint that the Antioch church's choice must first be submitted to a "higher council" of the mother church (Jerusalem).

Despite the ambiguities, however, some points in the passage are clear:

1. The laying on of hands is itself a reaction to the Spirit's inspiration mediated to an assembly gathered for prayer and fasting.

2. The laying on of hands is linked to a particular decision (the choice of Paul and Barnabas for missionary work).

3. No "office" is said to result from the laying on of hands (Paul and Barnabas are not said to have been "ordained" apostles).

Given all this, can Acts 13:1-3 in any way be construed as an ordination, and does it shed any light on the "ritual of appointment" in 1 Tim 4:14? One must admit that there are some interesting parallels between the two texts. Both Paul/Barnabas and Timothy are perceived as persons who have some kind of mandate for *missionary* work. And although "bishop" is a term never directly applied to Timothy either in Paul's letters or in the Pastorals, he could still be considered a "presbyter" in Powell's status-title sense and a "deacon" in the functional-ministerial sense. Indeed, Timothy is described as "God's co-worker" (1 Thess 3:2), as an "evangelist" (2 Tim 4:5), and as a deacon (1 Tim 4:6). As our previous discussions have shown, all three of these latter terms are related in the New Testament to Christians with missionary responsibility. Is there any significance to the fact that in both Acts 13:1-3 and 1 Tim 4:14, laying on of hands is linked with persons engaged in missionary activity? I believe there is, and will attempt to show why in the paragraphs that follow.

As used in the New Testament, the phrases "to lay on hands" (Greek, *epitithēmi tas cheiras*) or "the laying on of hands" (Greek, *hē epithesis tōn cheirōn*) do not have any essential connection with appointment to a ministry. Both verb and noun forms are used to describe a variety of actions: e.g., Jesus' healing of others (Mk 8:23), his "blessing" of children (Mt 19:13-15), the reception of the Spirit through laying on of hands by the apostles (Acts 8:17; 19:6).[65] It would be difficult to argue, therefore, that in the New Testament "laying on of hands" has already acquired the technical and precise meaning of "ordination". At the same time it is hard to dismiss passages like 1 Tim 4:14 as having no significance beyond a mere "pat of approval" for a mission undertaken or a task well done.

The solution to this apparent dilemma about the meaning of the laying on of hands in the New Testament can, I believe, be resolved if we pay closer attention to the larger context that, in each case, specifies the gesture's significance. That the gesture can convey meanings like "healing", "blessing" or "gift of the Spirit" need not conflict with a more specialized meaning in passages like Acts 13:1-3 or 1 Tim 1:14. In these latter two passages, as I have indicated, the gesture is directed toward persons who are missionaries. The same pattern, less apparent because of Luke's theological agenda, is found in Acts 6:6 (the seven Hellenists, Stephen and his group). As we have noted in Chapter Two, these Hellenists were almost certainly missionaries who carried the gospel message to places like Samaria and to hellenized Jews living outside Palestine. All three of these passages, then, make a connection between laying on of hands and the choice, election or appointment of missionar-

[65]See Adela Yarbro Collins, "The Ministry of Women in the Apostolic Generation," in Leonard and Arlene Swidler, eds., *Women Priests*. A Catholic Commentary on the Vatican Declaration, (New York: Paulist Press, 1977), pp. 159-166.

ies. By contrast, residential leaders like "bishops" are never described in the New Testament as having hands laid upon them. In 1 Tim 4:14, however, it is the *presbytery* that lays hands on the "deacon" Timothy — an action which would make sense if Powell's contention about the meaning of presbyterate (a status-title) in the Pastorals is correct. There would be nothing astonishing if the presbyters commissioned one of their own number (Timothy, a man recognized as among the first-fruits of Paul's labor and thus a presbyter in status) for the ministerial function of deacon. And if the deacon's function were missionary in nature, the presbyter's action of laying on hands in 1 Tim 4:14 would be entirely consistent with the other passages we have examined (Acts 6:6; 13:1-3).[66]

But what of a passage like Acts 14:23, where the presbyters themselves are said to be "appointed", and the Greek verb used to describe this action is *"cheirotonein"*, a word that later assumed the technical significance of "ordaining" someone? It should be noted first that although the Greek word for "hand" (*cheir*) appears in *cheirotonein*, the verb did not originally mean "to lay on hand(s)", but rather "to choose, elect by raising hands".[67] Or as we might express it today, the verb means to elect someone by having a "show of hands".[68] Acts 14:23 does not, therefore, speak of Paul and Barnabas "ordaining" presbyters through a "laying on of hands". If presbyters are "first-fruits", "first" in conversion and thus "senior" in status, then the passage makes greater sense. Paul and Barnabas are depicted by Luke as designating (through a "show of hands") those persons in the newly-founded churches whose conversion and faith exemplify a

[66]One might suggest that the earliest Christian "deacons" more closely resembled the missionary apostle (e.g., Paul) or the apostle's "co-worker".

[67]See Walter Bauer, *A Greek-English Lexicon of the New Testament*, translated from the fifth German edition by W.F. Arndt and F.W. Gingrich, (Second edition; Chicago: University of Chicago Press, 1958), p. 881.

[68]See Henry Liddell and Robert Scott, *A Greek-English Lexicon*, (New edition revised and augmented by H.S. Jones and R. McKenzie; 2 vols; Oxford: Clarendon Press, 1948), Vol. 2, p. 1986.

maturity worthy of imitation by all. Such "presbyters" would become the logical leaders (in status, though not necessarily in ministerial function) after the missionary apostles had moved on.

One other text needs to be considered in this connection. In 1 Tim 5:22, Timothy is warned "not to be hasty in the laying-on of hands". Catholic commentators have frequently taken this passage as evidence for ordination through the laying on of hands, on the anachronistic assumption that Timothy was somehow a "bishop" who ordained "presbyters".[69] As we have already noted, it cannot be assumed that Timothy was a bishop in the functional-ministerial sense, though he is explicitly called a "deacon". Even if Timothy were a "bishop", the Pastorals nowhere connect episcopal ministry with "sacramental" acts like "ordination". The larger context of 1 Tim 5:22 suggests instead that the warning is addressed to Timothy precisely because he implicitly belongs to that status-titled group, the "presbyters". Because he is a *presbyter*, and because presbyters are linked with laying hands on those chosen for functional ministries (see 1 Tim 4:14), Timothy is advised to be cautious.[70]

It is my conviction, then, that the laying on of hands as a "commissioning" gesture has very restricted significance in the New Testament. It seems linked to the special circumstances of people who are designated for missionary work (e.g., "apostles" like Paul and Barnabas, a "deacon" like Timothy, the "Seven" hellenist-missionaries of Acts 6:6). Nowhere are bishops described as having hands laid on them for their ministry in the local church. Nor do presby-

---

[69]See, for example, George Denzer, "The Pastoral Letters," in *The Jerome Biblical Commentary*, edited by Raymond Brown, Joseph Fitzmyer, and Roland Murphy, (Englewood Cliffs, New Jersey: Prentice-Hall, Inc., 1968), Vol. II, p. 356 (57:29).

[70]See further discussion of the passage in Fred Gealy and Morgan Noyes, "The First and Second Epistles to Timothy, and The Epistle to Titus," in: *The Interpreter's Bible*, edited by George A. Buttrick *et. al.*, (12 vols.; Nashville: Abingdon Press, 1951), Vol. 11, pp. 444-445.

ters appear to receive their status in the community through a ritual laying on of hands, though the presbyters themselves may employ this gesture on some occasions (1 Tim 4:14).

But why would missionary workers need some "ritual" form of designation for their ministry? The question can be answered, I think, if we recall the crisis of leadership that beset second- and third-generation Christians. We noted earlier that after 70 C.E. many Christians became suspicious of those wandering charismatics and prophets who claimed to speak in the name of the Risen Lord. One can assume that the behavior and doctrine of a functioning residential minister (e.g., a bishop) would be well known in a community, but the itinerant missionary's status was more difficult to assess. Thus Matthew warns against "wolves in sheeps' clothing" (Mt 7:15), while the *Didache*, a manual of catechesis and church practice produced probably in the late-first and early-second centuries, outlines criteria by which a true prophet can be distinguished from a false one (*Didache* 12, 13). The laying on of hands by those "first" in conversion and senior in status in the local church (the presbyters) might have provided legitimation for a missionary who would travel to distant congregations.

In summary, the question "does ordination exist in the New Testament?" is poorly posed. It would be preferable to ask how Christian communities of the first, second and third generations recognized leaders, and how those leaders gained authoritative status through their ministerial service. That recognized leadership existed in earliest Christianity is clear, for example, from the relation between Paul and his missionary communities (e.g., Corinth, Galatia). Paul obviously thought of himself as an authority to be reckoned with, and he legitimated his position by appealing to a mandate from the Risen One (see Gal 1:1, 11-17). By the second and third generations, however, it was more difficult to discern who might legitimately claim a "mandate" for ministry. In local churches, resident leaders could be chosen, probably through election, because their quality of life and teaching were well known and long observed.

(Recall that 1 Tim 3:6 excludes from leadership those *recently* converted and baptized.) Increasingly, however, the "missionary" presented a problem. The old apostles, in both the Pauline and Lukan senses, had passed on; the prophets were a source of increasing anxiety to those — like Matthew — who wanted to fix and preserve the tradition of Jesus' sayings. Sources of the second (Luke/Acts) and third (the Pastorals) generations reveal a tendency to limit or control the innovative impulses linked with missionary figures like the Pauline apostle or the wandering prophet. Paul, certainly an innovator in his own lifetime, is thus pictured by Luke as chosen and ritually designated for his work through a laying on of hands (Acts 13:1-3); Timothy is similarly depicted in the Pastorals (1 Tim 4:14).

In the New Testament, therefore, the gesture of laying on hands for ministry should be viewed in relation to the pastoral problems and leadership-crisis which second- and third-generation Christianity faced. We cannot speak of a general custom of "ordaining" leaders at this period, but we can say that in some situations, persons chosen for a special task (e.g., missionary work) received a laying on of hands within the "liturgical" context of assembly, prayer and prophecy.

LEADERSHIP AND EUCHARISTIC MINISTRY

A final point needs discussion before we conclude our section on ministry in second- and third-generation Christianity: the relation between church leadership and eucharistic presidency. This issue, like that of "ordination", is perhaps beside the point. In the New Testament, ministry does not organize itself around the liturgy but around building up the community's life. Preaching, admonition and leadership are more central than questions about "who presides" at baptism or eucharist.[71] The fundamental pur-

---

[71]See Schillebeeckx, *Ministry*, pp. 29-30.

pose of ministry, as the New Testament understands it, is to preserve the community's self-identity as the *community of Jesus*, to help it discover the *gospel* amid the changing circumstances of its life.

For this reason the literature of the New Testament shows little interest in questions of "presidency" or leadership at the eucharist. Paul seems to be cast in this role by Luke in Acts 20:11, but the apostle himself never mentions presiding at eucharist. The Pastorals, as we have seen, say a good deal about "bishops" and "deacons", but never list "leading the church at eucharist" among their tasks. There is absolutely nothing in the New Testament about a "chain of sacramental power" passed from Jesus to the Twelve, to the Missionary apostles, to the bishops.[72] The most we can say, as Raymond Brown notes, is that *someone* must have led the community when it gathered for the Lord's Supper — and that this "someone's" leadership must have been acknowledged by those assembled.[73] Beyond that, our knowledge is meager indeed. We are never told *how* someone acquired such a position, nor whether it was permanent or merely "ad hoc". Nor are we told by the New Testament sources that presiding at eucharist is an exclusively male prerogative. It seems likely, for example, that in house churches, the host or hostess presided, and the New Testament refers explicitly to women whose houses were used for Christian meetings (see, e.g., Col 4:15).[74]

Nowhere in the New Testament, then is an explicit connection made between ministry in the church and the act of presiding at eucharist. This probably does not mean, however, that anyone at all could lead the community in the celebration of the meal. As Edward Schillebeeckx has observed, the New Testament seems to assume that anyone competent to serve the church in matters of public responsibility would, *ipso facto*, be competent to preside at eucha-

---

[72]See Brown, *Priest and Bishop*, p. 41.

[73]*Ibid.*

[74]See Schillebeeckx, *Ministry*, p. 30.

rist.[75] For this reason, no "separate authorization" (e.g., a laying on of hands) would have been needed in order to legitimate the ministry of leading the church at the Lord's Supper.[76]

By the end of the first or beginning of the second century, however, this situation seems to have begun changing. In non-canonical sources contemporary with the late New Testament writings, one can detect a change of practice with regard to who presides at eucharist. The *Didache*, for example, speaks of permitting prophets to "make eucharist" (Greek, *eucharistein*) (Did 10:7), but later the document speaks of choosing "bishops and deacons" who can fulfill the "ministry" (Greek, *leitourgian*) of the "prophets and teachers" (Did 15:1). The two chapters of the *Didache* date from different decades, with Chapter 15 being a later addition. This probably reveals a change in practice. As itinerants, prophets could not always be counted on to be present when the community gathered for worship on Sunday (Did 14:1). It would thus have been necessary for others to lead the community in the breaking of bread. These "others" were probably the "bishops and deacons" of Did 15:1).[77]

A similar shift can be detected in the so-called "First Letter of Clement", actually a letter from the church in Rome to the church in Corinth, written about 95 C.E.[78] 1 Clem 44:4 refers to those "of the episcopate" who offer "sacrificial gifts."[79] The reference may well be to local leaders (bishops or presbyter-bishops) who preside at eucharist.[80] 1 Clement appears to distinguish, in fact, between presbyters who are "*episkopoi*" and those who are not. The

[75]*Ibid.*

[76]*Ibid.*

[77]See Brown, *Priest and Bishop*, p. 42.

[78]The Greek text and an English translation of 1 Clement may be found in Kirsopp Lake, *The Apostolic Fathers*, (The Loeb Classical Library; 2 vols.; Cambridge, Massachusetts: Harvard University Press, 1977), Vol. I, pp. 8-121.

[79]Text and translation in Lake, *The Apostolic Fathers*, Vol. I, pp. 84-85.

[80]See Brown, *Priest and Bishop*, p. 42.

ministry of those presbyters who are "bishops" seems to include "celebrating the sacrifices" (see 1 Clem 40:2).[81] Further, 1 Clement seems to introduce a distinction, unknown earlier, between the church leaders who constitute a "*klēros*" ("clergy") and other believers who form the "*laos*" ("people") (see 1 Clem 40:5).[82]

By the time we reach the letters of Ignatius of Antioch, it is quite clear that bishops are eucharistic presiders: "Let that be considered a valid eucharist which is celebrated by the bishop, or by one whom he appoints. . . . It is not lawful either to baptise or to hold an 'agape' without the bishop" (Smyrnaeans 7:1-2).[83] While this text reveals that others besides the bishop could lead the church at eucharist, Ignatius' clear preference is for the *one* bishop to preside. It should be noted, too, that Ignatius thinks of a single bishop for each church. For this reason Ignatius has sometimes been considered the first example of a movement toward "monarchic" episcopate, though it is more accurate to speak of Ignatian "mono-episcopate" (one church, one bishop).

We can say, then, that although the New Testament does not link ministry to eucharistic presidency, other documents from the late-first and early-second centuries have begun making this connection. It is not clear, however, whether sources like the *Didache*, 1 Clement, and the letters of Ignatius presumed that presiders needed some ritual authorization (e.g., laying on of hands) in order to lead the community in the breaking of bread. In the section of this chapter which follows, we will need to ask when and how churches chose to connect the "office" of bishop with eucharistic presidency and with a ritual authorization mediated through the laying on of hands by others who were similarly "ordained".

[81]Text and translation in Lake, *The Apostolic Fathers*, Vol. I, pp. 76-77.

[82]Text and translation in Lake, *The Apostolic Fathers*, Vol. I, pp. 78-79.

[83]Text and translation in Lake, *The Apostolic Fathers*, Vol. I, pp. 260-261.

II

Second Century Christianity

It is quite clear that by the beginning of the *third* century, three distinct offices — bishop, presbyter and deacon — had emerged in the Christian churches, and that these officers ordinarily attained their position through some form of election, together with a ritual of ordination that included prayer and the laying on of hands. This is precisely what we find in the *Apostolic Tradition* of Hippolytus (ca. 215), a document that may reflect customs of the church at Rome. Ordination prayers for bishop, presbyter and deacon are found in *Apostolic Tradition*, and in each case the ritual includes an imposition of hands by a bishop or (in the case of episcopal ordination) by several bishops. "Let him be ordained bishop," the *Apostolic Tradition* instructs, "who has been chosen by all the people; and when he has been named and accepted by all, let the people assemble, together with the presbyters and those bishops who are present, on the Lord's day."[84] The text goes on to describe the laying on of hands and the prayer of ordination. Similar provisions are found for presbyters and deacons in the *Apostolic Tradition*: "And when a presbyter is ordained, the bishop shall lay his hand on his head, the presbyters also touching him .... And when a deacon is ordained, let him be chosen according to what was said above, the bishop alone laying on hands... "[85]

This full-blown liturgical description from the early third century has led scholars to ask what led to the custom of laying on hands as an ordination gesture. As we have seen, the New Testament passages which speak of laying on hands cannot be taken as evidence for a general practice commonly used whenever residential church leaders were

---

[84]Text cited from Geoffrey Cuming, trans., *Hippolytus: A Text for Students*, (Grobe Liturgical Study, No. 8; Bramcote, Notts., England: Grobe Books, 1976), p. 8.

[85]*Apostolic Tradition*, pp. 7-8; cited from Cuming (note 84, above), pp. 12-13.

chosen. Furthermore, non-scriptural sources of the late-first and early-second centuries like the *Didache, First Clement* and the letters of Ignatius never mention "imposition of hands", even though they refer explicitly to the election or appointment of bishops and deacons.[86]

Later Christian literature of the second century is also silent about any ritual of ordination for local church leaders. In his famous description of Sunday worship, Justin Martyr (ca. 150) outlines the eucharistic celebration and speaks of "one who presides" at it, but says nothing about this presider's position (bishop?) nor about an ordination which qualifies him for this ministry. Toward the latter part of the second century, Irenaeus of Lyons (ca. 180), in his work *Against Heresies*, provides us with a list of "bishops" of the Roman church, but never alludes to an "imposition of hands" through which the office was transmitted from one incumbent to another.[87]

Some scholars have seen a reference to the practice of laying on hands in the apocryphal *Acts of Peter*, which was probably written in Asia Minor toward the end of the second century (ca. 190-200).[88] In a section of this document which describes the call of the apostles, we are told that Christ "chose and laid hands on them".[89] Since Jesus is not represented in the Scripture as having used this gesture in calling the apostles, some have argued that it reflects the

[86]See Johannes Behm, *Die Handauflegung im Urchristentum*, (Darmstadt: Wissenschaftliche Buchgesellschaft, 1968; reprint of the 1911 edition), pp. 72-73.

[87]See Irenaeus, *Adversus Haereses*, III.2-2; Latin text, with French translation, in Adelin Rousseau and Louis Doutreleau, eds., *Irenee de Lyons, Contre les Heresies*, Livre III, (2 vols.; Sources chretiennes, pp. 210-211; Paris; Cerf, 1974), Vol. II, pp. 32-39. The list of Roman "bishops" in Irenaeus is complicated; for further discussion on the list and its meaning, see Rousseau and Doutreleau, Vol. I (Sources chretiennes, 210), pp. 222-236.

[88]See Pierre Galtier, "Imposition des Mains," *Dictionnaire de Theologie Catholique*, edited by A. Vacant et al., (15 vols.; Paris: Libraire Letouzey et Ane, 1930-1950), Vol. VII/2, col. 1331.

[89]Acts of Peter, Chapter 10; Latin text with French translation in Leon Vouaux, ed., *Les Actes de Pierre*: Documents pour servir a l'etude des origines chretiennes, (Paris: Librarie Letouzey et Ane, 1922), pp. 296-297.

common custom at ordination in the late second century.[90] But as Edward Kilmartin has noted, the larger context of the *Acts of Peter* does not really support this interpretation.[91] More probably the laying on of hands signifies Jesus' forgiveness of the apostles (who had doubted him) and his subsequent choice of them as collaborators in his mission.

Second century sources thus appear to be silent about the use of laying on hands as a way to "ordain" or commission local leaders. One might, of course, argue from silence and maintain that laying on hands was so common that it needed no comment. But such arguments are notoriously unreliable, and in this case they may be quite misleading. It is curious, for example, that nowhere in the second-century sources we have studies do we find an allusion to the so-called "ordination ritual" of the Pastoral Letters as a basis for Christian practice. This may be due, in part, to the slow process by which churches gradually determined what writings belong to the "canon" of inspired Scripture. The Pastorals may not have been perceived by some second-century Christians as belonging to the Bible, while other documents later considered non-scriptural — e.g., the letters of Ignatius — may have been accepted and read in many churches. In any case it is clear that in orthodox Christian writings of the second century, texts like 1 Tim 4:14 or Acts 13:1-3 are not invoked to support laying on of hands as an "ordination gesture".

There is, moreover, evidence that some churches developed customs for commissioning or designating local leaders that did not include a laying on of hands. In Letter 146 of St. Jerome, written to the presbyter Evangelus sometime during the episcopate of Pope Damasus (366-384), there is a description of an earlier custom used at Alexandria for the selection of its bishop. Jerome writes:

> At Alexandria, from the time of Mark the evangelist until the time of bishops Heraclas (232-247) and Denis

[90]See Behm, *Die Handaufelgung*, p. 73.

[91]See Kilmartin, "Ministere et Ordination," pp. 79-80.

(247-264), the presbyters always installed one elected from among themselves as bishop, whom they then enthroned—much like soldiers designate their "emperor" or deacons elect as archdeacon one of their own number well known for his industriousness....[92]

It will be noted that Jerome does not mention a laying on of hands either by the presbyters or by bishops from neighboring churches. Apparently, the very act of seating ("enthroning") the bishop-elect was considered sufficient. The Alexandrian custom would thus resemble a form of installation commonly used for public officials (e.g., the consul, the praetor) in the ancient Roman world. By taking his seat (his *cathedra* or episcopal chair), the bishop-elect performed his first public episcopal act and thus effectively *became bishop*.[93] Jerome would have us believe, moreover, that this was the custom followed in Alexandria from earliest Christian times (in popular legend the evangelist Mark was regarded as that city's first bishop) until past the middle of the third century.

 (handwritten margin note: "or a does he just not mention it?")

It is difficult, however, to confirm the accuracy of Jerome's report. No other early Christian writer mentions this Alexandrian custom, and it is certainly contrary to the procedures we find in the *Apostolic Tradition*, where there is a clear distinction between the bishop's *election* "by all the people" and his *ordination* by the "bishops who are present". Besides, Jerome's vigorously anti-episcopal feeling and his contempt for customs attached to ordination are well known.[94] There is a growing consensus among recent scholars, however, that Jerome was probably not fabricat-

[92]Jerome, Letter 146; Latin text in Isidore Hilberg, ed., *Sancti Eusebii Hieronymi Epistulae*, (3 vols.; Corpus Scriptorum Ecclesiasticorum Latinorum, 54-56; Vienna: F. Tempsky, 1910-1918), Vol. 3 (CSEL 56), p. 310; my translation.

[93]See the discussion in Cyrille Vogel, *Ordinations inconsistantes et Caractere inamissible*, (Etudes d'histoire du culte et des institutions chretiennes, Vol. 1; Turin: Bottega d'Erasmo, 1978), pp. (78)-(80).

[94]*Ibid.*, p. (79).

ing history when he spoke of the manner in which early Alexandrian bishops entered upon their ministry.[95] Although the question has not been completely settled, the evidence points toward the fundamental accuracy of Jerome's report, and there is reason to believe that a similar custom may have been followed at an early period in churches like those of Antioch, Rome and Lyons.[96]

To persons familiar with the long tradition that regards laying on of hands as an element essential for valid ordination, the practice of the Alexandrian church (and of other churches too, perhaps) may seem astonishing. One must remember, however, that "ritual validation" is only one of several means which churches have historically used to designate ministers.[97] As Cyril Vogel has noted, the ultimately essential item in the choice and designation of ministers is *the mandate of the church*, i.e., the mission which the church entrusts to one or another of the faithful in view of a ministry to be carried out.[98] Liturgically, this mandate is ordinarily transmitted to a candidate — in the traditions of both the East and the West — through the ritual gesture of imposing hands; at least this appears to be the case from the third century onward. But there is no overwhelming reason why churches would need to use this gesture alone in order to "ordain" someone. The Alexandrian church's early custom — "ordination" of the bishop by seating him in the episcopal chair — would also have been a legitimate way to entrust the church's mandate to an individual.

Even after the beginning of the third century, individuals were sometimes accorded official ministerial status (usually as presbyters) without any ritual intervention such as a

---

[95]See W. Telfer, "Episcopal Succession in Egypt," *Journal of Ecclesiastical History* 3 (1952), pp. 1-13.

[96]See Kilian McDonnell, "Ways of Validating Ministry," *Journal of Ecumenical Studies* 7 (1970), pp. 209-265, especially 231-234.

[97]Other forms of ministerial validation, such as the "charismatic" and the "ecclesiological", are discussed by Kilian McDonnell in the article cited in the preceding note.

[98]See Vogel, *Ordinations inconsistantes*, p. (113), cf. pp. (82)-(83).

liturgy of ordination or the imposition of hands. The same Hippolytus who gave us our earliest ordination prayers also knew of "confessors" (persons persecuted for the faith) who became deacons or presbyters without any laying on of hands:

> A confessor, if he was in chains for the name of the Lord, shall not have hands laid on him for the diaconate or the presbyterate, for he has the honour of the presbyterate by his confession. But if he is appointed bishop, hands shall be laid on him.[99]

Similarly, in Cyprian's letter defending the election of Cornelius as bishop of Rome (written about 251), nothing is said about laying on of hands.[100] While it is true that Cyprian did not intend to provide a complete dossier of all circumstances surrounding Cornelius's election, it is curious that he would have overlooked the laying on of hands, since this gesture might have supported his arguments in favor of Cornelius's legitimacy as bishop. Elsewhere, moreover, Cyprian explicitly refers to the imposition of hands as one of the factors that constitute valid episcopal ordination.[101]

It is possible, of course, that Rome simply did not use the laying on of hands in the ordination of its bishops in the mid-third century. This may seem startling in the light of the evidence we have seen in *Apostolic Tradition*, purportedly a Roman document. It must be remembered, however, that the Hippolytus responsible for the *Apostolic Tradition* was leader of a *dissident* group within the Roman church and that his views were not necessarily those of the party in

[99]*Apostolic Tradition*, 9; translation from Cuming (note 84, above), p. 14.

[100]Cyprian, Letter 55.8. Latin text in G. Hartel, ed., *S. Thasci Caecili Cypriani Epistulae*, (Corpus Scriptorum Ecclesiasticorum Latinorum, III/2; Vienna, 1871), pp. 629-630. English translation of the letter in Rose Bernard Donna, trans., *St. Cyprian: Letters 1-81*, (Fathers of the Church, Vol. 51; Washington, D.C.: Catholic University of American Press, 1964), pp. 138-139.

[101]See Cyprian, Letter 67.5. Latin text in CSEL III/2 (ed. Hartel), p. 739; English translation in Donna, *St. Cyprian: Letters 1-81*, pp. 235-236.

power.[102] Furthermore, in the earliest Roman ordination ritual written in Latin, contained in Ordo Romanus 34 (manuscript copied ca. 700-750), absolutely nothing is said about the imposition of hands for a bishop, presbyter or deacon.[103] Commenting on *Ordo Romanus* 34, Michael Andrieu argued that the author omitted reference to the laying on of hands because he was merely providing a "summary description" of the ordination rite.[104] But in recent studies Cyril Vogel has called Andrieu's judgment on this point into question.[105] Vogel comments:

> In spite of this booklet's rusticity of language and its evident brevity, one finds gathered there a number of details relating to gestures, vestments, prostrations, and chants. Under these conditions it is difficult to believe that if, during the period when the redactor of *Ordo* 34 compiled his directory in a decadent Rome, the rite of imposing hands had had the least prominence, it would not have been mentioned.[106]

As astonishing as it may seem, therefore, our evidence for imposition of hands as a prominent element in the ordination rites of the Roman church is rather scanty — at least during the first several centuries of the Christian era. We are forced to conclude, then, that in the second cen-

---

[102]On Hippolytus's career and its relation to the Roman bishops of the early third century, see G.L. Prestige, *Fathers and Heretics*, (The Bampton Lectures for 1940; London: S.P.C.K., 1963, paperback edition), pp. 23-42.

[103]Latin text of Ordo Romanus 34 in Michel Andrieu, ed., *Les Ordines Romani du haut moyen age*, (4 vols.; Louvain, 1951), Vol. III, pp. 603-613. The original language of the Apostolic Tradition was Greek, though the document survives in a partial Latin translation and in other languages or dialects (e.g., Ethiopic, Sahidic). The "Leonine" (or "Verona") Sacramentary, composed in Latin and copied ca. 600, provides prayers for ordination but does not give us a description of the ritual. For its ordination prayers, see L. Cunibert Mohlberg, ed., *Sacramentarium Veronense*, (Rerum Ecclesiasticarum Documenta, Series Maior, Fontes, I; Rome: Herder, 1956), nn. 942-954, pp. 118-122.

[104]See Andrieu, *Les Ordines Romani*, III, pp. 559, 569.

[105]See Vogel, *Ordinations inconsistantes*, pp. (131)-(132).

[106]*Ibid.*, p. (131); my translation.

tury — and even later, in some churches — laying on hands does not seem to have been a prominent feature in the commissioning or "ordaining" of church leaders. On this point arguments from silence are not persuasive, especially since there is reasonably good evidence that some churches (e.g., Alexandria) devised other methods for installing persons in an ecclesiastical ministry (e.g., that of bishop). Not until the early third century do we encounter a document, Hippolytus's *Apostolic Tradition*, which insists upon imposition of hands as part of the ordination rite for bishops, presbyters and deacons. And even then it is impossible to conclude that *all* churches would have regarded Hippolytus's rite as essential in all circumstances.

PRESBYTERS, BISHOPS AND DEACONS — AGAIN

Earlier in this chapter, our discussion of church order in the Pastorals led us to conclude that in the later literature of the New Testament there is no evidence for a hierarchically arranged system of ministerial "orders" composed of bishop, presbyter and deacon. Following the suggestion of Douglas Powell, however, we noted a distinction between persons of authoritative status (the presbyters, first in conversion and thus "senior" in the community) and persons with a ministerial function (the bishops and deacons). The two categories — status and function — are not exclusive; indeed, it seems likely that those who performed episcopal or diaconal ministry were drawn from among the *presbyteroi*. This distinction will prove useful, as well, when we examine the non-biblical literature of the late-first and early-second centuries, particularly the so-called "First Letter of Clement" (ca. 95) and the letters of Ignatius of Antioch (ca. 110).

1 Clement, a letter written from the church at Rome to the church at Corinth, has been the topic of enormous debate among scholars of the late-nineteenth and twentieth centuries.[107] Its importance derives not only from its early date (it is contemporary with New Testament sources like the Gospel of John), but also from its information about church order and the advisory role of the Roman community in matters affecting the internal affairs of other churches. The immediate occasion that prompted the writing of *1 Clement* was a rebellion against the "presbyters" at Corinth (1 Clem 47:6). The author insists that the rebels must repent and submit to the presbyters (1 Clem 57:1), since these latter are part of that God-willed order which has been handed on from Christ through the apostles (1 Clem 44).

Who were these Corinthian presbyters and what was their role in the life of the church there? At first glance their exact identity in 1 Clement seems confusing, for we are first told that the apostles "appointed their first converts, testing them by the Spirit, to be *bishops and deacons* of the future believers" (42:4-5), while later we read that the contentious Corinthians have removed some of the *presbyters* "in spite of their good service" (44:5-6).[108] Here we find the same kind of shifting references to bishops, deacons and presbyters which we observed in the Pastoral letters. If we bear in mind the distinction between status-title and function-title proposed by Powell, however, the situation in the Corinthian church becomes much clearer. The presbyters of 1 Clement, like those of the Pastorals, are persons senior in status and authority, worthy of respect and imitation by all. *Some* of these presbyters have specific ministries to fulfill: the deacons and bishops. In other words, the Corinthian bishops and deacons (function-titles) belong to that larger class, the presbyterate (status-title).[109] Among the ministerial responsibilities of the bishops is the task of offering the community's gifts and sacrifices — almost surely a reference to

[107]For a recent summary of this scholarship, see John Fuellenbach, *Ecclesiastical Office and the Primacy of Rome*, (Studies in Christian Antiquity, No. 20; Washington, D.C.: Catholic University of America Press, 1980).

[108]Text and translation in Lake, *The Apostolic Fathers*, Vol. I, pp. 80-81, 84-85.

[109]See Powell, "Ordo Presbyterii," p. 306.

presiding at eucharist (see 1 Clem 40:2-5; 44:4).[110]

In this order of status (presbyterate) and ministries (episcopal, diaconal), the author of 1 Clement sees a divinely-willed "succession". The apostles received the gospel from Christ; they in turn transmitted it to their "first converts", the "bishops and deacons of the future believers" (1 Clem 42:1-5).[111] The reference to "first converts" fits in perfectly with the notion of presbyters as the first-fruits of the apostolic mission, provided we remember that 1 Clement's functioning ministers (bishops and deacons) belong to the authoritative status-group (presbyterate).[112] This order of authority and ministry is also similar, 1 Clement argues, to the ordinances of Jewish life and worship, where high priest, priests, Levites, and laity each had a proper service to perform (40:4-5).[113]

In 1 Clement, therefore, church order, status and ministry are not merely practical conveniences but divinely-willed realities that form part of the tradition transmitted by Christ's apostles. The ministry of bishops and deacons is defended by appeal to the Scriptures (1 Clem 42:5); rebellion against the presbyters is tantamount to rebellion against Christ and God (44:4-5; 54:1-4; 57:1-7). An incipient theology of church order and ministry has already begun to emerge in this document, and we will see further theological development in letters of Ignatius of Antioch.

Turning to those letters, we find a pattern of local church leadership that both resembles and differs from 1 Clement. The most striking feature of Ignatian church order is the role of the bishop. From 1 Clement, one gets the impression that several "*episkopoi*" minister in the Corinthian community (1 Clem 42:4, 44:4), but in Ignatius's letters the bishop is a single individual who can be greeted by name: "I

---

[110]Text and translation in Lake, *The Apostolic Fathers*, Vol. I, pp. 76-79, 84-85.

[111]Text and translation in Lake, *The Apostolic Fathers*, Vol. I, pp. 78-81.

[112]See Schillebeeckx, *Ministry*, p. 19, for 1 Clement's view that church order is a divinely-willed institution.

[113]Text and translation in Lake, *The Apostolic Fathers*, Vol. I, pp. 76-79.

received in the name of God your whole congregation in the person of Onesimus. . . . your bishop" (Eph 1:3); "I was permitted to see you in the person of Damas, your godly bishop." (Magn 2:1); "I know that your bishop obtained the ministry. . . . in the love of God the Father and the Lord Jesus Christ" (Philad 1:1).[114] Only in his letter to the Romans does Ignatius omit references to the bishop.

While he was not a monarch, the Ignatian bishop was very clearly a person of authority. Likened to God the Father (Trall 3:1; Magn 6:1; 13:1-2; Eph 5:2), the bishop is also the visible representative of Jesus Christ, who is every church's "unseen bishop." Apart from the bishop, no legitimate eucharist is possible (Smyrn 8:1-2), and he is the leader who gathers the Christian assembly, writes to other churches, supervises marriage arrangements, and watches over widows (Ign to Polyc 7:2; 8:1; 5:2; 3:4).

Deacons, too, are important ministers in Ignatius's letters. They frequently act as itinerant emissaries or "ambassadors" from one church to another (Philip 4:1; Smyrn 10:1; 11:2-3; 12:1). One is reminded of the missionary Timothy, Paul's co-worker and a "deacon" (1 Tim 4:6). In his letter to the Trallians 2:3, Ignatius insists that the deacon's work is not limited to "food and drink" (i.e., to waiting tables). Deacons are, he insists, true servants of the church of God (Trall 2:3). It is perhaps significant that the word Ignatius uses to describe deacons as "servants" is *hyperetai,* a Pauline term linked to the ministry of missionary apostles (1 Cor 4:1). The Ignatian deacon's work is not restricted to service in the local church but includes participation in missionary tasks.[115]

The Ignatian portrait of bishop and deacon is, then, reasonably clear. But once again we have to ask who the *presbyters* were. That they are persons held in high esteem is

---

[114]Text and translation of Ignatius's letters in Lake, *The Apostolic Fathers*, Vol. I, pp. 172-277.

[115]More detailed discussion will be found in Lemaire, *Les Ministeres*, pp. 177-178.

obvious. Consistently they are compared to the "council of the apostles" (Magn 6:1, Trall 3:1, Smyrn 8:1), and in fact the apostles themselves are called the "presbyters of the church" (Philad 5:1). Deacons are expected to be subject to the bishop and to the presbytery (Magn 2:1). In Magnesians 3:1-2, Ignatius counsels the "holy presbyters" of that church not to presume on the youth of the bishop, but to render him all respect.... (and) yield to him in their godly prudence."

Does this mean that the Ignatian presbyters are a "college" of *ministers*, superior in authority to the deacons but inferior to the bishop? The answer is probably no. Like the presbyters of the Pastorals and 1 Clement, the ones referred to by Ignatius seem to constitute a group distinguished by status but not by function. The functional titles of ministry belong to the bishop and the deacons, while those authoritative leaders "with no functional title" remain simple presbyters.[116] This helps explain the consistency of Ignatius's typology for the presbyters: They are always the "type" of the *apostles*, those "first disciples" of Jesus. One could say, perhaps, that the presbyters are distinguished in status precisely because they are premiere examples of discipleship, types of those who first heard the gospel, believed its message, and grew fruitful in faith and conversion of life. The presbyters are esteemed not because they perform a "ministry" or have a "job to do", but because their lives reveal the deep maturity of faith. They are "types" in the radical sense of that word (used, e.g., in 1 Pet 5:3, Rom 5:14): not examples *we* choose to follow, but examples guaranteed and authenticated by *God*, as the first apostles were.[117]

There appears to be, then, a parallelism of pattern between 1 Clement and the letters of Ignatius. In both cases, "presbyter" seems to be a title of status or condition rather than a descriptive term for ministerial function. The persons who carry out tasks of ministry in both 1 Clement and

---

[116]See Powell, "Ordo Presbyterii," p. 307.

[117]For this meaning of "type", see *ibid.*, pp. 324-325.

Ignatius are "bishops and deacons," though the Ignatian bishop is a single individual in each church. Part of the episcopal ministry is liturgical: Clement's bishops offer the community's gifts and sacrifices, while Ignatius's bishop presides at eucharist.

It does not seem, therefore, that in the early second century presbyters were regarded as "ministerial" figures or as a "college" of leaders with specialized tasks to perform. Still, there may be exceptions to this pattern. In the greeting of Polycarp's letter to the Philippians, the author never refers to himself as a "bishop" (though he is so addressed by Ignatius); he speaks instead of "Polycarp and the presbyters with him".[118] Later in the same letter, Polycarp outlines the presbyters' duties: They are to bring back the straying, visit the sick, care for widows, orphans and the poor, serve as "judges" and avoid avarice.[119] These duties resemble the tasks of an Ignatian bishop, and this has led some to suggest that Polycarp's presbyters are really "*episkopoi*" — or that Polycarp's church (Smyrna) knew only a collegial ministry of presbyters or "presbyter-bishops") and had not yet adopted Ignatius's model of "mono-episcopacy".

Here again, the distinction between status-title and function-title is useful. Ignatius clearly assumes that Polycarp is "bishop of the Church of the Smyrnaeans" (Ign to Polyc, greeting).[120] Further, in his letter to the Smyrnaeans, Ignatius employs the same consistent typology he uses elsewhere: "See that you all follow the bishop, as Jesus Christ follows the Father, and the presbytery as if it were the Apostles" (Smyrn 8:1).[121] There is nothing in the greeting of Polycarp's own letter to the Philippians that would deny the author's episcopal function — especially since "presbyterate" is, as we have seen, a status-title which can include

---

[118]Text and translation in Lake, *The Apostolic Fathers*, Vol. I, pp. 282-283.

[119]Polycarp to the Philippians, 6; text and translation in Lake, *The Apostolic Fathers*, Vol. I, pp. 290-291.

[120]Text and translation *ibid.*, Vol. I, pp. 266-267.

[121]Text and translation *ibid.*, Vol. I, pp. 260-261.

persons who also have a function-title (bishops and deacons). Nor is there any special difficulty in the duties Polycarp links with the "presbyters", since none of them involve
actions which 1 Clement and Ignatius "reserve" to bishops
(offering sacrifices, presiding at eucharist). It would thus be
hard to argue that Polycarp's presbyters are equivalent to
Clement's *episkopoi* or Ignatius's solitary bishop. More
probably, Polycarp is a "bishop", while Smyrna's presbytery is the "council of apostles", the "type" of those first
disciples who believed and converted.

To repeat: There is little in these second century sources
that indicates any specialized ministerial function attached
to presbyters as such. They are neither emissaries from one
church to another (like Ignatius's deacons), nor presiding
ministers of the eucharist (as Clement's and Ignatius's
bishop(s) appear to be). Throughout the second century, in
fact, one gets the impression that presbyter remains a
"status-title" rather than one denoting ministry and function. Irenaeus of Lyons (ca. 180), for example, speaks of
presbyters as "disciples of the apostles" (*Against Heresies*,
II:33:3).[122] This would make the presbyters authoritative
ancestors in the faith who had had immediate contact with
Christ's apostles, the "first disciples". Since Polycarp was
supposed to have been acquainted with "John the apostle",
status-title would be perfectly logical even if (as seems
likely) Polycarp was *functionally* a bishop.[123] For Irenaeus,
the importance of presbyters lay in their role as teaching
authorities responsible for the authentic exposition of
Scripture and Christian doctrine. This understanding of
presbyterate is one Irenaeus may have derived from Papias
(ca. 60-130), who was supposedly bishop of Hierapolis in
Asia Minor and whose five books entitled *Exegesis of the
Lord's Gospel*, though lost, are quoted in Eusebius's *Eccle-*

[122]Text in W. Wigan Harvey, ed., *Sancti Irenaei Libros quinque Adversus
Haereses*, (2 vols.; Cambridge, 1857), Vol. I, p. 331.

[123]Text will be found *ibid.*, Vol II, p. 254.

siastical History (III:39).[124] Though the exact meaning of "presbyter" in Papias's fragments has been disputed, it appears to signify "an old and reverend person who is cited with respect, whether he is an ecclesiastical writer, or the source of an oral tradition, or one who hands on an earlier tradition."[125] In borrowing "presbyter" from Papias, Irenaeus seems to have narrowed its meaning. A Papian presbyter might have been any ancient disciple (an apostle, an apostle's pupil, a bearer of early traditions about Jesus); the Irenaean presbyter seems to have been strictly an apostle's pupil and thus a vital link in that chain of doctrine which constitutes "apostolic succession." One can understand why Irenaeus, combatting heresy, was anxious to link these ancient presbyters with the ecclesiastical office of bishop, since this helped establish an unbroken line of authoritative teaching in the church: Christ, the apostles, the presbyters (apostle's pupils), bishops. And in light of the distinction between status and function which we have been using, Irenaeus's linkage makes historical sense. Bishops do, in fact, seem to have emerged as a differentiated functional ministry from among the status-title-bearing presbyters.[126]

Were the second-century presbyters or the ministerial "bishops and deacons" regarded as priests? The sources indicate a lingering reluctance to apply the vocabulary of priesthood to Christians who guide or serve the churches. Ignatius, for example, never calls the bishop a priest (Greek, *hiereus*), though he does allude to the Jewish priests (Philad 9:1), as does 1 Clement (25:5). Later in the second century, Irenaeus uses "priest(s)" in reference to heretical groups (followers of Simon Magus, AH I.16:3; followers of the

---

[124]An English translation of the fragments of Papias's work may be found in James Kleist, trans., *The Didache, The Epistle of Barnabas, The Epistles and the Martyrdom of St. Polycarp, The Fragments of Papias, The Epistle of Diognetus,* (Ancient Christian Writers; Westminster, Maryland: The Newman Press, 1948), pp. 114-124.

[125]See Johannes Munck, "Presbyters and Disciples of the Lord in Papias," *Harvard Theological Review* 52 (1959), 233; full article, pp. 224-243.

[126]See Powell, "Ordo Presbyterii," p. 327.

gnostic Valentinus, AH II.31:2), but he never applies the word to orthodox Christian bishops.[127] High priesthood is occasionally mentioned in these sources (e.g., Ignatius, Philad 9:1), and it is possible that 1 Clem (40:5) uses this term for bishops. Ordinarily, however, the high priest is either Christ (1 Clem 61:3) or the Jewish incumbent in that office (1 Clem 41:2). There is, though, an unambiguous application of the term "high priests" to Christian ministers in the *Didache*, and we shall examine this reference in the section that follows.

THE PERSISTENCE OF PROPHECY

Didache 13:3 reads: "You shall take the firstfruit of the produce of the winepress and of the threshing-floor and of oxen and sheep, and shall give them as the firstfruits to the prophets, for they are your high priests."[128] It will be noticed immediately that the high priests of the *Didache* are not the bishops and deacons of 15:1, but the prophets. These same prophets are apparently the preferred presiders at the eucharist (11:7), which is the community's "sacrifice" (Greek, *thusia*; 14:2). This is one of the earliest examples we possess of the adaptation of Jewish priestly and cultic vocabulary to Christian worship and ministry. The *Didache* also reveals that in the later-first and early-second centuries, prophets were still recognized leaders in some churches.

But here we encounter a difficulty, especially if we compare the church order of the *Didache* to that of 1 Clement and the letters of Ignatius. Like these latter two, the *Didache* mentions bishops and deacons (15:1), but unlike them, it never alludes to presbyters. Further, *Didache* 9-10 links eucharist with the prophets, while *Didache* 15:1 remarks that the bishops and deacons minister the "liturgy" of the prophets and teachers. We are thus faced with two questions: Exactly

[127]Texts of Irenaeus in Harvey (note 122, above), Vol. I, p. 194, p. 320.

[128]Text and translation in Lake, *The Apostolic Fathers*, Vol. I, p. 329. I have altered the translation slightly.

who are the prophets, and what is their relation to the bishops and deacons?

It is tempting to answer the first question by suggesting that *Didache's* prophets are roughly the equivalent of the presbyters found in 1 Clement, Ignatius, Papias and Irenaeus. First of all, prophets are clearly esteemed authorities whose teaching must be taken seriously; if they are genuine, no one in the community may judge them (Did 11:11). Secondly, the *Didache* seems to use three words — prophet, apostle, teacher — for the same class of people (Did 11:3-12). This sounds very much like Papias's presbyters, who could include a variety of ancient and honored disciples: apostles, apostles' pupils, teachers who transmitted early traditions about Jesus. Perhaps, then, "apostles and prophets" (Did 11:3) or "prophets and teachers" (15:2) are simply those senior persons whose authoritative status, like that of Irenaeus's presbyters, comes from a proven ability to interpret Scripture and doctrine authentically.

Two factors, however, stand against the interpretation of *Didache's* prophets as "presbyters". It is clear, first, that the prophets are itinerants, though the *Didache* does make provision for them to settle in a community (12:3). By contrast, the presbyters of 1 Clement and Ignatius appear to form a stable group who reside permanently in the local church. Secondly, the prophets are linked with a liturgical ministry in *Didache* 10:7, whereas we have seen that in the other sources, presbyter is a title of status rather than one of ministry or function.

The identity of the prophets may be illumined, however, if we follow an interpretation recently proposed by Edward Schillebeeckx.[129] As others have also done, Schillebeeckx argues that the *Didache* represents a community whose patterns of ministry and worship are undergoing transition. Earlier sections of the *Didache* (9-10) describe the breaking of bread and link "making eucharist" with the prophets, while sections of the document added later outline Sunday

[129]See Schillebeeckx, *Ministry*, p. 23.

worship and mention bishops and deacons along with the prophets (14-15). The differences in these sections, Schillebeeckx suggests, reflect a development in the community's liturgy. The earlier sections (Did 9-10) say nothing about frequency or day of the week for the breaking of bread, but the later additions (Did 14-15) reveal a liturgy that has become more elaborate and now includes a weekly meeting on Sunday, a "communal penance service", followed by a eucharist. In a word, the community's liturgy has now become more regular, perhaps more frequent, and more extended than it had been earlier. For this reason, Schillebeeckx argues, "newcomers" (bishops and deacons) have been added to assist the prophets and teachers who still "preside" at the liturgy.[130]

If we compare the ministries mentioned in the *Didache* with those of 1 Clement and Ignatius, therefore, there may be less difference than first meets the eye. All three sources know the bishops/deacons pattern of ministry, though in the *Didache* these appear to be "new people on the block". The *Didache's* prophets are similar — if not identical — in status to the presbyters of Clement and Ignatius: Prophets are uniquely authoritative guides who have the "behavior of the Lord" (Did 11:8), and are thus worthy of imitation. And like the presbyters of 1 Tim 5:17-20, the *Didache's* prophets are not to be judged too swiftly or rashly (Did 11:7, 11).

It is important to note that in the church represented by the *Didache*, changes in ministry and worship led not to the suppression of prophets but to the addition of others (bishops and deacons) to help meet pastoral needs. Many scholars believe that the *Didache* may have been produced in Antioch prior to the end of the first century, and this invites a further comparison with Ignatius. Two striking differences emerge. The *Didache* speaks of "bishops" (plural), while Ignatius clearly thinks of a single bishop for each church. And while Ignatius does refer to the "prophets whom we love" because they "proclaimed the gospel" and

[130]*Ibid.*

are hoping and waiting for Jesus Christ (Philad 5:2), he does not give them the attention he lavishes on the bishop, presbytery and deacons. One gets the impression that for Ignatius, prophets are already part of the church's *past*, a vanishing breed that once commanded esteem but is now virtually extinct.

We know from other sources, however, that prophets did not utterly disappear from second-century Christianity. The *Shepherd of Hermas* (ca. 140-150) is the work of a Christian prophet who belonged to the church at Rome.[131] Divided into a series of "Visions", "Mandates" and "Similitudes", the *Shepherd* contains valuable information about Christian prophets and prophecy in a community of the mid-second century. In Mandate XI, Hermas outlines criteria for discerning true prophets from false.[132] False prophets are avaricious; they seek the "first places" (XI:2), accept money in exchange for prophecy (XI:12), and do not join in the Christian assembly (XI:13). True prophets, by contrast, are modest and calm, seeking always the "lower places" (XI:8-9). It is likely that these prophets, like those of the *Didache*, had some officially recognized role in the liturgical assembly.

What does a mid-second century prophet like Hermas tell us about church order at Rome? It is ordinarily assumed that "from the beginning" the Roman church had a single bishop of the Ignatian type. Irenaeus of Lyons even provides an episcopal list, as we have noted earlier. But other early sources are strangely silent about this point. A quick run-down of the evidence makes this clear:

• *1 Clement* (ca. 95): no reference to a bishop of Rome; the *episkopoi* are apparently a *group* at Corinth.

• *Ignatius* (ca. 110): no reference to a bishop in his letter to the Romans, though in every other letter the bishop of the church is mentioned, usually by name.

---

[131]On the date, provenance and authorship of the Shepherd of Hermas, see Robert Joly, ed., *Hermas: Le Pasteur*, (Sources chretiennes, 53; Paris: Cerf, 1958), pp. 11-16, 46-57.

[132]Text and translation in Joly (preceding note), pp. 192-199.

• *Justin Martyr* (ca. 150): uses a generic word (*proestos*) for the one who presides at eucharist in his description of Sunday worship (*First Apology* 65-67), though he does refer to deacons.

• *The Shepherd of Hermas* (ca. 140-150): does not refer to "the bishop" of the Roman church, though he does mention "bishops" who "sheltered the destitute and widows" (Sim IX.27:2), as well as "apostles and bishops and teachers and deacons who have walked according to the holiness of God, and who have sincerely and reverently served the elect of God" (Vis III:5:1).[133]

Hermas's references to bishops (plural) do not suggest a single leader of the Ignatian type, and indeed elsewhere Hermas speaks of the "presbyters who direct the church" (Vis II:4:3).[134] What we may have here is a pattern similar to the one we found in 1 Clement: The ultimate authorities in the church are presbyters (status-title), some of whom exercise their leadership ministerially as "bishops" and "deacons" (function-titles). The parallelism of pattern would not be surprising, since both 1 Clement and Hermas come from Rome. What is mildly astonishing, of course, is the consistent absence of any reference to a single bishop for the Roman church. Later in the second century (ca. 180), Irenaeus found it impossible to conceive of more than one bishop in one church, though he clearly thought of that bishop as a "presbyter", i.e., as an authoritative teacher and reliable guide in a long "succession" that stretched back to the apostles. (Powell, 316-317). In short, Irenaeus accepts the Ignatian model of mono-episcopate, while Hermas appears to be unfamiliar with it.

We are left here with some unanswered questions. When, for example, did Rome move definitively toward the Ignatian model of a single bishop? In his report of the Quartodeciman controversy, Eusebius (*Ecclesiastical History* V.

---

[133]Translation from Jack Sparks, ed., *The Apostolic Fathers*, (Nashville: Thomas Nelson Publishers, 1978), pp. 252, 171; Greek text in Joly (Sources chretiennes, 53), pp. 346, 110.

[134]Greek text in Joly (Sources chretiennes, 53), p. 96.

23-25) speaks of the dispute over the date of Easter between bishop Anicetus (Rome) and bishop Polycarp (Smyrna) (ca. 155), and of a similar dispute between bishop Victor (Rome) and bishop Polycrates (Ephesus) (ca. 185-195). But Eusebius's report is from the early fourth century, and its exact historical reliability is difficult to assess. What seems quite clear is that by the time of Hippolytus's *Apostolic Tradition* (ca. 215), Rome had adopted the mono-episcopal pattern of ministry. What seems equally clear is that the prophet Hermas did not know such a pattern. (140-150)

Hermas is thus an important source both for what he says and for what he does not say. Prophecy is still a vital force in the church for Hermas, and it does not appear to conflict with either the "apostles and bishops and teachers and deacons" or the "presbyters who direct the church". In Hermas, as in the *Didache*, the presence of other functional ministries does not appear to have eliminated the prophet's role. Still, suspicion about these prophets is evident even in the sources that describe and approve their activities. Both the *Didache* (12) and Hermas (Man XI) warn against false prophets and offer tests for their legitimation. And some writers like Ignatius and Irenaeus seem to consign prophecy to the church's past.

THE THREAT OF HERESY

In Similitude V. 7:4 of the *Shepherd of Hermas*, there is a passage that reads: "Be on the watch, lest the notion enter your heart that your flesh is perishable; be on guard lest you abuse it with some defilement. If you defile your flesh, you will also defile the Holy Spirit, and if you defile your flesh, you will not live."[135] On the surface this text sounds like a familiar moral exhortation against impurity or sexual irresponsibility. But if one places Hermas in his historical context (Rome in the 140's and 150's), the passage assumes another significance. As Robert Joly has noted, Hermas is

[135]Greek text *ibid.*, pp. 240-241.

almost certainly attacking a specific group — the Gnostics, whose dualistic tendencies often led to a denigration of the human body and its role in salvation.[136]

The origins and early evolution of Gnosticism, which specialized in secret saving knowledge (Greek, *gnōsis*) revealed to select initiates, are anything but clear. The questions about it are legion: Did it develop before or after the emergency of Christianity? Is it indebted to hellenistic or Jewish speculation — or to both? Was it a coherent movement, a systematic "religion", or merely a "*Zeitgeist*", the "spirit of an age"? Debate on all these questions has literally filled volumes, and the results are largely inconclusive, even though modern scholars have been greatly aided by the discovery of a Gnostic "library" at Nag Hammadi (Egypt) in 1946. Prior to this discovery, our information about Gnosticism was chiefly second-hand, and had to be pieced together from quotations contained in the works of heresiologists like Irenaeus. The Nag Hammadi library has made it possible to read Gnostic sources first-hand and has also revealed how diversified Gnosticism actually was.[137] Our purpose here will not be to discuss Gnosticism in any detail, but to show, if possible, how the crisis induced by second-century Gnostic speculators affected the development of Christian ministry.[138]

In her recent study *The Gnostic Gospels*, Professor Elaine Pagels has proposed that the conflict between Gnostics and orthodox Christians in the second century involved not only differences in doctrine but differences in church order and spiritual authority as well.[139] It has often been assumed that

---

[136]See *ibid.*, pp. 37-39.

[137]An English translation of the Nag Hammadi documents may be found in James M. Robinson, ed., *The Nag Hammadi Library*, (San Francisco: Harper and Row, 1977; paperback edition, 1981).

[138]For a succinct, lucid account of Gnostic origins, evolution and literature, see Pheme Perkins, *The Gnostic Dialogue*. The Early Church and the Crisis of Gnosticism, (New York: Paulist Press, 1980), especially pp. 1-22.

[139]See Elaine Pagels, *The Gnostic Gospels*, (New York: Random House, 1979), pp. 28-47 ("The Politics of Monotheism").

Gnostic doctrine was based on metaphysical dualism: two irreconcilable principles-of-being — one good, the other malevolent — are locked in everlasting combat. Thus, for instance, the heretic Marcion is sometimes accused of Gnosticism because he distinguished between a God of love and compassion revealed by Jesus in the New Testament and an avenging creator-God revealed in the Old. Against Marcion's view, Christians of more orthodox mind insisted that God is one and unique, the "maker of heaven and earth" and the "Father" of Jesus Christ.[140] Although Marcion's own views may have been dualistic, the Nag Hammadi library has revealed that some forms of Gnostic speculation were not really dualistic at all. The Valentinians, for example, whose "first teacher" Valentinus was active in Rome when Hermas was composing the *Shepherd*, stressed God's unity, though they wanted to distinguish between the ordinary images used to represent God (e.g., creator, king, lord) and the deeper truth of a God who is the unfathomable source of being.[141]

This kind of distinction sounds innocent enough, and even Irenaeus admitted in his *Against Heresies* (III 16:8) that most Christians couldn't tell the difference between Valentinian and orthodox teaching. Why then all the fuss? Why were orthodox writers like Irenaeus so unsparing in their attacks against "blasphemous heretics" like the Valentinians and other Gnostic groups? It must be said first that although the Valentinians shared many doctrinal views in common with orthodox Christianity, other Gnostic groups were more flamboyant in their speculations. To speak of God as a "malicious envier" who capriciously punished Adam would surely have been offensive to orthodox ears, as would have been the view that Jesus' humanity was a mere chimera and that the "real Jesus" stood laughing while his persecutors tried to crucify him.[142]

---

[140]See *ibid.*, pp. 28-29 for discussion.

[141]*Ibid.*, pp. 31-34.

[142]See texts in Perkins, *The Gnostic Dialogue*, pp. 16-17; James Robinson, ed., *The Nag Hammadi Library*, pp. 344-345.

But as Professor Pagels has observed, doctrinal differences alone cannot account for the bitter debate between
Gnostics and orthodox Christians in the second century.
Political and social motivations helped exacerbate the conflict. To speak of God's nature is, after all, to speak of
spiritual authority — and of who possesses that authority in
the human community called "church".[143] This issue is
directly linked with church order, the recognition of qualified ministers, and judgments about who may legitimately
speak and teach in the community. The Valentinians, for
example, appear to have favored a church order devoid of
ministers who hold "permanent office" and wield ultimate
authority in matters of doctrine and morality.[144] Other
Gnostics ridiculed orthodox leaders:

> . . . .there shall be others of those who are outside our
> number who name themselves bishop and also deacons,
> as if they have received their authority from God. They
> bend themselves under the judgment of the leaders.
> Those people are dry canals.[145]

At stake in the battle between Gnosticism and orthodoxy
was thus not only doctrine but authority and ministry.
Gnostic Christians appear to have resisted the second-
century trend to organize members into "superior" and
"inferior" ranks within a "hierarchy" of ministers; thus
anyone might be selected *ad hoc* as a "bishop", "presbyter",
"deacon" or "prophet".[146] This helps to explain why early
bishops like Ignatius of Antioch insisted on "one God, one
church, one eucharist, one bishop." One can also see why
prophets — who by their very nature did not fit well into a

---

[143]See Pagels, *The Gnostic Gospels*, pp. 34-35.

[144]*Ibid.*, pp. 37-43.

[145]Apocalypse of Peter, 79.24-30; text from James Robinson, *The Nag Hammadi Library*, p. 343.

[146]See Pagels, *The Gnostic Gospels*, p. 41.

hierarchical structure of permanent officers — were
regarded with increasing suspicion.

ANTI-
WOMEN

The crisis induced by Gnosticism may also throw light on
the orthodox churches' increasing tendency to limit or
exclude women from positions of leadership. It is reasonably certain that some, though not all, Gnostic groups
encouraged women leaders, especially as prophets.[147]
Orthodox bishops like Irenaeus reacted almost fanatically
to this phenomenon, probably because members of their
own congregations had become involved. Indeed, Irenaeus
complains that the wife of one of his deacons had been
seduced and corrupted in mind and body by a gnostic group
associated with Marcus, a disciple of Valentinus (*Against
Heresies*, I. 13:5).[148] While one must take Irenaeus's polemi-
cal report with a grain of salt, it reveals that orthodox
leaders frowned on the gnostic habit of admitting women to
positions of leadership. Irenaeus explicitly remarks, in fact,
that Marcus invites women to assist him in presiding at
gnostic celebrations of the eucharist (*Against Heresies*, I.
13:1-2).[149] Such a eucharist, the bishop declared, is really
debauchery and magic.

Not all orthodox Christians of this period resisted the full
participation of women in the life and work of the church.
Irenaeus's contemporary Clement of Alexandria stressed
the complete equality of women and men as human beings
and as Christian believers. In his *Paidagogos*, Clement
wrote that "one life, one hope, one knowledge and one love"
are available to women and men, who also share in the "one
church" where grace and salvation are possessed in common.[150] Later on in the same work, Clement used very

---

[147]*Ibid.*, pp. 48-69, especially p. 59.

[148]For the text, see Rousseau/Doutreleau, ed., (note 87, above), Vol. II, pp.
200-201.

[149]*Ibid.*, Vol. II, pp. 188-193.

[150]Clement, *Paidagogos* I.4:1-2; text in Henri-Irénée Marrou and Marguerite
Harl, ed., *Clément d'Alexandrie: Le Pédagogue*, (3 vols.; Sources chretiennes, 70;
108; 158; Paris: Cerf, 1960), Vol. I, pp. 128-129.

explicit feminine imagery to describe the "breasts of the Father's goodness" which supply milk to nourish Christians.[151] It seems, further, that women were among Clement's students at the catechetical school which he headed in Alexandria. This suggests that Clement did not exclude women from the intellectual life of the community or from the more sophisticated "Christian philosophy" which his school promoted.

But Clement was an exception. A more typical view, strongly anti-feminist, was represented by the acerbic Christian convert, Tertullian, who wrote:

> It is not permitted for a woman to speak in the church, nor is it permitted for her to teach, nor to baptize, nor to offer (the eucharist), not to claim for herself a share in any masculine function — least of all, in priestly office.[152]

Whether these remarks of Tertullian were formulated as veiled objections to gnostic practice is not clear, though elsewhere he complains that the "heretics" (probably followers of Marcion) are wholly capricious in their choice of ministries:

> What impudence exists among the women heretics! They do not hesitate to teach, debate, offer healing, and perhaps even baptize. Their ordinations are rash. . . . Today, one person is a bishop, tomorrow, another; today a deacon — tomorrow a lector; today a presbyter — tomorrow a layperson. For even the laity fulfill sacerdotal functions.[153]

---

[151]Clement, *Paidagogos*, I.6:46; text in Marrou/Harl, ed., (preceding note), Vol. I, pp. 192-195.

[152]Tertullian, *De Virginibus Velandis*, 9; text cited from Pagels, *The Gnostic Gospels*, p. 69.

[153]Tertullian, *De Praescriptione*, 41; text in R.F. Refoule and P. de Labriolle, eds., *Tertullien: Traite de la Prescription contre les Heretiques*, (Sources chretiennes, 46; Paris: Cerf, 1957), pp. 147-148; my translation.

This last quotation from Tertullian is revealing on several levels. Taken from his *De Praescriptione*, probably written about the year 200, it shows not only his objections to women in ministry, but his distinction between "laity" and "clergy" and his view of "ordination" as well. Ordination already appears to have acquired a technical meaning for Tertullian, and it is intimately linked with the offices of bishop, presbyter and deacon.[154] These offices are, moreover, permanent — thus Tertullian's complaint that among the "heretics" one who is a deacon today may be merely a lector tomorrow. Finally, Tertullian excludes laity from "sacerdotal" functions, and the context suggests that these functions are didactic (teaching, debating) and sacramental (baptism, eucharist) in nature.

Ironically, Tertullian himself eventually joined the heretics by siding with the Montanists, probably in 212 or 213. As a further irony, the Montanists were charismatic enthusiasts who supported the renewal of Christian prophecy and so opposed the ordained leadership's exclusive claim to teaching authority. Tertullian's own biography thus reflects many of the internal tensions that pressed on Christians in the late-second and early-third centuries: the nature of spiritual authority, the role of women in church life, the meaning of ecclesiastical office and "ordination", the relation between prophetic charism and episcopal structure in the community. These tensions were heightened by the ongoing doctrinal struggles between adherents of Gnosticism (in any of its myriad forms) and adherents of "catholic orthodoxy".

Conclusion

To conclude, it will be useful to summarize the evolution of Christian ministry between the period of late New Testa-

---

[154]See discussion in Refoule/Labriolle, eds., (preceding note), pp. 147-148, note 5.

ment literature (after 70) and the end of the second century (ca. 200).

1. Second and third generation Christians faced a crisis of leadership brought on by several factors: the fall of Jerusalem, the unexpected delay of Jesus' coming, the death of those early pioneers who had been privileged proclaimers of the gospel and founders of churches. Reactions to this situation varied greatly — from the Matthean impulse to "freeze" the Jesus-tradition in a fixed gospel narrative to the Johannine insistence on the "other Paraclete" who would lead believers to all truth.

2. No uniform pattern of ministry and leadership is discernible in the later New Testament literature, though the Pastorals seem to reflect a trend in some churches toward authoritative residential leaders of the "presbyter-bishop" variety.

3. The New Testament offers no unambiguous evidence for "ordination", though the gesture of laying on hands is found in contexts that suggest commissioning for a missionary task. Similarly, the New Testament does not link ministry with sacramental leadership (e.g., eucharistic presidency).

4. By the early second century a rather clearly defined "hierarchy" of local leaders is evident in the letters of Ignatius of Antioch. Bishops, presbyters and deacons are authoritative, and other members of the community must be submissive to them. Though the Ignatian model was not immediately accepted by all church, it gained ever greater popularity, and by the later second century it appears to have become the ordinary pattern in most orthodox communities.

5. Earlier forms of Christian ministry continued, however, to exist. The prophet's role is still prominent in the *Didache* and, it seems, in mid-second century Rome (Hermas).

6. The direct application of priestly or cultic vocabulary to Christian ministers is rather rare in second century sources, though parallels are sometimes drawn between priests

of the Hebrew covenant and those Christian ministers who offer the community's "gifts and sacrifices" (1 Clement). Similarly, these sources tell us next to nothing about "liturgies of ordination" or "imposition of hands" as essential elements in the commissioning of church leaders.

7. Theological attempts to link Christian ministry with an "order willed by God" are evident in the writings of this period. 1 Clement connects church order with Christ and the apostles and with the cosmic order of creation itself. Irenaeus connects the episcopal ministry with a "succession" of authoritative teaching that can be traced back to the "apostles".

8. During this period we witness the emergence of bishops and deacons as functional ministers in virtually all the churches. "Presbyter", on the other hand, seems to remain primarily a "status-title" for those in the community who are acknowledged as God-given exemplars worthy of imitation. They constitute primarily a "hierarchy" of prestige based on fruitfulness of life and maturity of conversion, though some presbyters doubtless functioned as episcopal or diaconal ministers.

By the end of the period studied in this chapter, a turning-point in the evolution of Christian ministry has been reached. There begins to emerge clear evidence for such things as ordination liturgies, ranks of Christian "priesthood", and the consolidation of one bishop's authority in each church. We will begin the next chapter by examining these important developments.

Recommended Reading

Käsemann, Ernst. "Ministry and Community in the New Testament," in: Essays on New Testament Themes. Translated by W.J. Montague. Studies in Biblical Theology, Vol. 41. Naperville, Illinois: Alec R. Allenson, Inc., 1964. A classic essay that deals with Paul's notion of "charism" and ministry — and that shows how the later New Testament literature altered Paul's notion.

McDonnell, Kilian. "Ways of Validating Ministry," *Journal of Ecumenical Studies* 7 (1970), 209-265. An important contribution to the contemporary ecumenical study of ministry among Christians.

Pagels, Elaine. *The Gnostic Gospels.* New York: Random House, 1979, pp. 28-47 —("The Politics of Monotheism"). Provacative discussion of Gnosticism and its impact on what became "orthodox" Christianity. Of special interest is the author's discussion of the exclusion of women from leadership among "orthodox" Christians.

Perrin, Norman. *The New Testament: An Introduction.* New York: Harcourt, Brace, Jovanovich, 1974. A comprehensive survey of the New Testament: its formation, growth and interpretation.

Powell, Douglas, "Ordo Presbyterii," *Journal of Theological Studies* 26 (New Series, 1975), 290-328. Offers a new interpretation of the meaning of "presbyter" in both New Testament and early Christian sources.

Schillebeeckx, Edward, *Ministry.* Leadership in the Community of Jesus Christ. Translated by John Bowden. New York: Crossroad Publishing Company, 1981. An historical and theological study of ministry, with some challenging critiques of contemporary practice.

CHAPTER FOUR
A CHRISTIAN PRIESTHOOD

Introduction

In the rubrics that accompany the ritual of ordination contained in the *Apostolic Tradition* of Hippolytus (ca. 215), the following is said about deacons:

> And when a deacon is ordained. . . . the bishop alone shall lay on hands, because he is not being ordained to the priesthood, but to the service of the bishop. . . . For he does not share in the counsel of the presbyterate, but administers and informs the bishop of what is fitting; he does not receive the common spirit of seniority in which the presbyters share, but that which is entrusted to him under the bishop's authority.[1]

This text reveals a distinction between the bishop and presbyters, who share a "priesthood", and the deacon, who is ordained to "service". Further, the presbyter belongs to a (priestly) "order" that is subordinate to the bishop's: ". . . . a presbyter has authority only to receive; he has not authority

<hr/>

[1]Apostolic Tradition, 8; translation from Geoffrey Cuming, trans., *Hippolytus: A Text for Students,* (Grove Liturgical Study, No. 8; Bramcote, Notts., England: Grove Books, 1976), p. 13.

to give. For this reason he does not ordain the clergy, but at the ordination of a presbyter he seals, while the bishop ordains."[2]

These passages outline a carefully defined pattern of Christian service that includes a "priesthood" composed of two ranks (bishop and presbyter) and a "ministry" whose members, the deacons, are not priestly. We are told that ordination of the clergy belongs exclusively to the bishop, and that the deacon's service is intimately linked to the bishop's role in the community. This pattern, in most of its features, is extremely familiar to Roman Catholics, since it includes a threefold ranking of ordained persons whose positions reflect superior and inferior status. And when one adds the *Apostolic Tradition's* description of the eucharist, the picture is even more familiar: "Then the deacons shall present the offering to him (the bishop); and he, laying his hands on it with all the presbytery, shall give thanks, saying: 'The Lord be with you;' and all shall say: 'And with your spirit'. . . . "[3] The eucharist described here is "concelebrated" by bishop and presbyters, while the deacons are responsible for "preparing the table".

While all this sounds familiar to us today, it reveals something rather different from the patterns of ministry we have studied in the previous two chapters. Ignatius of Antioch, for example, thought deacons should be submissive to the bishop, and the presbytery (Magn 2:1), but in the *Apostolic Tradition*, deacons are not merely "subordinate", they are *different*. Theirs is not a priesthood (*sacerdotium*) but a "service" or "ministry" (*ministerium*); they do not share in the "counsel of the presbyterate", nor do they receive "the common spirit of seniority in which the presbyters share". The presbyters, too, have taken on a different significance, or at least a more formal one.[4] In *Apostolic Tradition* they are ordained personnel whose "seniority" in the community

[2]*Ibid.*

[3]Apostolic Tradition, 4; translation from Cuming (Note 1, above), p. 10.

[4]See Douglas Powell, "Ordo Presbyterii," *Journal of Theological Studies* 26 (New Series, 1975), 320-321.

is ritually acknowledged through laying on of hands by the bishop, who alone has the right to "ordain the clergy".

Compared to the still somewhat fluid situation of the second century, the *Apostolic Tradition* confronts us with a rather exact outline of clerical ranks, rituals of ordination, and a hierarchical system of subordination. Still, it is possible even in the *Apostolic Tradition* to discern elements of an earlier situation. Although Hippolytus reckons deacons as "clergy", he excludes them from the "counsel" of the presbyterate and denies them "priesthood". This exclusion is not sheer arbitrariness, for in the Hippolytan view deacons lack an essential qualification: They do not share the "spirit of seniority" common to presbyters and bishop. We can see here traces of that view of presbyterate found in second-century sources and examined in the preceding chapter. In the *Apostolic Tradition* there is still a hint that the presbyterate is a status, a condition of *seniority* based not on the chronology of one's age or conversion but on the "spiritual maturity" that renders one an authoritative guide and a God-given example to be imitated.

But changes in the notion of presbyterate are also evident in Hippolytus. Second century deacons were regarded as "third grade" (subordinate to bishop and presbytery), and as Douglas Powell notes, "there is no second-century evidence that they were regarded as holding a different kind of office, and as lacking the necessary experience, sagacity and spirit of wisdom to form part of the consilium".[5] Second-century deacons, in other words, were still considered part of the "presbyterate" and so shared in its "counsel" (its advisory and deliberative responsibilities). In Hippolytus, however, the situation has changed. Deacons are not only "third grade", they are *a different kind of office*, non-presbyteral and thus "non-priestly". They lack that "spirit of seniority" with which Moses's seventy "elders" were filled (Num 11:16-17), with which Jesus was anointed by the Father, and which Christ in turn gave to his apostles. This is

[5] *Ibid.,* 309-310.

the "spirit" prayed for in Hippolytus's rite of ordination for bishops and presbyters:

> *Bishop:*
> .... now pour forth that power which is from you, of the princely Spirit which you granted through your beloved Son Jesus Christ to your holy apostles who established the Church in every place as your sanctuary....[6]

> *Presbyter:*
> God and Father of our Lord Jesus Christ, look upon this your servant, and impart the Spirit of grace and counsel of the presbyterate, that he may help and govern your people with a pure heart; just as you looked upon your chosen people and commanded Moses to choose presbyters whom you filled with your Spirit....[7]

In the prayer for ordaining a deacon, however, the "spirit" invoked is simply "the holy Spirit of grace and caring and diligence".[8]

One will note that in both the bishop's and presbyter's prayers, the "spirit" is related to notions of seniority and "first-fruits". The spirit that filled Jesus and the apostles (the first-fruits of his preaching) is petitioned for the bishop; the spirit that filled Moses and the elders (first-fruits of that people newly fashioned after Exodus and Sinai) is invoked upon the presbyters. But nothing is said about a share in this spirit of seniority for the deacon, though if he serves "blamelessly and purely" he may "attain the rank of a higher order".[9]

In Hippolytus's mind the spirit of seniority shared by bishop and presbyters is related to *priesthood*. This is clear from the first part of the *Apostolic Tradition's* prayer for episcopal ordination:

[6]Apostolic Tradition, 3; translation from Cuming, p. 9.
[7]Apostolic Tradition, 7; translation from Cuming, p. 12.
[8]Apostolic Tradition, 8; translation from Cuming, p. 13.
[9]*Ibid.*

....you foreordained from the beginning a race of
righteous men from Abraham; you appointed princes
and priests, and did not leave your sanctuary without a
ministry....

The prayer continues:

You who know the hearts of all, bestow upon this your
servant, whom you have chosen for the episcopate, to
feed your holy flock and to exercise the high-priesthood
before you blamelessly.... [10]

The bishop's priesthood is closely linked in these prayers to
the "ministry" (Greek, *leitourgia*, "liturgy") he performed,
and it is significant that immediately following the bishop's
ordination the eucharist is celebrated.[11] At this eucharist,
the *priests*, bishop and presbyters, lay hands on the offerings, while the deacons simply prepare the bread and wine.
    The *Apostolic Tradition* thus combines the old and the
new. The earlier notion of presbyterate as "senior-status"
survives, but is now restricted to those who share its "spirit"
(bishop and presbyters). These latter constitute a "higher
order" of priesthood which is intimately connected with the
"ministry of the sanctuary". The deacon's service is linked to
the "high priest" (bishop), "to do what is ordered by him,"[12]
and this reflects a trend toward regarding deacons as liturgical, financial and administrative officers of the bishop.[13]
    Two things should be noted here. First, the ranks of
priestly and non-priestly clergy in Hippolytus did not
monopolize all ministry. The only function which the
ordained controlled was a ritual and sacramental one (the
liturgy, especially the eucharist): "Ordination is for the
clergy on account of their liturgical duties."[14] The Hippoly-

---

[10]Apostolic Tradition, 3; translation from Cuming, p. 9.
[11]See Apostolic Tradition, 4; translation in Cuming, pp. 10-11.
[12]Apostolic Tradition, 8; translation from Cuming, p. 13.
[13]See Powell, "Ordo Presbyterii," 309.
[14]Apostolic Tradition, 10; translation from Cuming, p. 14.

tan clergy monopolize *leitourgia,* but not *diakonia* (service, ministry).[15] Ministry is also carried out by non-ordained persons in the community: widows, virgins, readers, sub-deacons, those with gifts of healing.[16] Secondly, Hippolytus's understanding of who belonged to the "priesthood" was not universally accepted. Optatus of Miletum (ca. 370), for example, considered deacons the third rank of *priesthood*. Writing against the Donatist schismatics whose bishops he accused of buckling several decades earlier under the pressure of persecution, Optatus remarked: "What can I say about the laity in the church who at this time were deprived of support (by those who held positions of) dignity? What can I say about the many ministers, the deacons in the third and the presbyters in the second (rank of) priesthood? For their higher-ups and leaders — certain bishops of that period — wickedly handed over the instruments of divine law so they could buy a little extra time in this life while they forfeited everlasting life."[17] Optatus' position was held by others too, for there are fourth-century conciliar prohibitions against deacons exercising priestly functions like celebrating the eucharist.[18]

But the fourth-century objections to deacons exercising the priesthood were based on a principle different from the one we find in Hippolytus. The question in the fourth century was "who has the right to offer the eucharist?", while for Hippolytus the question was "who possesses the 'spirit of seniority' common to the presbyterate?". Hippolytus, as we have suggested, was still working from the older notion of presbyter as one who possesses senior-status in the community and so is qualified to belong to the *sacerdotium*. Since deacons lack this status, they cannot be considered

[15]See Powell, "Ordo Presbyterii," 323.

[16]Apostolic Tradition, 10-14; translation in Cuming, pp. 14-15.

[17]Text in Carolus Ziwsa, ed., *S. Optati Milevitani Libri VII.* (Corpus Scriptorum Ecclesiasticorum Latinorum, Vol. 26; Vienna : F. Tempsky, 1893), p. 15; my translation.

[18]See Council of Arles, canon 15; Council of Nicaea, canon 18. Texts in Hermann T. Bruns, ed., *Canones Apostolorum et Conciliorum Seaculorum IV - VII,* (2 vols; Bibliotheca Ecclesiastica; Berlin: G. Reimeri, 1839; reprint, Turin: Bottega d'Erasmo, 1959), II, p. 109 (Arles); I, p. 19 (Nicaea).

one of the priestly orders. Eventually in the western church's history, Hippolytus's view triumphed, though for reasons different from the ones he proposed in the *Apostolic Tradition*. After the fourth century, especially, the presbyters' power expanded and deacons were increasingly restricted in their activities. The idea that priesthood comprises two "orders" — bishop and presbyter — while deacons, though clergy, are non-priestly, became deeply embedded in the liturgical and theological tradition of the West.

This chapter will explore these developments in three sections. First, we will examine the appearance of a distinctive vocabulary associated with those who minister in "holy orders". Secondly, our attention will turn to the earlier and later history of ordination as a liturgical rite. Finally, we will see how the notion of priesthood developed in the church — and how theologians came to understand it as a sacrament.

I

Succession, Order, Holy Orders

On several occasions earlier in this book we have noted that the first Christians were reluctant to call their senior members or ministerial leaders "priests". Gradually, though, the Hebrew Bible's vocabulary of "priest" and "high priest" was appropriated by Christian writers. The *Didache's* prophets are called "high priests", while Hippolytus's bishop is said to exercise the "high priesthood." By the middle of the third century, the equation "bishop=priest" was fully established in the writings of a Latin theologian and pastor like Cyprian of Carthage (+258). In a passionate and sarcastic letter written to bishop Florentius Puppian, Cyprian defended his own conduct as bishop of Carthage and explicitly called himself a "priest" (*sacerdos*).[19] He

[19]Letter 66.5; translation in Rose Bernard Donna, trans., *St. Cyprian: Letters 1-81,* (Fathers of the Church, Vol. 51; Washington, D.C.: Catholic University of America Press, 1964), p. 226.

insisted, further, that it is "God who makes bishops."[20]
Elsewhere Cyprian appears to include presbyters among the
sacerdotes, since he speaks of them as "joined with the
bishop in the sacerdotal honor."[21] The priesthood, in Cyprian's thinking, is especially linked to service at the altar and
thus demands a purity similar to that required of those who
"come forward to offer gifts" in Leviticus.[22]

For this reason Cyprian is sometimes accused of contributing to "sacerdotalism."[23] There is some truth to this
charge. An embattled pastor, Cyprian fought a war on two
fronts: One theatre was occupied by the battle between
North African Christians and the Emperor Decius; the
other, by an internal struggle between orthodox believers
and schismatics like the Novatianists. At stake on both
fronts was the unity of the church catholic:

> . . . . Although the stubborn and proud multitude of
> those unwilling to obey withdraw, yet the Church does
> not withdraw from Christ, and the people united to their
> bishop and the flock clinging to their shepherd are the
> Church. . . . You ought to know that the bishop is in the
> Church and the Church is in the bishop and, if there is
> anyone who is not with the bishop, he is not in the
> Church.[24]

Cyprian continues his vigorous insistence on unity with the
bishop by reminding his readers once more that bishops are
"priests of God," that they are the "solder" which unites the
church, that they are in collegial communion with one
another, and finally, that it is God "who ordains priests of
Christ."[25]

[20]Letter 66.1; translation in Donna, pp. 223-224.

[21]Letter 61.3; translation in Donna, p. 198.

[22]See Letter 67.1; translation in Donna, pp. 231-232.

[23]See James A. Mohler, *The Origin and Evolution of the Priesthood,* (New
York: Alba house, 1969), p. 61.

[24]Letter 66.8; translation in Donna, p. 229.

[25]Letter 66.8-9; translation in Donna, p. 229.

To modern readers, Cyprian's dogged defense of sacerdo-tal dignity may sound like clericalism of the worst sort. But one must remember that for Cyprian the priesthood was not a personal honor that brought a bishop privileges, but a shared responsibility whose ultimate purpose was the church's unity. In order to undestand this point better we need to investigate briefly the rise of notions like episcopal "succession" and "sacerdotal order" (*ordo sacerdotalis*).

SUCCESSION AND ORDER

Today, words like "succession" and "order" project strongly institutional images. Succession, as applied to bishops, suggests a relay-game in which an object (the epis-copal office) is passed from one incumbent to another in a line that stretches back to Christ and the apostles. Similarly, order conveys the sense of a regimented college or club whose members hold the franchise on an important role or right (the episcopate, the presbyterate as "orders" of clergy). As they were first used by Christian writers, however, "suc-cession" and "order" were meant to describe *theological* realities rather than socio-political ones like "power" or the "authority of government".

Irenaeus of Lyons (fl. ca. 180), for instance, appealed to both "succession" (Greek, *diadoche*) and "order" (Greek, *taxis*) in his *Against Heresies*.[26] As Irenaeus used them, the two terms were virtually interchangeable. They refer *not* to an instituted "college" of ministers (e.g., an "order" of presbyters or bishops), nor to the handing down of an "office" from one person to another (e.g., a "succession" of bishops in a church), but to the qualities which trustworthy leaders exhibit: fidelity to the tradition of teaching that comes from the apostles, blameless conduct, sound doctrine uncontaminated by heretical views. In short, order and

---

[26]See, for example, *Adversus Haereses* IV.41:1; IV.40:2; IV. 42:1; theses texts are discussed by Powell, "Ordo Presbyterii," 290-291.

succession are what result in the church when the apostolic teaching is authentically transmitted. Recognized leaders are especially responsible for this transmission, and so they have a unique and authoritative role to play in the church's "order." But order is not an office that belongs to a college of these leaders, nor is it something they monopolize to the exclusion of all others. If order and succession are closely linked with "presbyters" or with "bishops and deacons," it is because their lives — more than anyone else's — must exhibit that maturity of faith and conversion which characterized the "first-fruits" of Christ's mission (i.e., the apostles). The church manifests order and succession when its behavior imitates the Lord's, when its teaching is faithful to the apostles' message, and when its leaders are trusted exemplars worthy of imitation by all.

Early Latin theologians also seem to have interpreted order and succession in the senses outlined above. During his Catholic period, for example, Tertullian used the expression "*ordo episcoporum*" (literally, "order of bishops") not for a college of bishops but for an episcopal list which authenticates a church's fidelity to the doctrinal tradition handed on from the apostles.[27] It is also true, however, that in his later career, Tertullian used expressions like "*ordo ecclesiae*" (literally, "order of the church") in the narrower sense of "those who govern or direct the church", i.e., of the clergy.[28] In a much-disputed passage of his semi-Montanist *Exhortation to Chastity* (VII. 2-3), he spoke of both *ordo sacerdotalis* ("sacerdotal order") and *ordo ecclesiasticus* ("ecclesiastical order"). Both phrases seem to refer to the *clergy* in its various ranks, as distinguished from the *people*.[29] If this is the case, then we have one of the first clear

---

[27]See Tertullian *De Praescriptione Haereticorum*, 32:1; Text in R.F. Refoulé and P. de Labriolle, eds., *Tertullien. Traité de la Prescription contre les Hérétiques*, (Sources chrétiennes, 46; Paris: Cerf, 1957), p. 130. For more detailed discussion of this text, see Pierre van Beneden, *Aux Origines d'une Terminologie sacramentelle*. Ordo, Ordinare, Ordinatio dans la Littérature chrétienne avant 313, (Louvain: Spicilegium Sacrum Lovaniense, 1974), pp. 19-20.

[28]See texts and commentary in van Beneden, *Aux Origines d'une Terminologie sacramentelle*, pp. 22-24.

[29]*Ibid.* pp. 24-24.

examples in Latin theology of the technical distinction between clerics (*ordo*) and laity (*plebs*).

But here we have to tread carefully: first, because Tertullian's views were complicated by his increasing attraction to Montanism; and secondly, because he chose his language very precisely. As a Catholic, Tertullian certainly believed that there were "priestly functions" (*sacerdotalia munera*) from which laypersons were excluded.[30] But it is also clear that he saw these functions not as sources of clerical power, but as actions that needed authentication or sanction in order to preserve the church's integrity. Writing as a Catholic *On Baptism* (17:1-2), Tertullian commented:

> The supreme right of giving (baptism) belongs to the high priest, which is the bishop: after him, to the presbyters and deacons, yet not without commission from the bishop, on account of the Church's dignity: for when this is safe, peace is safe. Except for that, even laymen have the right: 'for that which is received on equal terms can be given on equal terms: unless perhaps you are prepared to allege that our Lord's disciples were already bishops or presbyters or deacons....'[31]

Two points in this passage deserve comment. The first is that Tertullian's use of "laymen" seems almost derogatory; he concedes their right to baptize grudgingly.[32] The second is the author's use of "high priest" for the bishop, whose "commission" (*auctoriatas*) is necessary if presbyters and deacons are to baptize — out of concern for the church's "dignity" (*honor*). We are confronted here by a constellation of terms that seem to smack of high sacerdotalism: laymen (at the bottom of a hierarchical totem-pole), a high-priestly bishop, and concern for "authority" and "honor".

---

[30]See Tertullian, *De Praescriptione* 41:8; text in Refoulé/de Labriolle (note 27, above), p. 148.

[31]Ernest Evans, ed., trans., *Tertullian's Homily on Baptism,* (London: S.P.C.K., 1964), p. 35.

[32]See comments in Evans, *Tertullian's Homily on Baptism,* p. 98.

We need to recall, however, that in this passage Tertullian is speaking *theologically* rather than socio-politically.[33] His chief concern is neither to promote a power-play by the clergy nor to put down the laity, but to safeguard "the Church's dignity". The bishop's "commission" (literally, his *auctoriatas*, "authority") is not the power to bark out orders and issue commands; it is rather a "guarantee of authenticity." Douglas Powell has summarized this point well:

> For Tertullian, when he is speaking theologically, *auctoritas* belongs to the *auctor* — Christ is the head of man because he is the author and creator of man. The bishops, presbyters and deacons are themselves *auctores*, since ecclesiastical *auctoritas* springs from the apostles, and every Catholic bishop finds his original *auctor et antecessor* in some apostle or apostolic man.[34]

Seen in this light, the bishop's authority is the community's guarantee that its important actions — like baptism — are rooted in Christ, whose authority is always supreme in the church. Similarly, the church's dignity (or "honor") is not the bishop's or another cleric's possession, but rather "the respect owed to the church" by all, including its leaders. This respect maintains the church's unity. Dignity and honor belong to the *whole* church; they are not, in the first instance, obligations owed to the clergy. This helps clarify the distinction between "clergy" (*ordo*) and "laity" (*plebs*) found in Tertullian's *Exhortation to Chastity*. The purpose of the distinction was not to create first- and second-class citizens in the church, nor to give clergy a monopoly over everything "priestly," but to preserve the church's identity and integrity. If we recall Edward Schillebeeckx's point that the ultimate purpose of ministry is to preserve the church's identity as the *community of Jesus* — and not some other human collectivity — then the motive for Tertullian's dis-

---

[33]See Powell, "Ordo Presbyterii," 293.
[34]*Ibid.*

tinction becomes clearer. Unlike other human groups, Tertullian implies, the church, rooted in Christ and built on
apostolic teaching, manifests the dignity and authority that
come from God. "Order" is thus not a sociological term
based upon human patterns of government or upon relations of superior and inferior, but a theological reality that
expresses the church's origin in Christ and its final goal in
God.

Despite its pagan roots in Roman law and civil administration, the word "order" (*ordo*) became, in early Latin
theology, a theological term.[35] One may even say it became a
metaphor for the new understanding of all human and
divine-human relationships revealed in Christ. As a theological metaphor, order in the Christian community manifests that "new situation" which results from Jesus' mission
in the world: the last are first, leaders are servants, the
foolish are wise, the weak are strong, the cross is salvation.
Even in its narrower sense (*ordo* = "clergy"), the term signifies not the status of "master" versus "slave" or "management" versus "labor," but the recognized authority of
persons whose lives and teachings guarantee the community's rootedness in Christ.

This also helps explain why the "priestly order" (*ordo
sacerdotalis*, the clergy) was the group responsible for leading the community's worship. This pattern, as we saw in the
preceding chapter, emerged quite early, even though the
New Testament makes no explicit connection between ministry and liturgical leadership. In 1 Clement, the letters of
Ignatius and the later sections of the *Didache*, bishops are
linked with liturgy, with the church's "gifts and sacrifices,"
its eucharist. Later on, Irenaeus, Tertullian and Hippolytus
make the same connection. This "clerical monopoly" of the
church's liturgy — though not of its ministry (*diakonia*) —
was based not upon an ideological theory of priestly power
but upon the nature of the church's relationship to Christ. In

[35]For the pre-Christian significance of *ordo,* see van Beneden, Aux Origines
d'une Terminologie sacramentelle, pp. 1-11.

Paul's theology, Christ is the first-fruits of them that sleep, the first-born among many sisters and brothers; we are the crop growing to harvest (see 1 Cor 15:20-23; Rom 8:29). Jesus' destiny is ours, for as church we too are "first fruits" of God's creatures (see James 1:18). And within the church, as well, there are first-fruits, "elders" (presbyters) by reason of their mature faith and exemplary conversion. From among these emerge those "bishops and deacons" who preside when the community offers its life, its bread and wine, its first-fruits in a sacrifice of thanksgiving.

The root-metaphor that underlies the primitive Christian notion of "order" is thus the Pauline one of first-fruits and crop/harvest.[36] Order is a theological reality rather than an ideological (priestly power and dominance) or sociological (good government in a group) one. When the church exhibits order and succession — the two terms are nearly interchangeable in their original meaning — its basic relation to Christ is revealed. As first-fruits of a new creation, of the new order of things in the world, Jesus becomes the one who guarantees the crop, insures its final gathering in the Father's harvest (see 1 Cor 15:23-24). One can see why Paul insisted so vigorously on the absolute necessity of faith in this Jesus — and why later Christians could draw the conclusion that those who best exemplified this faith, those "seniors" in conversion, should lead the community at its eucharist, where the promise of a fruitful, final harvest was celebrated.

Perhaps it is no accident that the earliest eucharistic prayer we possess (*Didache* 9-10) is dominated by metaphors of vine and fruit, crop and harvest. The gathering-in of grain to make bread is metaphorically expanded to include the church's being gathered into the kingdom: "As this broken bread was scattered upon the mountains, but was brought together and became one, so let thy Church be gathered together from the ends of the earth into thy king-

---

[36]See Powell, "Ordo Presbyterii," 301.

dom...."[37] The eucharist itself is a gathering-in of God's people, the first fruits of the new order manifested in Jesus; and the people's own first-fruits — the prophets (*Didache* 10), the bishops and deacons (*Didache* 15) — lead the celebration of that in-gathering.

Even when it was restricted to clergy, as it sometimes was by Tertullian, order was not an "object" (something the cleric receives) nor even a "college" (something the cleric enters into). It was what resulted, like succession, when the church, led by its ministers, adhered faithfully to a Christ-like way of life and to the apostles' teaching. This order is especially manifest when the community celebrates its hope of final fruitful harvest at the eucharist, where the *ordo sacerdotalis* (= clergy) presides. The honor and authority that attach to *ordo*, even in its restricted meaning, are not obligations owed to clerics, but qualities of the church itself, where all relationships — human and divine — are made new in Christ, the first-born among many sisters and brothers.

HOLY ORDERS

Our discussion of "order" in the preceding paragraphs reveals that from the beginning, Latin theology used the term "*ordo*" flexibly. We have seen, for example, that in Tertullian's writings "order" could mean a variety of things: a list of bishops that testifies to a church's "succession" in the life and doctrine of the apostles (*ordo episcoporum*); members of the clergy (*ordo sacerdotalis*); others in the community who have a recognized status or role (e.g., the order of virgins or widows). This flexible use of *ordo* continued for centuries in the Latin West.

But the Latin theology did not adopt Tertullian's termi-

---

[37]Didache 9,4; text and translation in Kirsopp Lake, ed., trans., *The Apostolic Fathers,* (2 vols.; Loeb Classical Library; Cambridge, Massachusetts: Harvard University Press, 1977), Vol. I, p. 323.

nology immediately. Cyprian (+258), bishop of Carthage and avid reader of Tertullian's works, avoided the use of *ordo*. The word appears only eight times in Cyprian, and in only one of these instances can "order" possibly be construed as "clergy" or "priests".[38] In a letter written to Pompey, a fellow-bishop in Africa, Cyprian urged a return to "the divine precepts" and to "the apostolic tradition... whence both our order (*ordo*) and our origin have arisen."[39]. Some scholars have seen in this passage a reference to the "order" of bishops, with its "origin" in apostolic tradition, but a more likely interpretation is that Cyprian sees apostolic tradition as the fundamental principle that "orders" Christian life and conduct.[40] In this, Cyprian would represent the ancient notion, discussed above, which understood order as a quality exhibited by the church (and by the church's leaders) when its behavior and faith follow the example of the apostles, the first-fruits of Christ's preaching.

Other third century sources were also reluctant to use the term "*ordo*" as a special designation for clergy. The *Apostolic Tradition* of Hippolytus is clearly familiar with "ranks" or "grades" of clergy, as well as with rituals of ordination, but *ordo* as a technical term for a "college" of ministers does not appear in the Latin versions of that document.[41] A recent study of Pierre van Beneden shows, in fact, that virtually no Latin writer before the fourth century picked up Tertullian's specialized use of *ordo* for ecclesiastical institutions like the clergy.[42] This does not mean that writers of the period failed to distinguish between clerical responsibilities (e.g., presiding at liturgy) and those which laypersons could fulfill. Cyprian, for instance, clearly had a high regard for bishops as "God's priests," and he jealously guarded their

---

[38]See van Beneden, *Aux Origines d'une Terminologie sacramentelle*, pp. 46-49 for discussion.

[39]Cyprian, Letter 74:10; translation in Donna, p. 293.

[40]See van Beneden, *Aux Origines d'une Terminologie sacramentelle*, p. 47.

[41]The oldest Latin versions of Hippolytus were probably made about the middle of the fourth century; see the edition of Cuming (note 1, above), p. 6.

[42]See van Beneden, *Aux Origines d'une Terminologie sacramentelle*, p. 140.

role against intrusions. But there is no evidence that Cyprian and his contemporaries spoke of "orders" or "holy orders" in the technical sense of a collegiate body of bishops, presbyters and deacons. They did, however, speak of "ordination" (*ordinatio*), a word to which we shall return.

In the fourth and fifth centuries "order" (*ordo*) and "orders" (*ordines*) appear more regularly, especially — though not exclusively — as designations for a college of ministers. In his commentary on the book of Isaiah, for example, St. Jerome spoke of "five orders in the church: bishops, presbyters, deacons, the faithful, catechumens."[43] Here again we can discern the ancient meaning of order as a quality characterizing the *entire church*, from catechumen to bishop. To belong to the church, Jerome implies, is to belong to an *ordo*. Further, though Jerome does not say it, each of these *ordines* has a distinctive role to play in the church's worship. Even public penitents temporarily excluded from full participation in the eucharist constitute an "*ordo*," according to Jerome, and they too have a "liturgy" to perform.[44]

i.e., not alienated

This connection between *ordo* and liturgy should be underscored. The church exhibits "order" most fully when it is gathered for eucharist, where each of the *ordines* — from bishop to penitent — exercises its ministry. The order exhibited at worship is not a sociological phenomenon (in the sense of "keeping good order" in a large group) but a theological statement. At stake here, as we noted earlier, is not the domination of one group over another, nor even the expression of a "hierarchy" willed by God, but what Tertullian called "the church's dignity." To repeat: the ancient meaning of *ordo* is *theological*; it expresses that particular way of being-in-the-world called "church," a communion of persons who constitute God's crop growing to harvest and who celebrate that growth around the Lord's table. The

[43]See M. Adriaen, ed., *S. Hieronymi Presbyteri Commentariorum in Esaiam Libri I-IX,* (Corpus Christianorum, 73; Turnholti: Brepols, 1963), p. 198.

[44]Texts and commentary may be found in Paul Palmer, *Sacraments and Forgiveness,* (Westminister, Maryland: Newman Press, 1960), pp. 109-110, 121.

church's dignity, its authenticity and integrity as the *community of Jesus*, require that all members, including catechumens and penitents, *belong*. The sign of that belonging is membership in an *ordo*. Everyone in the church, including those publicly designated for penance, belongs to an order and exercises a ministry, for there is no such thing — according to the view of a writer like Jerome — as a Christian who lacks an "order" or a ministry.

This use of "order(s)" as a comprehensive term that shows how *all* Christians belong to the church requires us to look again at the distinction, already found in Tertullian, between "*ordo*" (= clergy) and "*plebs*" (laity, people). The original purpose of this distinction was not to promote clericalism. Indeed, when Tertullian alluded to "the difference between clergy and laity" in the *Exhortation to Chastity*, his intentions were quite the opposite. As a Christian increasingly attracted to Montanism, Tertullian sought to *limit*, rather than expand, the clergy's role in the church. And so, though he recognized a "difference" — e.g., clergy are elected by the community's mandate and "ordained" by other clerics for their work — Tertullian wanted to minimize its importance. He argued, in fact, that since Christ has made *all* Christians priests (Rev 1:6), the absence of clergy does not mean the absence of the church. If Christians find themselves without clerical leaders, they may still celebrate baptism and eucharist, since "where there are three, even if they are laity, there is the church" (*Exhortation to Chastity*, VII:3).

This may help explain why Latin Christian writers who followed Tertullian were reluctant to adopt his "*ordo/plebs*" vocabulary. These writers clearly recognized a distinction between clergy and people, but they avoided using "order" to mark the difference. Thus Cyprian, whose avoidance of *ordo* we have already noted, spoke of "clergy and people" (Latin, *clerus et plebs*), as did Ambrose, Augustine and Leo the Great.[45] And Jerome kept the meaning of *ordo*

---

[45]References may be found in Albert Blaise, *Dictionnaire Latin-Francais des Auteurs chrétiens,* (Turnhout: Brepols, 1954), s.v. "Plebs", p. 629.

broad by using it of all who belong to the church, from catechumen and penitent to presbyter and bishop.

Gradually, the phrase *"holy* order(s)" emerged as a specific designation for members of the clergy. Leo I, bishop of Rome from 440 to 461, complained of persons who are admitted to a "holy order" (*admittuntur. . . . ad ordinem sacrum*) even though they lack the proper endowments of nature and grace.[46] Leo also spoke of the "order of clerics" (*ordo clericorum*), among whom are subdeacons ("fourth from the top"), deacons (third), presbyters (second), and bishops (first). Reference to holy orders also appears in Roman sources like the Verona Sacramentary, which contains liturgical texts from the fifth and sixth centuries, and which mentions the "God whose glory is served by holy orders (*sacratis ordinibus*)" in its prayer for the ordination of bishops.[47] In the late sixth century, one of Leo's successors, Gregory I, also referred to holy orders (*ordines sacros*).[48] At this period, however, the phrase was not yet reserved exclusively for the clergy, since in the sixth century the Roman senate was similarly designated as a *"sacer ordo."*[49]

The vocabulary of holy orders thus remained quite flexible in the Latin West for many centuries. Writers disagreed both about how many clerical orders existed in the church and about which persons actually constituted an *ordo*. In Jerome's list of five orders in the church, three are clerical (bishops, presbyters and deacons), while the remaining two are not (the faithful, catechumens). Leo I included subdea-

---

[46]Leo the Great, Letter 4:1; Latin Text in PL 54:611.

[47]Text in Leo Cunibert Mohlberg, ed., *Sacramentarium Veronese,* (Rerum Ecclasiasticarum Documenta, Series Maior, Fontes, I; Rome: Herder, 1956), p. 119, n. 947.

[48]Gregory the Great, Letter 8:17; Latin text in Louis Hartmann, ed., *Gregorii I Papae Registrum Epistolarum* (2 vols.; second edition; Monumenta Germaniae Historica, Epistolae; Berlin: 1899), II, p. 19.

[49]See the discussion in P.M. Gy, "Notes on the Early Terminology of Christian Priesthood," in: *The Sacrament of Holy Orders.* Papers Given at a Session of the Centre de Pastorale liturgique, 1955; translator not given, (Collegeville, Minnesota: The Liturgical Press, 1962), pp. 98-115.

cons as a "fourth order" among clerics, while Isidore of
Seville (+636) refrained from calling them an *ordo*.[50]

These differences indicate that Latin ecclesiastical writers
did not yet possess a commonly agreed-upon system for
naming the ranks of clergy in the church. The *Statuta
Ecclesiae Antiqua*, compiled in southern Gaul sometime
after the middle of the fifth century, uses the term *ordo* only
once in reference to clergy, though it frequently speaks of
ordaining clerics. Among the eight ranks (*gradus*) mentioned by the *Statuta* are bishops, presbyters, deacons, sub-
oned by the *Statuta* are bishops, presbyters, deacons, subdeacons, acolytes, exorcists, lectors, and door-keepers
("porters").[51] But this list does not exactly coincide with
what we find in Isidore of Seville's *Etymologies*, which
includes a ninth rank among the clergy, the "psalmist" (or
"chief cantor," *princeps cantorum*).[52] Elsewhere, other ministers — like grave-diggers — were sometimes referred to as
an *ordo* and numbered among the ranks of clergy. This is
what we find, for instance, in a work entitled "On the Seven
Orders of the Church," which many consider to be the work
of a fifth-century Pelagian author.[53]

Medieval theologians also had difficulty deciding what
ministries should be included among the orders and how the
ranks of clergy should be distinguished from one another.
Hugh of St. Victor (+1142), like many of his contemporaries, believed that *ordo* was a single sacrament embracing
seven ranks of clergy from door-keeper (*ostiarius*) to priest.[54]
But since by this period "priest" generally meant "presbyter", Hugh and others had to search for a way to understand
the exact difference between the presbyter's priesthood and

---

[50]See Isidore, *De Ecclesiasticis Officiis*, II:7:1 (Latin text: PL 83:787); II:8:1 (PL
83:788); II;11:1 (PL 83:791); *Etymologiae*, VII. 12:4 (PL 82:290).

[51]See Charles Munier, ed., *Les Statuta Ecclesiae Antiqua*, (Bibliothèque de
l'Institut de Droit canonique de l'Université de Strasbourg, V; Paris: Presses
Universitaires de France, 1960), pp. 95-98.

[52]Isidore, *Etymologiae*, VII.12:3 (PL 82:290).

[53]See *De Septem Ordinibus Ecclesiae* (PL 30:155).

[54]The notion of *ordo* as a sacrament of the church will be discussed in greater
detail below.

that of the bishop. This they often did by distinguishing between an "order" (e.g., lector, deacon, presbyter) and a "dignity within an order" (e.g., the archdeacon of a diocese). Hugh thus argued that while priest and bishop constitute "one rank in the sacrament" of order, they have different powers in the exercise of their ministry.[55] The difference between bishop and priest is one of *dignity*, Hugh insisted, rather than one of rank or order: "the difference of ranks in holy orders is one thing, but the difference of dignities within the same rank is another."[56] This distinction implied, of course, that bishops do not constitute a separate order in the church, but rather a "dignity within the order" of priesthood.[57] In short, medieval theology could no longer make sense of the earlier tradition, widespread in both East and West that bishops and presbyters differ precisely because they belong to two distinct *ordines* in the church.[58] In Hugh's thinking, the *single order* common to bishops and presbyters is *priesthood*, with the episcopate being merely a dignity or "excellence" within the priesthood.

Hugh of St. Victor's distinction between "order" and "dignity within an order" became commonplace in medieval theology. It was accepted by Peter Lombard, whose *Sentences* became the standard theological text in medieval universities, and it appears in the work of theologians like Thomas Aquinas. Commenting on Lombard's *Sentences*, Aquinas —like Hugh a century earlier — argued that the episcopate was not an order, though he noted that the bishop's "spiritual power" exceeds that of other priests (= presbyters).[59] Aquinas's argument was based on the notion that distinctions among the various ranks of clergy — which ranks *together* constitute the single sacrament of *ordo* — were to

---

[55] Hugh of St. Victor, *De Sacramentis*, II:2:5 (PL 176:419).

[56] Text in PL 176:419.

[57] Further discussion in Gy, "Notes on the Early Terminology of Christian Priesthood," p. 102.

[58] On the earlier understanding of *ordo*, see Bernard Botte, " 'Presbyterium' et Ordo Episcoporum," *Irenikon* 29 (1956), 5-27.

[59] See Thomas Aquinas, *Summa Theologiae* IIIa Pars, Supplementum, Q. 40, art. 5.

be understood in relation to the eucharist. Since both bishop and priest possess the same power of celebrating the eucharist, the difference between the two could not be a strictly sacramental one.[60]

Throughout the middle ages no clear-cut solution to the question of orders and who belonged to them was forthcoming. Even the Council of Trent avoided resolving the question, though it insisted that *ordo* was truly and properly a sacrament. Nor is it entirely clear, even among theologians today, how the difference between the orders of bishop and presbyter ought to be expressed in theological terms.[61] We shall thus return to this complex question later in the chapter, when the issue of orders as a "sacrament" is discussed.

At this point, however, it will be useful to summarize our discussion of succession, order and holy orders.

1. In their earliest Christian usage, succession (= episcopal succession) and order were virtually interchangeable terms. Both expressed a quality exhibited by the church and its leadership when the apostles' teaching and way of life are faithfully followed. At this stage, order was neither a "college" of ministers nor a socio-political concept, but a theological notion that reflected the new way of being-in-the-world called "church." Occasionally, however, writers like Tertullian did use *ordo* in the more restricted sense of "clergy."

2. In the fourth and fifth centuries *ordo* began to appear more frequently among writers in the Latin West. As used broadly by Jerome, *orders* included all who belong to the church: bishops, presbyters, deacons, the faithful, catechumens, penitents.

3. Increasingly, however, *ordo* was becoming a technical term for ranks (*gradus*) of the clergy. Writers did not always agree, however, on exactly how many ranks constituted the *ordo clericorum*.

[60]See *ibid.,* Q. 37, art. 2; further discussion may be found in Paul Palmer, *Sacraments of Healing and Vocation,* (Foundations of Catholic Theology Series; Englewood Cliffs, New Jersey: Prentice-Hall, 1963), p. 65.

[61]See Karl Rahner, *Bishops: Their Status and Function,* translated by Edward Quinn, (Baltimore: Helicon, 1963, paperback).

4. In the fifth and sixth centuries, the phrase "*holy* orders" appeared, though it was not reserved exclusively to clergy. We find the phrase in the works of bishops like Leo I, Gregory I and Isidore of Seville, as well as in liturgical sources like the Verona Sacramentary.

5. During this period, too, the first allusions to *ordo* as a *sacramentum* emerge. The fifth-century treaties "On the Seven Orders of the Church," mentioned above, speaks of the deacons who constitute the "fifth order of the sacrament" and mentions the "sacrament of the sevenfold church" in its discussion of the clergy.

6. Despite these developments, however, theologians could not agree on exactly how *ordo* should be interpreted. Hugh of St. Victor, Peter Lombard and Thomas Aquinas regarded order as a single comprehensive sacrament that included *all* the ranks of ordained clergy: door-keepers, exorcists, acolytes, lectors, subdeacons, deacons and priests. Within the single priestly order these theologians distinguished a "dignity" or "spiritual power" that belonged to bishops, though they denied that episcopate is a distinct *ordo*.

7. Later theologians, from the Council of Trent to the twentieth century, have also been unsure about how *ordo* should be understood theologically and applied to ranks of the clergy. Since Vatican Council II, "order" — as a technical term — has been reserved exclusively to deacons, presbyters and bishops. All other offices — even those for which liturgical rites of designation exist (e.g., lector, acolyte) —are called "ministries."

It seems fair to say, then, that throughout the church's history the vocabulary of *ordo* has been characterized by ambiguity. Theologians have struggled to clarify its meaning — as theological reality, as designation for ranks of clergy, as "sacrament" — but without complete success. Similar ambiguity has surrounded the notion of ordination and even of priesthood, as we shall discover in the section that follows.

II

Ordination

We have noted earlier that by the beginning of the third century, in the *Apostolic Tradition* of Hippolytus, "ordination" already appears to have acquired a technical and familiar meaning. It is used there exclusively for bishops, presbyters and deacons, and it involves the ritual of laying on hands with prayer. Hippolytus also tells us that the Christian people have an indispensable role in the choice and election of their clergy — a point strongly reiterated more than two centuries later by Leo I, who insisted that no bishop is to be ordained "against the wishes of the people and without their consenting to it."[62] As described by the *Apostolic Tradition*, then, ordination involves two distinct but related procedures: choice and election by the people, and a liturgical rite whose principal elements are the laying on of hands and prayer.

Hippolytus's description of ordination is the earliest surviving one in Christian literature — unless, of course, one chooses to construe the Pastoral Letters of the New Testament as evidence for a primitive rite of ordination. Our next detailed information appears nearly a century and a half later in works such as the *Apostolic Constitutions* (ca. 350-400), *The Testament of our Lord* (ca. 400), and the *Prayerbook of Serapion*, bishop of Thmuis in Egypt (ca. 350). The ordination rites for bishop, presbyter and deacon in the *Apostolic Constitutions* are a re-working and expansion of the liturgies found in Hippolytus, as the following chart indicates:[63]

[62]Leo the Great, Letter 14; English translation in Edmund Hunt, trans., *St. Leo the Great: Letters,* (Fathers of the Church, Vol. 34; New York:Fathers of the Church, Inc., 1957), p. 63.

[63]Texts in F.X. Funk, ed., *Didascalia et Constitutiones Apostolorum,* (2 vols.; Paderborn: F. Schoeningh, 1905), I, pp. 473-525 (= *Apostolic Constitutions,* VIII.4:2 - 18:3).

Apostolic Tradition	**Apostolic Constitutions**
BISHOP	BISHOP
—Election by people	—Election by people
—Ordination on Sunday	—Ordination on Sunday
	—Interrogations and testimony to candidate's worthiness by people and clergy
—Imposition of hands	—Gospels held open over candidate's head
—Prayer of ordination	—Prayer of ordination
—Celebration of eucharist	—Celebration of eucharist
PRESBYTER	PRESBYTER
—Imposition of hands by bishop and presbytery	—Imposition of hands by bishop; presbyters and deacons stand by
—Prayer of ordination	—Prayer of ordination
DEACON	DEACON
—Imposition of hands by bishop	—Imposition of hands by bishop; presbyters and deacons stand by
—Prayer of ordination	—Prayer of ordination

The parallelism of pattern between these two sources is immediately evident. The *Apostolic Constitutions* do, however, reveal some ritual innovations: in the ordination of a bishop the holding open of the gospels over the candidate's head is mentioned, while reference to a laying on of hands is omitted; in the ordination of a presbyter the bishop acts alone, without the presbytery, in imposing hands. Unlike the *Apostolic Tradition*, further, the *Apostolic Constitutions* explicitly describe the ordination — with imposition of hands and prayer — of deaconesses, subdeacons and lectors. Other ministers are mentioned, too, in *Apostolic Constitutions*, but these — confessors, virgins, widows, exorcists — are not ordained.[64]

The same ritual pattern for ordaining bishops, presbyters and deacons is found in *The Testament of Our Lord*, without, however, the innovations contained in the *Apostolic Constitutions*.[65] Other ministers are also named in the *Testament* — confessors, widows, subdeacons, lectors, virgins — but these do not receive a laying on of hands.[66] The *Prayerbook of Serapion* provides prayers for the ordination of bishop, presbyter and deacon, but gives no information about the liturgical rites themselves.[67] The titles attached to the prayers in Serapion indicate the use of laying on hands (*cheirothesia*), though these titles may have been added later and do not necessarily have a technical meaning.[68]

After Hippolytus, the earliest western liturgical rites and prayers for ordaining bishops, presbyters and deacons are contained in the Verona Sacramentary, a Roman book that assumed its present shape around the year 600. Its contents vary in antiquity; some of the material may derive from as early as the mid-third century, though much of it is later (ca. 400-590). The ordination material probably dates from the sixth century, though it may come from the end of the fifth, during the episcopate of Gelasius I (+ 496).[69] The ritual pattern for ordinations is still quite simple, though it contains some elements not found earlier in the *Apostolic Tradition*, the *Apostolic Constitutions* or *The Testament of Our Lord*. Since the Verona Sacramentary contains few rubrics, we must attempt to reconstruct the rites of ordination from the prayer texts it provides. In the case of episcopal ordination, the Verona first gives a set of prayers for use

[64]See *Apostolic Constitutions* 23:1 - 26:3; ed. Funk (preceding note), I, pp. 527-529.

[65]See Ignatius Ephraem II Rahmani, ed.. *Testamentum Domini Nostri Jesu Christi*, (Mainz: F. Kirchheim, 1899; reprint, Hildesheim: Georg Olms Verlagsbuchhandlung, 1968), pp. 29-93.

[66]See *ibid.*, pp. 95-109.

[67]See Funk, *Didascalia et Constitutiones Apostolorum*, II, pp. 188-190 for texts.

[68]See notes in Funk, *Didascalia et Constitutiones Apostolorum*, II, pp. 188-199.

[69]See D.M. Hope, *The Leonine Sacramentary*. A Reassessment of its Nature and Purpose, (Oxford: Oxford University Press, 1971), pp. 110, 116.

at the eucharist during which the bishop is ordained.[70] These include an opening collect, a prayer over the gifts, a special form of the "*Hanc igitur*" to be inserted into the eucharistic prayer, and a prayer after communion. Following these texts, two formulas for the ordination itself are provided: a prayer that appears to serve as a concluding collect to a litany, and the ordination prayer proper.[71] A similar pattern — though without a full set of prayers for the eucharistic liturgy — is followed for the ordination of deacons and presbyters.[72] The Verona Sacramentary's pattern for ordination may thus be outlined as follows:

Bishop
—(Invitation to the litany?)
—(Litany?)
—Concluding prayer of the litany
—Prayer of ordination

Presbyter
—Invitation to the litany
—(Litany)
—Concluding prayer of the litany
—Prayer of ordination

Deacon
—Invitation to the litany
—(Litany)
—Concluding prayer of the litany
—Prayer of ordination

The ancient and simple pattern for ordination found in the *Apostolic Tradition* is clearly reproduced here as well. The only ritual addition made in the Verona appears to be the litany, with its initial invitation (a "bidding" formula probably said by the deacon) and its concluding collect. None of the ritual additions characteristic of later ordi-

---

[70]See *Sacramentarium Veronense*, ed. Mohlberg, nn. 942-945, pp. 118-119.
[71]See *ibid.*, nn. 946-947, pp. 119-120.
[72]See *ibid.*, nn. 948-951, pp. 120-212 (deacon); nn. 952-954, pp. 121-122 (presbyter).

nation liturgies is found in the Verona; nothing is said about special vesture for the candidates, anointings, or presentation with the "signs of office" (e.g., stole, chalice and paten, book of the gospels). For that matter, nothing is explicitly said about the laying on of hands, either. Scholars ordinarily assume that the gesture was known and used in Rome during this period, though Cyrille Vogel has recently questioned the legitimacy of this assumption.[73] Vogel notes that the *Ordines Romani* — small booklets containing rubrics and ceremonial details designed for use in conjunction with the sacramentaries — are strangely silent about the gesture of imposing hands at ordination. *Ordo Romanus* 34 (manuscript, ca. 700-750) is a case in point. A Roman document, it contains numerous details about the ordination ritual for bishops, presbyters and deacons, but says nothing about imposing hands.[74]

There is, however, other evidence from western sources that indicates familiarity with the ritual gesture of imposing hands at the ordination of bishops, presbyters and deacons. The fifth-century *Statuta Ecclesiae Antiqua*, mentioned earlier in this chapter, clearly testify to this custom:

> When a bishop is ordained, two bishops place and hold the book of the gospels over his neck, and while one of them says the prayer of ordination....all the other bishops who are present touch his head with their hands.
>
> When a presbyter is ordained, the bishop says the prayer of ordination and imposes hands on his head, while all the other presbyters who are present hold their hands over his head next to the hand of the bishop.
>
> When a deacon is ordained, the bishop alone....imposes his hand, because the deacon is consecrated not for the priesthood but for the ministry.[75]

[73]See Cyrille Vogel, *Ordinations inconsistantes et Caractère inamissible, (Études d'Histoire du culte et des institutions chrétiennes*, I; Turin: Bottega d'Erasmo, 1978), p. (131).

[74]Latin text of Ordo Romanus 34 in Michel Andrieu, ed., *Les Ordines Romani du haut moyen age*, (4 vols.; Louvain: 1951), III, pp. 603-613.

[75]Texts in Munier, ed., *Les Statuta Ecclesiae Antiqua*, pp. 95-96; my translation.

We have already encountered most of the elements contained in the *Statuta's* description of ordination: the use of the gospel-book in the ordination of bishops (*Apostolic Constitutions*); imposition of hands by the presbytery in the ordination of presbyters, and the observation that deacons are ordained "for the ministry," not for the priesthood (*Apostolic Tradition*).

Despite the lack of reference to laying on hands in the Verona Sacramentary and *Ordo Romanus* 34, it is reasonable to conclude that from the early third century onward, most eastern and western churches — if not all of them —are familiar with this gesture as part of the ordination ritual for bishops, presbyters and deacons. We can conclude, too, that from this same period onward, rites of ordination were the usual means of designating ministries in the churches. We need to ask, though, exactly what such an ordination meant — and how it was related to the other important element in the appointment of clergy, viz., election and choice by the people.

ORDINATION BEFORE THE FOURTH CENTURY

Catholics today automatically think of ordination as a *sacramental* event, parallel in importance and effect to other ecclesial actions such as baptism or eucharist. But our discussions thus far make it clear that the perception of "holy orders" as a "sacrament" developed very slowly. In the earliest sources, sacramental language is not used to describe the significance or effects of ordaining someone to a clerical ministry. We thus need to examine more carefully how words like "ordain" (*ordinare*) and "ordination" (*ordinatio*) made their appearance in Latin theology — and what the authors who used them meant.

Once again, Tertullian is the writer in whose works words like "ordain/ordination", as applied to ecclesial functions, first appear. But while in Tertullian's writings these words assumed a distinctly *theological* significance, they did not lose their ordinary, non-technical meaning. According to a recent study by Pierre van Beneden, Tertullian used "ordain" in at least three different senses:[76]

1. In the general sense of "directing" or "orienting" a person or object toward something else. This use resembles popular English expressions like "She is orienting her life toward new goals" or "His life was always directed toward higher achievements."

2. In the sense of installing or establishing someone in a position, role or rank. This meaning of "ordain" is slightly more technical than the first and does imply an authoritative action with public consequences. Here the use would resemble English sentences like "Mrs. Thatcher was installed as Prime Minister" or "Ronald Reagan was inaugurated as President". These examples imply authoritative action with public repercussions, but they do not suggest permanent or unalterable "states of being".

3. In the sense of "ratifying" an event or a person's role. Here again the meaning is more technical. The ratification of a treaty, for instance, is not only authoritative but implies responsibilities closely linked to national honor, peace between peoples, etc.

As Tertullian used them, "ordain" and "ordination" clearly had consequences for the church's life, unity and integrity. But the words did not refer primarily to the liturgical or "sacramental" acts of designating clergy, still less to some "indelible sacerdotal character" possessed by persons ordained.[77] Still, it is true that Tertullian recognized in ordination a "hierarchical" pattern of ministry with its own system of regulations. To ordain someone did, in fact, imply a serious commissioning, the giving and receiving of a ministerial charge, a mandate to serve the local church. But the giving of this mandate was not restricted to a rite or a liturgy; it included both the admission of a person to a ministerial function through election by the people (*adlectio in ordinem*), and the public ratification or "consecration" of

---

[76]See van Beneden, *Aux Origines d'une Terminologie sacramentelle*, pp. 53-62.
[77]*Ibid.*, pp. 57, 144-145.

that person by the church's leadership. This latter act is what we customarily think of today when we say "ordination", but in Tertullian's view the rite was less important than the mandate for service, while the ratification was quite impossible if the candidate had not been chosen by the people.

This view is also reflected in the works of Cyprian and his contemporaries, though by the middle of the third century ordination had acquired further precision as a theological term. According to Cyprian, ordination is both an action of God and an action of the church.[78] God is ultimately the One who "ordains", who destines or orients persons toward an ecclesial post, but this ordination must be mediated through the church's action. Several distinct elements comprise this twofold activity of ordaining:[79]

1. *Election:* In the case of a bishop, Cyprian insists that election to the office must involve the people, the local clergy, and bishops from neighboring churches.

2. *Divine investiture:* Cyprian sees, further, an intimate linkage between the call to ecclesial office (mediated by the church) and God's choice of the minister. This is why he argues, as we noted earlier, that "*God* ordains priests (= bishops)".

3. *Ecclesial investiture:* The church is the concrete historical agent that calls a person to ministry. But the actual installation of persons in ministry requires action by the bishops. Although the power to call persons to ministerial service belongs to the whole church, the "right" to ordain them belongs to bishops.

4. *Imposition of hands:* Apart from liturgical sources like the *Apostolic Tradition,* Cyprian is the first Latin writer who explicitly mentions laying on hands as the recognized ritural for episcopal investiture (Letter 67:5).

5. *Conditions:* The validity and legitimacy of an ordination require fulfillment of two basic conditions in Cyprian's thinking: it must first be in accord with "apostolic

[78]*Ibid.,* pp. 63-66.
[79]*Ibid.,* pp. 147-162.

tradition"—i.e., the church and the candidate for ministry must live and believe according to the tradition handed on from those "first witnesses to Christ's mission"; secondly, the ordination must occur in a community that lives in communion with the whole church. Apart from these two conditions—"apostolicity" and "catholicity"—no valid ordination can occur. A schismatic community, thus, cannot have authentic ministers, since any group that damages the church's unity could not fulfill the conditions mentioned above.

6. *Effects:* Cyprian clearly believes that certain effects follow from ecclesiastical ordination. Ordained persons form the *clerus* (clergy) and have an authoritative role in directing the community's life. These persons possess "honor" and "dignity" in the church (Letter 55:24), though their powers are *spiritual* in nature, rather than socio-political. Bishops, specifically, possess power related to liturgical functions: baptism, reconciliation of penitents, investiture of others in an ecclesial office (= ordination), presiding at eucharist. Such powers are, however, radically rooted in the church itself—of which bishops and others are *ministers.*

7. *Loss of ecclesial mandate:* Cyprian vigorously believed that the people have the right not only to choose worthy bishops, but also to reject unworthy ones (Letter 67:3). Ordination does not, therefore, create an "indelible mark" on the person ordained. An ecclesial mandate can be lost through the minister's unworthiness; the effects of ordination are not irrevocable. Since the mandate for ministerial service is mediated by the *church,* the community can revoke the mandate. In this Cyprian accurately reflects the pre-Constantinian theology of ordination. That theology did not distinguish between the "power of order(s)" (an irrevocable, indelible quality belonging to the ordained person) and the "power of jurisdiction" (the actual exercise of a ministry, which can be revoked).

8. *Approval by others:* Because of his concern for catholic (i.e., inter-church) unity, Cyprian insisted that a local

bishop's installation must be approved not only by the local community but also by bishops in other regions. The purpose of such approval was to safeguard the unity of all churches in love—and at the same time to show that episcopal ministry is a *collegial* responsibility shared by many.

All these elements constitute the meaning of "ordination for Cyprian. It is clear that the ritual act of commissioning ministers—though important—is but one element of a much larger process. Indeed, the ritual is obviously subordinate to other actions: election by people, local clergy and bishops; fulfillment of the conditions of "apostolicity" and "catholicity"; continued evidence of the minister's worthiness. There is nothing in Cyprian's thinking that resembles later theories of "indelible character" or "ontological change" in the ordained person. For Cyprian, as for Tertullian, ordination is primarily a *functional* term that expresses a many-staged process by which a local community chooses, legitimates, and ritually installs its clergy.

Prior to the fourth century, therefore, Latin theology had developed a rather precise theological understanding of ordination. A *process* involving several closely-related elements, it also had public effects and consequences. The ritual part of the ordination process appears to have included, at least from the early third century onward, the layng on of hands for bishops, presbyters and deacons. Still, ordination was not considered an inviolable "possession"of the ordained. The mandate to serve, given by the church, could also be revoked by the church—and in that case the minister simply returned to the ranks of the laity.

ORDINATION: LATER EVOLUTION

The church's acceptance as a licit religion by Constantine (ca. 312) produced far-reaching changes in its life and in the development of its ministries. These changes have been chronicled by others, and there is little reason to repeat them here.[80] Our focus will concern the shifts of understanding that eventually contributed to a theology of ordination which emphasized the "personal powers" and "unalterable character" attached to ordained ministers.

We have seen that in Latin theology before Constantine, the essential "core" of ordination was the *mandate of the church*—i.e., the mission entrusted to a minister through an ecclesial process that involved election, discernment of God's choice of the candidate, ritual action (laying on hands and prayer), fulfillment of certain conditions (apostolicity, catholicity), and attention to inter-church communion (e.g., the approval of a local church's bishop by other bishops in the region). Although liturgical ritual was one component of this process, it was neither the only nor the most important one. In short, the imposition of hands was not, in itself, sufficient to make one a bishop, presbyter or deacon. Much more fundamental was the church's *recognition* of ministry—a recognition which could (e.g., in the case of the "confessors") take forms other than laying on hands.

Early Christianity was also convinced that ordination involved attachment to a concrete community. No one could be ordained "in general" or "absolutely", i.e., without some specific attachment to a church and its people. A bishop had to be attached to a city or (later) to a diocese or province; a presbyter had to be linked with an urban or rural church, a monastery, or some other officially recognized community. In later terminology, this attachment to a concrete church was referred to as the ordinand's "title" (*titulus*). So strong was the conviction that an ordinand must have a title that the Council of Chalcedon (451) utterly prohibited "absolute" ordinations. If a person is ordained without title, Chalcedon declared, it renders the ordination not only "null and void" but utterly non-existent.[81]

Chalcedon's prohibition is another example of Christian

---

[80]See, for example, Bernrad Cooke, *Ministry to Word and Sacrament,* (Philadelphia: Fortress press, 1976).
[81]See text, French translation and discussion of canon 6 of Chalcedon in Vogel, *Ordinations inconsistantes,* pp. (134)-(139).

attitudes toward ordination in the earlier centuries of the church's life. The mere liturgical act of laying on hands did not guarantee the existence or the validity of an ordination; other ecclesial and juridical conditions had to be met as well. In the East, the Chalcedonian rule has been maintained until the present.[82] In the West, too, for many centuries the principle prohibiting absolute ordinations was honored by both theologians and canonists. But toward the end of the twelfth century an important shift in Latin thinking on the subject occurred. At the Third Lateran Council in 1179, Pope Alexander III reinterpreted the "title" of ordination, suggesting that it merely meant a cleric should be assured of sufficient revenue to live on.[83] This "economic" reinterpretation differed vastly from the earlier meaning of the title as attachment to a specific church's life and people. A further step toward reinterpretation occurred ca. 1198, when Innocent III argued that even a presbyter ordained "absolutely" still possessed and retained his "presbyteral" quality. This meant, in effect, that the ritual act of ordination was, in and of itself, sufficient to make one a minister—a point that would have been hotly denied by the Council of Chalcedon.[84]

This shift of attitude about what is essential for valid ordination resulted, in large part, from the West's rediscovery of a principle contained in the works of Augustine. In his battle against the Donatists (ca. 400-420), Augustine had put forward the notion of *"character dominicus"*, which might be roughly translated as in "indelible quality" that results from the Christian's sacramental incorporation into Christ's body, the church.[85] The Donatists insisted that since personal holiness is essential for membership in the "true church", an unworthy Christian or an unworthy minister should, upon re-conversion, be re-baptized or re-ordained. As a corollary, Donatist theology argued that

[82]See *ibid.,* p. (133).
[83]*Ibid.,* p. (140).
[84]*Ibid.,* pp. (140)-(141).
[85]*Ibid.,* pp. (54)-(59).

only holy ministers celebrate valid and efficacious sacraments: "*nemo dat quod non habet*"—"nobody gives what he doesn't have".

Donatist theology presented a serious challenge to Augustine. He had to admit that Donatists, though heterodox, still validly celebrated sacraments like baptism and ordination—otherwise he would have implicitly affirmed their principle of re-baptizing and re-ordaining. At the same time, however, Augustine argued that a "valid" sacrament is not always a *fruitful* one. This distinction between "validity" and "fruitfulness" permitted Augustine to affirm three things:

1. A sacrament may be valid and fruitful even if its minister is unworthy or heretical, since God does not penalize people simply because their leaders are corrupt.

2. Because even heterodox communities celebrate valid sacraments, one need not re-baptize or re-ordain if those communities return to communion with orthodox churches. A Donatist bishop or presbyter is truly (i.e., validly) ordained, though the ordination remains unfruitful as long as the person persists in heresy.

3. Even a heterodox community's sacraments create a "*character dominicus*"; i.e., they permanently claim and mark the individual as one who belongs to Christ—even if that claim remains unfruitful in the individual's life.

None of this surprises Catholics today. We are familiar with the distinction between validity and fruitfulness, as well as with the idea of an "indelible character" that permanently marks the Christian as one who belongs to Christ. But Augustine's thinking on these matters was, in his own time, rather innovative. For almost eight centuries, Latin theologians generally ignored his distinction and his notion of a permanent "character".[86] Implicit in the shift that occurred in the late twelfth century, however, was a revival of Augustinian theology. If ordination produces a permanent and inviolable "mark" on the minister—and if ordina-

---

[86] See *ibid.,* pp. (61)-(63) for some exceptions.

tion is essentially a *ritual act*—then it makes little difference whether an ordinand meets other conditions (e.g., attachment to a specific church, election, a genuine mandate for ministry).

In the thirteenth century, Thomas Aquinas gave systematic expression to the revived Augustinian notion of an "indelible character" attached to ordination. Defining "character" as a "spiritual power" (*spiritualis potestas*), Thomas noted that it is especially related to empowering the Christian for participation in worship.[87] "Character" was not, therefore, an object or thing but a new *relationship* established between God and the Christian, particularly through the sacraments of baptism and confirmation. On the basis of this new relationship, a Christian is joined to the unique priesthood of Christ and is thus equipped to offer the Father that true worship which Jesus brought to perfection in the sacrifice of the cross. In a word, "character" is an empowerment that permanently changes Christians, making them radically capable of authentic worship through union with the priesthood of Christ.

According to Aquinas the root of sacramental "character" is baptism, though two other sacraments are perceived as producing a similar effect in the Christian's life: confirmation, in which persons are empowered to witness in mature faith; and holy orders, in which persons are empowered for a new kind of service in the community.[88] The character of orders is not, according to Aquinas, limited to diaconate, presbyterate and episcopate. *All* the ministries, including those sometimes called "minor orders" (e.g., lector, acolyte), result in that empowering relationship referred to by the word "character".[89] At the same time, Aquinas placed emphasis on the liturgical rites of ordination as the "moment " when the new relationship or character is established.[90]

[87]See Thomas Aquinas, *Summa Theologiae,* IIIa Pars, Q. 63, arts. 1-2.
[88]*Ibid.,* IIIa Pars, Q. 72, art. 5; Q. 35, art. 2.
[89]*Ibid.,* IIIa pars, Q. 35, art. 2.
[90]*Ibid.,* IIIa Pars, Q. 37, art. 5.

By the thirteenth century, then, the notion of a permanent character attached to holy orders and "conferred" in the rites of ordination was firmly entrenched in Latin theology. So permanent was this character that in Aquinas's view it survived even death.[91] Eventually this position worked its way into official documents of the church's magisterium. At the Council of Florence in 1439, the permanent character established through holy orders was spoken of in the "Decree for the Armenians".[92] The Council of Trent reiterated this position in its twenty-third session (15 July, 1563) and anathematized anyone who would contend that an ordained priest could ever again be considered a "layman."[93]

The medieval conviction about the absolute permanence and the indelible character attached to holy orders was a profound departure from the earlier Christian understanding of ordination. Writers like Cyprian and ecumenical councils like Chalcedon clearly attached great importance to ordination, but they did not restrict its significance to liturgical rites and indelible marks. Nor did Cyprian and Chalcedon believe that the mere fact of being ritually ordained was sufficient to make one "a priest forever". The church had the right to reject unworthy ministers, and those rejected could no longer lay claim to priesthood.

It was, however, the theology of persons like Aquinas and the magisterial decisions of Councils like Florence and Trent that shaped the modern Latin understanding of ordination. As a result, the ritual of ordination has come to be regarded as THE determining factor in the valid transmission of ministries, to the exclusion of virtually every other consideration (e.g., participation of the people in the choice and election of ministers, their right to reject unworthy candidates, the ancient meaning of the "title" of ordination). This has created special difficulties in ecumenical discussions, since the Roman Church has generally insisted that

[91]*Ibid.,* IIIa Pars, Q. 50, art. 4, ad 3.
[92]Texts may be found in H. Denzinger and A. Schoemetzer, eds., *Enchiridion Symbolorum,* (33rd edition; Rome: Herder, 1965), n. 1313, p. 333.
[93]See Vogel, *Ordinations inconsistantes,* pp. (1)-(2) for texts and commentary.

ministers of other churches are not truly ordained because their liturgies of ordination are "invalid".[94]

The later history of ordination in the West is thus a history of increasing emphasis on the liturgical action which, if validly celebrated by the competent minister (the bishop), effects an "ontological change" in the ordinand and "imprints an indelible character on his soul". Given this view, it is not surprising that the ordained person's priesthood was thought to differ *essentially* (and not merely in degree) from the baptismal priesthood of the laity. Nor is it surprising that the ordained were believed to have sacred powers—e.g., the power to consecrate the eucharist—which could be exercised quite independently of a concrete community and its pastoral needs. This explains, too, why a person who resigns his ministry or is dispensed from its obligations is still regarded as possessing the "indelible priestly character", even though he no longer exercises the office.

III

Priesthood and Sacrament

Closely connected to the Latin church's later understanding of ordination was its interpretation of priesthood. In Chapter Two we noted that the first generation of Christians seem consciously to have avoided using categories of priesthood to identify their ministers. Paul, for example, spoke of many kinds of mutual service in the churches, but preferred to name these services by terms like "co-workers"," apostle", "helper" (*diakonos*), "prophet". Not

[94]This was the basis for rejecting the validity of Anglican orders in the late nineteenth century: see Denzinger/Schoenmetzer, eds., *Enchiridion Symbolorum*, nn., 3315-3319, pp. 648-650. In recent years, some Roman Catholic theologians have begun to suggest alternative ways of recognizing ministries in the churches; see, e.g., Kilian McDonnell, "Ways of Validating Ministry," *Journal of Ecumenical Studies* 7 (1970), 209-265.

even the later New Testament literature—the Pastoral Letters, for example—chose to speak of Christian leaders as "priests". Rather early on, however, Christian writers began appropriating the vocabulary of Israelite priesthood and applying it to their own leaders. The *Didache* 13:3 calls Christian prophets "high priests" and announces that they are entitled to receive tithes from the community—just as Israel's priests were. In a similar vein, *I Clement* 40 implicitly compares the Christian leaders who offer the community's gifts and sacrifices with the Israelite high priesthood.

James A. Mohler has suggested that one reason for Christianity's appropriation of priestly terminology was the emergence, in the late-first and early-second centuries, of a "New Israel" theology.[95] This theology is evident in works like the *Epistle of Barnabas* (ca. 100), which describes the church as the true Israel that has inherited the covenant and now celebrates a perfect worship in a spiritual temple.[96] As Christians became increasingly conscious of themselves as a new religion rather than a sectarian group within Judaism, it was natural for them to interpret the Hebrew Scriptures in a new light. Temple, cult and priesthood were thus regarded as "types" now fulfilled in Jesus and in the mutual ministry and "spiritual sacrifices" of Christians.

Still, the reluctance to call Christian leaders priests lingered. Not until the early third century do we begin finding a consistent pattern of priestly vocabulary applied to Christian ministers. As noted earlier in this chapter, both the *Apostolic Tradition* (ca. 215) and Cyprian of Carthage (+ 258) call the bishop a "priest", though Cyprian seems deliberately to have extended the term to include presbyters. Generally, however, the community's "priest" or "high priest" is its bishop, at least in Christian literature up to the sixth century.[97] Here, our attention will center on

[95]See Mohler, *The Origin and Evolution of the Priesthood,* p. 49.

[96]See Barnabas, 13-16; text and translation in Lake, *The Apostolic Fathers,* Vol. I, pp. 386-399.

[97]See Gy, "Notes on the Early Terminology of Christian Priesthood," pp. 109-112.

the way in which "priest" eventually became synonymous with "presbyter".

PRESBYTERS AS PRIESTS

As they are described in third-century sources, presbyters function primarily as a body of advisors to the bishop, who is pastor of the local community. With him they share a role in certain liturgical actions, such as celebration of the eucharist, but their pastoral activity seems quite limited. Third-century bishops like Cornelius (Rome, 251-253) and Cyprian speak about consulting the *presbyterium* in important church matters, but these same bishops resisted any movement toward presbyteral independence from the bishop.[98] As Cornelius put it, "There is one true God and one Lord Christ whom we confess, and there should be one Holy Spirit and one bishop in the church."[99]

Even after the Constantinian era began in the early fourth century, presbyters were not recognized as an independent body with "distinct powers" of their own over against those of the bishop. The bishop's role as liturgical president, teacher, reconciler of penitents and local pastor was maintained, at least in principle. But the increasing number of urban and rural churches in the fourth century meant that the bishop's presence at all community functions was impossible. Presbyters began to be deputed as pastors of rural congregations, and in large metropolitan areas like Rome they might also serve churches within the city or its suburbs. This is what we find, for example, in a letter of Innocent I, written about the year 416 to Decentius, bishop of Gubbio. Innocent explains that the entire community at Rome cannot be accommodated on Sundays in a single church; as a result, presbyters preside at eucharists in other churches and a fragment of consecrated bread from the

[98]See Botte, " 'Presbyterium' et ordo Episcoporum," 7-9.
[99]Cornelius's letter is contained in Cyprian's correspondence (Letter 49:2); cited by Botte, " 'Presbyterium' et Ordo Episcoporum," 8, note 4.

i.e. *spreading membership, which calls for office*

bishop's Mass is sent round to these churches as a sign of unity.[100]

But practical pastoral concerns were not the only reason why presbyters began to achieve greater prestige and independence at this period. In the later fourth century there arose what can be called a "presbyterian movement" rooted in the notion that, to all intents and purposes, presbyters are equal to bishops. St. Jerome was a proponent of this view, and it is also evident in fifth-century works like the *Statuta Ecclesiae Antiqua* and "On the Seven Orders of the church."[101] The *Statuta* clearly intend to limit the bishop's power: "In church, the bishop sits in a higher place than the college of presbyters, but at home, he should recognize that he is truly a colleague of the presbyters."[102] Again, the *Statuta* decree: "A bishop should not ordain clerics without the advice of his fellow-presbyters. . . "[103] The author of these regulations (probably Gennadius of Marseilles, a presbyter) appears to regard the bishop as simply "first among equals " within the presbytery. A similar point of view is found in the anonymous work "On the Seven Orders of the Church". Its author admits that the "*ordo episcopalis*" is highest among the orders, but presbyters are given the title "priests": "The sixth order is that of the seniors, which is given to priests, who are called 'presbyters'. These preside over the church of God and confect the sacraments of Christ."[104] The author continues with a defense of the eucharist celebrated by presbyters: "In confecting Christ's body and blood, no difference should be thought to exist between them (the presbyters) and the bishop. And if need demands, bishops should receive the eucharist already consecrated by presbyters. . . "[105]

[100]See discussion in Nathan Mitchell, *Cult and Controversy*, (Studies in the Reformed Rites of the Catholic Church, Volume IV; New York: Pueblo Publishing Company, 1982), pp. 34-37.

[101]See Botte, " 'Presbyterium' et Ordo Episcoporum, " 12.

[102]*Statuta Ecclesiae Antiqua*, Canon 2; text ed. Munier, p. 79; my translation.

[103]*Statuta Ecclesiae Antiqua*, Canon 10; text ed. Munier, p. 80; my translation.

[104]*De Septem Ordinibus Ecclesiae*; PL 30:159, 162.

[105]*Ibid*; PL 30:160.

By the early fifth century, therefore, representatives of the "presbyterian movement" had begun to insist that presbyters have as much right to the title "priest" as do bishops—and that, with the exception of ordination, presbyters can do essentially everything a bishop can. Not everyone, of course, supported the presbyters' claims. In the Verona Sacramentary, for example, the ordination prayers, possibly compiled by Gelasius I (+496), speak strongly of the sacerdotal office that belongs to bishops, who are "chosen for the ministry of the high priesthood."[106] The Verona's prayer for presbyters, on the other hand, makes it clear that while they cooperate with the "high priests" in the sacerdotal ministry, they remain "second in dignity".[107] This vocabulary of priesthood in Roman liturgical texts remained fairly stable at least until the eighth and ninth centuries, as one can see from a comparison of Verona's texts with those of the Gelasian and Gregorian sacramentaries.[108]

The Roman liturgical texts thus tried to maintain the ancient identification of "priest" (sacerdos) with "bishop". But outside Rome the vocabulary was shifting in another direction. During the Carolingian epoch (8th-9th centuries), Gallican sources increasingly identified presbyters as priests. In the Gallican sacramentaries of this period, for example, we find formulas for anointing the presbyter's hands and prayers that emphasize his power to consecrate the Lord's body and blood in the eucharist.[109] Theologians

---

[106]Sacramentarium Veronense, ed. Mohlberg, n. 947, p. 119; on Gelasius as the possible compiler of these prayers, see Hope, The Leonine Sacramentary, p. 110.

[107]Sacramentarium Veronense, ed. Mohlberg, n. 954, pp. 121-122.

[108]Both the Gelasian and the Gregorian books also contain material that is non-Roman in origin, but the nucleus of their ordination rites repeats material from the Verona ("Leonine") Sacramentary. See Leo Cunibert Mohlberg, ed., Liber Sacramentorum Romanae Aeclesiae Ordinis Anni Circuli, (Rerum Ecclesiasticarum Documenta, Series Maior, Fontes, IV; Rome: Herder, 1960), nn. 143-146 (for presbyters); nn. 769-771 (for bishops). See also Jean Deshusses, ed., Le Sacramentaire Grégorien, (Fribourg: Éditions universitaires, 1971), nn. 23a+b (for bishops); 29 a+b (for presbyters).

[109]See Leo Cunibert Mohlberg, ed., Missale Francorum, (Rerum Ecclesiasticarum Documenta, Series Maior, Fontes, II; Rome: Herder, 1957), nn. 32-34, pp. 9-10.

of the same era also stressed the legitimacy of calling presbyters "priests". Rabanus Maurus (+ 856), for instance, wrote that "presbyters are called priests because, like bishops, they give what is holy . . . .in confecting the Lord's body and blood, in baptism, and in the office of preaching".[110] Although Rabanus recognized that presbyters are priests of the "second order", subordinate to bishops, he explicitly linked the presbyterate to the Aaronic priesthood of the Old Testament: "The order of presbyters took its origin from the sons, as it is said, of Aaron. For those who were called priests in the Old Testament are those whom we now call presbyters; and the one who was then called 'chief priest' is now called bishop."[111]

In Rabanus's theology the later vocabulary of Israelite priesthood is fully and explicitly applied to presbyters. Like the sons of Aaron, Christian Presbyters offer sacrifice (eucharist) and thus have a relation to the altar that parallels that of the "chief priest" (bishop). From the ninth century onward, therefore, "priest" is essentially equivalent to presbyter, though theologians still recognized that the term technically applies, in the first instance, to bishops. The trend toward identifying priest with presbyter received a further boost in the eleventh century in the work of influential theologians like Peter Damian (+ 1072). In his *Liber Gratissimus,* written to Archbishop Henry of Ravenna, Damian argued vehemently against re-ordaining bishops who had been consecrated by simoniacs (i.e., by bishops who had attained their ecclesiastical office through the payment of money). The basis for his argument was twofold: first, the effectiveness of ordination does not depend on the worthiness of its minister (a position strongly reminiscent of Augustine); and secondly, the episcopate is not in itself a new "order" (*ordo*) but simply a more "excellent" rank within the one order of *priesthood*.[112] Defining priest (*sacer-*

---

[110]See Rabanus Maurus, *De Clericorum Institutione,* I:6; PL 107:302.

[111]*Ibid.,* I:6; PL 107:301.

[112]See Peter Damian, *Liber Gratissiums,* cap. 15; PL 145:118.

dos) as one who "offers sacrifice to God", preeminently "in the mystery of the Lord's body and blood", Damian clearly assumed that priest = presbyter. Thus, though the notion that bishops also belonged to the priesthood persisted, the ancient equation (bishop = *sacerdos*) was well on the way to being lost.[113]

Peter Damian's definition of priest—one who has power to consecrate the eucharist—became the standard one in medieval theology. Two consequences followed from this. First, bishops are no longer an *ordo,* but an "excellence" or "dignity" added to the order of priesthood. This was, we have seen, the position held by Hugh of St. Victor in the twelfth century and by Thomas Aquinas in the thirteenth. Secondly, since bishops are not an *ordo* they are not "ordained" but "consecrated" to their new dignity. This was the language used, for example, by an eleventh-century writer who commented on the election of Hildebrand (Gregory VII) to the papacy in 1073. Since Hildebrand was only a deacon at his election, he was first "ordained priest" (*ordinatus est sacerdos*), and then "consecrated bishop" (*consecratus est in episcopum*).[114] This procedure was itself rather innovative, since in earlier centuries, a deacon elected bishop of Rome was immediately ordained to the episcopate, without first being ordained presbyter.[115]

By the beginning of the twelfth century, therefore, the equation "priest = presbyter" was firmly entrenched in theology. The priesthood was defined, moreover, primarily in reference to "powers" given at ordination. Chief among these was offering sacrifice, "consecrating" or "confecting" the Lord's body and blood in the eucharist. This power was perceived, further, as quite independent of any pastoral connection with a concrete community of Christians (the "title" of ordination in the ancient sense). By the end of the twelfth century, these powers were considered a permanent

---

[113]See Gy, "Notes on the Early Terminology of Christian Priesthood," p. 106.

[114]Texts cited *ibid.,* p. 105.

[115]See Michel Andrieu, "La carriére ecclésiastique des papes," *Revue des Sciences Religieuses* 21 (1947), 90-120, especially 106-107.

possession of the ordained person, who was "indelibly marked" with the "character" of priesthood. At the same time, the ministry of bishop was no longer regarded as an "*ordo*" (in the sense of a distinct college of responsible ministers) but as an ecclesiastical "excellence", a "dignity" added to priesthood. Bishops were thus "consecrated" rather than "ordained".

ORDER AND JURISDICTION

If priesthood is the highest order in the church, if it consists essentially in the power to consecrate the eucharist, and if this power is shared alike by the bishop and presbyter, then how does one distinguish between these two ministries? Some attempts by medieval theologians to answer this question have already been noted, e.g., Hugh of St. Victor's distinction between an "order" (priesthood) and ranks or dignities within that order (e.g., episcopate). But a distinction of this sort proved too fluid, especially for canon lawyers concerned about the exact status of priests and bishops. This concern was intensified by the medieval struggle between the powers of the state (the *imperium* of kings and secular rulers) and the powers of spiritual authority (the *sacerdotium* of bishops and priests). This struggle was not merely an ideological one, for some medieval writers considered kings—consecrated, anointed and vested in a liturgical rite—to be as fully "priests" as any ordained cleric. An anonymous author of the eleventh century, for example, insisted that a king should not be called a "layman" because he is the "anointed of the Lord" and so is able to remit sins and offer bread and wine in sacrifice, as indeed he does on the day he is crowned".[116] Such extravagant claims to sacerdotal power by sovereigns were by no means uncommon in the high middle ages.

---

[116]Text cited, with further discussion in Yves Congar, *Lay People in the Church,* translated by Donald Attwater, (Westminster. Maryland: The Newman Press, 1967), p. 252.

As a result of these conflicts and concerns, canonists of the twelfth and thirteenth century began to distinguish between the spiritual power that results from ordination itself (*potestas ordinis*) and the power to exercise ecclesiastical jurisdiction (*potestas jurisdictionis*). This distinction between "orders" and "jurisdiction" was possible, in part, because of factors we have discussed earlier in this chapter: the developing notion of an "indelible mark" attached to (1) holy orders, which remains even if the cleric is deposed or prevented from exercising the order; the reinterpretation of (2) "title" as a kind of legal fiction that insures income for clerics; and the idea that episcopate is a dignity or excellence (3) rather than an order in its own right. In theory, the two powers—orders and jurisdiction—are correlative principles, closely connected. But while the power of orders is permanent, the power of jurisdiction may be delegated, withheld, restricted or withdrawn by competent authority. Thus, for example, a presbyter's ordination gives him "power" to celebrate the eucharist; but the bishop may suspend the exercise of that power. In such a case, the presbyter radically retains the "*potestas ordinis,*" but lacks the proper mandate to exercise it (*potestas jurisdictionis*).

All this may sound like hopeless hairsplitting to us today, but the practical consequences of the medieval distinction were far-reaching. In effect, it resulted in a further split between the liturgical rite of ordination and the ancient significance of the "title" of ordination. For earlier writers like Cyprian it would have been unthinkable to ordain someone who had no mandate to serve among a specific people in a specific ministry. Indeed, the whole purpose of liturgical ordination was to give ritual expression to the transmission of that mandate ("title"). in Cyprian's view, one could not be a minister without a mandate, an ordained cleric without a title. But the distinction between orders and jurisdiction allowed for this possibility. One could, for instance, be a "titular bishop", ordained to the episcopate (and so possessing the power of orders) but without any people to serve (i.e., without the jurisdiction of a bishop).

This phenomenon of titular prelates in fact began to emerge after the twelfth century.[117] Similarly, one could be ordained to the presbyterate without ever assuming the work of pastoral care and ministry. In such cases the rite of ordination was considered effective, in and of itself, to produce the power of orders—even if that power were never exercised in a concrete pastoral situation.

Occasionally, this medieval distinction was invoked in extraordinary ways. There exists, for example, a fifteenth-century rescript from the pope (Boniface IX) to the Augustinian abbot and community of St. Osithae in the diocese of London, which grants the abbot and his successors the right to ordain members of the community to the subdeaconate, deaconate, and presbyterate.[118] Here is a case where the power of episcopal jurisdiction was granted to someone not a bishop (these abbots were presbyters). It was thus possible to possess both orders without jurisdiction and jurisdiction without orders. This explains, too, how some "prince-bishops" in the seventeenth and eighteenth century could for years exercise episcopal jurisdiction in a diocese without actually being ordained bishop. In this case, the prince could exercise the power of jurisdiction, but not the power of orders (e.g., could not ordain clerics or preside at eucharist).

We may return now to the question raised at the beginning of this section: How did medieval theology distinguish between the priesthood of presbyters and that of bishops? The difference was perceived primarily as one of authority and jurisdictional power, though theologians like Aquinas admitted that bishops were also superior to presbyters in the power of orders, i.e., bishops can perform some sacramental actions (confirmation, ordination) which presbyters cannot.[119] According to Thomas's view, then, the episcopate

[117]See F.J. Winslow, "Titular Bishop," *New Catholic Encyclopedia*, Vol 14, pp. 176-178.

[118]Text in Denzinger/Schoenmetzer, *Enchiridion Symbolorum*, n. 1145, pp. 313-314.

[119]See Thomas Aquinas, *Summa Theologiae* IIIa Pars, Supplementum, Q. 40, art. 5, ad 3.

was not a sacramental order but a hierarchical rank.[120] Or to put it another way, the episcopate is not a sacrament because, unlike priesthood, it is not an order; it is not an order because it does not "imprint" an "indelible character"; and it does not imprint character because, Aquinas said, the bishop's ministry is directed not primarily toward God but toward sanctifying and governing God's people.[121]

Although Aquinas's opinion may have been the prevailing one during the high middle ages, it was not the only one. The Franciscan theologian Duns Scotus (ca. 1265-1308) argued that episcopate is a true order conferred through the laying on of hands.[122] Later theologians like Gabriel Biel (ca. 1420-1495) and, more especially, Robert Bellarmine (1542-1621), followed Scotus's argument and held that episcopate is a genuine order and sacrament that makes a bishop different from a presbyter in both jurisdiction and sacramental powers.[123] In 1563 the Council of Trent took up the question of episcopal office, but did not reach a definitive decision about its precise sacramentality or about its status as an "order" distinct from priesthood.[124] Trent also discussed the relation between the power of orders and the power of jurisdiction in the episcopal office. Some bishops maintained that episcopal jurisdiction derives from papal appointment, while others argued that it comes directly from God. But this question too was not conclusively resolved.

The medieval distinction between orders and jurisdiction

---

[120]*Ibid.,* IIIa Pars, Supplementum, Q. 40, art. 4.

[121]*Ibid.,* IIIa pars, Supplementum, Q. 38, art. 2, ad 2. See also Geogre E. Dolan, *The Distinction between the Episcopate and the Presbyterate according to the Thomistic Opinion,* (Catholic University of America Studies in Sacred Theology, Second Series, no. 36; Washington, D.C.: Catholic University of America Press, 1950), p. 82.

[122]Aquinas and many other medieval theologians held that the essential act of conferring the order and character of priesthood consists in giving the chalice to the ordinand. See *Summa Theologiae,* IIIa pars, Supplementum, Q. 37, art. 5.

[123]For further detail on this point see Joseph H. Crehan, "Bishop," *A Catholic Dictionary of Theology,* (3 vols.; London: Thomas Nelson and Sons Ltd., 1962), Vol. 1, pp. 273-283.

[124]*Ibid.,* pp. 278-281.

thus represented both loss and gain. On the one hand, it contributed to the notion that ordination is permanent and effective despite any other consideration: a cleric without mandate for ministry or power of jurisdiction is still a cleric and still possess the "power of orders". This led, in some instances, to a view of ministry based on a model of personal power rather than on a model of pastoral service. On the other hand, the distinction had positive repercussions. It kept ministry from being totally identified with ordination. By insisting that one needed "jurisdiction" (i.e., a mandate for mission) in order to perform pastoral ministry, the distinction kept alive some of what was earlier implied by "title".

ORDER(S) AS SACRAMENT

In the background of the medieval discussions of priesthood, orders and jurisdiction lies the question of sacrament. Today we are so accustomed to thinking of orders as sacrament that we may be surprised to learn how long it took for theologians to reach this conclusion. As late as the twelfth century theologians were still debating just which actions of the church constituted sacraments. Hugh of St. Victor listed as many as thirty possibilities, while Peter Lombard enumerated the seven which became traditional. Lombard's list was adopted by Aquinas, affirmed at the Council of Florence in 1439, and accepted by the Council of Trent. Only from the thirteenth century onward, therefore, has there been anything like general agreement among theologians about the number and name of the sacraments. Here, our attention will be limited to the way in which the ordination of ministers came to be regarded as a sacramental action.

THE CHANGING MEANING OF "SACRAMENT"

As in the case of words like "order(s)", "priesthood", and "ordination", Christian use of the word "sacrament" developed over many centuries. In Latin theology, once again, Tertullian led the way in popularizing its application to distinctively Christian realities. A recent study of "sacrament" in the works of Tertullian shows that the word is richly complex.[125] Two fundamental sets of meanings are evident: sacrament as "oath/alliance/covenant", and sacrament as "sign". Both sets have influenced Christian interpretations of sacrament, and so deserve comment.

Underlying the Christian use of sacrament are ancient Roman military and legal customs. A soldier's "*sacramentum*" or "oath" bound him contractually to military service, required him to follow his general in combat, and forbade him to act contrary to law.[126] Violation of this oath was tantamount to sacrilege and resulted in severe sanctions. Besides military personnel, other Roman officials also entered upon their service by swearing a *sacramentum:* civil magistrates, consuls, tribunes.[127] In ancient Roman Law, moreover, *sacramentum* designated a legal process whereby two parties involved in litigation were expected to supply "proofs" that their testimony was trustworthy. Originally, these proofs consisted of formulas and ritual gestures whose correct performance was believed to indicate how the gods regarded the case. At a later period, the proof involved putting up a sum of money, similar, perhaps, to our legal custom of posting bail for persons awaiting arraignment and trial. It should be noted that in both military and legal language, *sacramentum* implied a series of *actions*—and that the word could be used for both *process* and *what resulted* from the process.

As a Christian, Tertullian appropriated the language of sacrament by investing it with theological significance. This is especially clear in the first set of meanings: sacrament as "oath/alliance/covenant". *Sacramentum* in this sense was a comprehensive term for all those transactions that join

---

[125]See Dimitri Michaelides, *Sacramentum chez Tertullien,* (Paris: Études Augustiniennes, 1970).
[126]*Ibid.,* pp. 25-26.
[127]*Ibid.,* p. 26.

humans with God, God with humans, Christians with one another. What results from this joining is a holy covenant between God and humankind, a "sacrament". This covenant is sealed in baptism, which reveals both God's promise of salvation to us and our fidelity to God as children and servants. Underlying this notion of sacrament as covenant is the ancient Roman legal sense of "contract". But Tertullian has personalized the meaning of contract by showing that Christians enter the baptismal covenant through the free choice and response of *faith*. The sacrament-covenant of baptism thus has eschatological (i.e., permanent, definitive) significance; it reveals God as the only and ultimate "future" of Christians.

A second set of meanings for sacrament is also apparent in Tertullian's works. *Sacramentum* is not only covenant, it is also *sign*. This provided Tertullian with a way to understand the relation between the prophetic signs (*sacramenta*) of Israel's religion and the ritual signs (*sacramenta*) of the Christian community (e.g., baptism and eucharist). As "sacraments", Israel's religious institutions provided a guarantee, in advance, of the salvation God promised humanity from the beginning. They looked forward, for completion, to the saving work of Jesus, which is now grasped by Christians through the ritual signs of baptism and eucharist. The sacraments of the Old Law and those of the New are thus related as "guarantee" and "completion", "foreshadowing" and "reality". It is significant that Tertullian does not limit the notion of sacrament as sign to Christian realities. Israel's religion was also a religion of "sacrament"—a point that later theologians like Aquinas also recognized.[128]

Tertullian's understanding of sacrament as simultaneously covenant and sign, divine action and human response, established a basic outline for later theological interpretation. At their heart, sacraments are not "things" but transactions, dialogues between a God who offers himself fully to humans and humans who yearn for God. Later writers like

---

[128]See Thomas Aquinas, *Summa Theologiæ,* IIIa Pars, Q. 70, art. 4.

Augustine understood the transactional character of sacraments and tried to clarify how the transaction takes place.
According to Augustine, several elements were involved,
each of them important: visible deeds, gestures and products of human activity; words; God's continuing action in
the world of space and time; faith. A sacrament is all these
elements as they interact with one another in the life, prayer
and ritual activity of a Christian community.[129]

One aspect of Augustine's sacramental theory became
especially significant in medieval theology: the notion that
sacraments have an objectivity and effectiveness that tran-
scend the personal qualities of their ministers or their recipients. This principle was clearly formulated in Augustine's
polemic against the Donatists.[130] Applied to both baptism
and ordination, the principle was closely linked to Augustine's notion of permanent "character", a point discussed
earlier in this chapter. Both baptism and ordination, Augustine argued, deserved the title of "sacrament", since they are
permanent endowments that cannot be lost even if one
becomes a heretic.[131]

This Augustinian view, ignored by many theologians for
centuries, was revived in the twelfth and thirteenth centuries, because it furnished clear patristic testimony that holy
orders are a) a "sacrament", b) an objective, permanent
reality; and c) still valid even if a person chooses to join an
heretical community. All three of these positions are found
in Aquinas, who accepted Peter Lombard's contention that
orders are one of *seven* sacraments.[132] But Aquinas went a
bit further. For him, the sacrament of order embraced all
seven clerical ranks: lector, acolyte, porter, exorcist, sub-

---

[129]For further discussion of Augustine's view of sacrament, see Paul Palmer,
Sacraments and Worship, (London: Darton, Longman and Todd, 1957, paperback edition), pp. 119-129.

[130]See *ibid.,* pp. 120-124 for relevant texts, translations and commentary.

[131]See Augustine, *Against the Letter of Parmenian,* II:13:38; English translation
in Palmer, *Sacraments and Worship,* pp. 125-126.

[132]See Thomas Aquinas, *Summa Theologiae,* IIIa Pars, Supplementum, QQ.
34-36.

deacon, deacon, and priest (= presbyter).[133] Tonsure and
episcopate are not orders, though the later is a further
dignity within the order of priesthood. The sacramental
"character", Aguinas argued, is "imprinted" on the individual at each of the seven order, though one may distinguish
between "sacred orders" (priest, deacon, subdeacon) and
lesser ones (the four "minor orders").[134]

In Aquinas's view, further, the difference between one
order and another was based on each rank's relation to the
eucharist. Here we can see the influence of Peter Damian's
definition of "priest" as one who "has power to consecrate
the eucharist". This is exactly the reason Aquinas gives for
ranking priesthood as the highest order.[135] All others are
ranked similarly: deacons have power to *dispense* the eucharist but not to consecrate it; subdeacons may touch the holy
vessels in which bread and wine are consecrated, but may
not dispense the sacrament; acolytes receive power to present the bread and wine for consecration, etc.[136] This view
implies, of course, that the holy orders consist essentially in
ritual powers directed toward the church's cult. Except for
the episcopate, which for him is not an order, Aquinas has
little to say about ordination as oriented toward pastoral
care, preaching the word, and witnessing the gospel—
though he obviously understood these activities as part of
the "priestly life".

Not until the fifteenth and sixteenth centuries did the
church's official teaching, expressed in ecumenical councils,
directly affirm the view that order is a sacrament which is
permanently effective and "imprints character". This was
the position taken at the Council of Florence (1439) and
reiterated by the Council of Trent (1562). Florence affirmed
that "among these (seven) sacraments are three—baptism,
confirmation, and order—that imprint an indelible charater
on the soul, that is, a certain spiritual sign different from all

133*Ibid.,* IIIa Pars, Supplementum, Q. 37, arts. 1-2.
134*Ibid.,* IIIa Pars, Supplementum, Q. 35, art. 2; Q. 37, art. 3.
135*Ibid.,* IIIa Pars, Supplementum, Q. 37, art. 2.
136*Ibid.,* IIIa Pars, Supplementum, Q. 37, art. 2.

others.[137] Trent, reacting against challenges from the reformers, insisted that the sacrament of order was "instituted by Christ", imparts the Spirit and imprints character.[138] It argued further that an ordained priest could never again be considered a layman, and that the office of bishop is superior to that of presbyter.[139] Trent stopped short, however, of defining the exact nature of the episcopate's superiority over the presbyterate.

One other point about order as a sacrament needs comment: the notions of "matter" and "form". As popularly explained, they are often defined as "material" (e.g., bread and wine as the "matter" of the eucharist) and "words" (e.g., "This is my body . . ." as the "form" of the eucharist). In fact, however, this is not a very accurate account of what these philosophical terms meant for theologians, like Aquinas, who used them. Matter and form, categories found in Aristotle's philosophy, are not things, objects, or materials but ways of expressing "potential" and "actuation". "Matter" implies potential—e.g., the capacity for change, for becoming, or for coming-to-be in the first place. Similarly, "form" implies actuation—"putting into action", the realization of something that was formerly only "potential". Philosophers and theologians used these terms in an effort to understand more exactly how and why things change, how something that didn't exist before *becomes* something actual and real. When Aquinas indicates that the "form" of a sacrament is a series of words said by its minister, he is not saying that ministers possess magical powers to pull rabbits out of hats. He means, instead, that the human language of the church at prayer is creative, that it is capable of revealing sacred reality in a human event (e.g., in the washing of a person at baptism, in the human sharing of food and drink at eucharist, in the prayerful designation of persons as ministers for the church). Similarly, when Aquinas says that bread and wine

---

[137]Text in Denzinger/Schoenmetzer, *Enchiridion Symbolorum* 1313, p. 333; my translation.

[138]*Ibid.,* 1773-1774, p. 414.

[139]*Ibid.,* 1774, 1777, pp. 414-415.

are the "matter" of eucharist, he implies that human products—the work of our hands—have the potential to disclose the presence and action of the Lord in our midst.

As Aquinas understood it, the sacrament of order can also be analyzed in terms of "matter" and "form". Human gestures ("matter") have the potential to reveal God's action and presence at ordination through the human language of the church gathered in prayer ("form"). The human gesture, Aquinas argued, involved giving the ordained what was needed for his ministry (e.g., the chalice and paten for eucharist at priesthood ordination). The church's language of prayer could vary, but it often included expressions like "Receive the Holy Spirit . . ."[140] In the twentieth century, Pius XII declared that the crucial gesture at ordination was the laying on of hands rather than the giving of utensils needed for ministry.[141]

Today, we may find this style of theological analysis pointless, not to say distressing. But we need to remember that underlying medieval discussions of "matter" and "form" were questions and convictions that are still relevant. It is still important, for example, to recognize that the human gestures and words of the church at prayer are creatively powerful ones that can bring us to recognize the Lord working in the midst of his people. Sacraments are neither human magic nor divine sleights-of-hand. At the risk of sounding too poetic, they are both dialogue and dance, word and gesture. Our human words and ritual "dances", worn and time-tattered as they are, retain their power to reveal God at work in the community gathered to name and send forth its ministers. That, ultimately, is what the language of the "matter and form" of ordination sought to affirm.

In sum, the conviction that order is a sacrament developed only very gradually in the church, even though early

---

[140]See Thomas Aquinas, *Summa Theologiae*, IIIa Pars, Q. 37, art. 5.
[141]See Denzinger/Schoenmetzer, *Enchiridion Symbolorum*, 3857-3861, pp. 765-766.

theologians like Tertullian introduced *sacramentum* into the Christian vocabulary. Even after the thirteenth century, theologians could still not agree about certain issues: e.g., the exact difference between priest and bishop; the ritual gestures essential for ordination. Many of these discussions seem remote today, but underlying them all is the conviction that the community's choice and designation of ministers is an act of central importance is its life and future.

CONCLUSION

The purpose of this chapter has been to explain the origin and evolution of a Christian priesthood by examining such ideas as "succession, order and holy orders", the liturgy of "ordination", and priesthood as "sacrament". Here it will be appropriate to summarize the results of our study.

1. In earliest Christian usage, "order" was understood as a quality exhibited by the whole church when it follows faithfully the apostles' teaching and way of life. But at a rather early period, in the works of Tertullian, "order" began to acquire the more technical and restricted meaning of "clergy". By the fifth and sixth centuries, "holy order(s)" has appeared, in both literary and liturgical sources, as a proper term for ordained ministers.

2. Ordination, too, acquired a rather precise and technical meaning by the beginning of the third century, in sources such as the *Apostolic Tradition*. This document provides both liturgical rites and prayers for ordaining bishops, presbyters and deacons, and restricts the function of ordination to the bishop. Increasingly, the gesture of laying on hands was seen as central to ordination, though medieval theologians like Aquinas appealed to a different action (e.g., giving the chalice and paten to a priest).

3. At an early period, in the time of Cyprian for example, ordination was closely connected with "title", i.e., with the mandate for ministry in a concrete community which

retains the right to choose worthy candidates and reject unworthy ones. Later, however, the West reinterpreted the meaning of "title", transforming it into a kind of legal fiction that guarantees an income for the ordinand.

4. For centuries, in both East and West, it was assumed that an ordained person, if proven incompetent and unworthy, could be removed from ministry. A person so deposed was no longer regarded as a bishop, presbyter or deacon. Late in the twelfth century, however, Latin theologians began reviving Augustine's notion of a permanent character attached to ordination. This "indelible quality" was understood to remain, even if a cleric were deposed from office and "reduced to the lay state".

5. The use of a "priestly" vocabulary for Christian ministers, though present in early documents like the *Didache* and I Clement, became far more common in the third century. Originally, the bishop was the Christian "priest" or "high priest", but from the Carolingian period onward, "priest"commonly meant "presbyter". Eventually, this shift in vocabulary was also reflected in theological assessments of the priesthood. The priest (= presbyter) is, above all, one with power to consecrate the eucharist. As a result, episcopate was no longer thought of as an order or "college" of ministers, but as a "dignity" added to the rank of priesthood.

6. The orders of Christian ministry were eventually perceived as constituting a sacrament. Tertullian introduced *sacramentum* into Latin theological language, though he did not restrict its meaning to the later technical sense. In both Augustine and the anonymous "On the Seven Orders of the Church" (fifth-century), sacrament was applied to orders. Theologians like Aquinas in the thirteenth century developed a systematic interpretation of order as one of the seven sacraments, distinguished by its permanent effect, its indelible character and its relation to the eucharist.

Our survey has shown that, over many centuries, the notions of holy orders and priesthood have been subject to numerous theological interpretations. The consistent fac-

tors underlying change have been the church's need for and
right to a ministry, the importance of fidelity to origins
("apostolic traditions", "succession"), the need to recognize
and commission ministers in a visible, public way ("ordination"), and the conviction that God works in the human
gestures and prayerful language of the community ("sacrament"). In our final chapter we shall probe more deeply into
the theological meaning of ministry, today and for the
future.

Recommended Reading

Cooke, Bernard. *Ministry to Word and Sacrament*. Philadelphia: Fortress Press, 1976. A thorough investigation
of ministry (especially that of the ordained) in its historical and theological aspects.

Mohler, James. *The Origin and Evolution of the Priesthood*. New York: Alba House, 1969. A fine short study of
the development of the priesthood, especially in the New
Testament and patristic periods.

The Sacrament of Holy Orders. Papers given at a Session of
the Centre de Pastorale liturgique, 1955. Translator not
identified. Collegeville, Minnesota: The Liturgical Press,
1962. Collection of essays by European scholars on a wide
variety of topics: the vocabulary of Christian priesthood;
the discussion about ministry at the Council of Trent, etc.

CHAPTER FIVE: A THEOLOGY OF HOLY ORDERS

Introduction

In the earlier chapters of this book, we have discussed the origins and evolution of ministry in the Christian church. We noted the gradual evolution of ministerial structures, the wide diversity of practice in the early Christian churches, the development of a mono-episcopate (a single bishop in each local church), and the emergence of a Christian "priesthood". We observed, also, how the church's ministry was accorded theological significance—and how the notion of holy orders as a "sacrament" evolved.

This chapter will attempt to deal with a problem that often afflicts modern Roman Catholics. How can we relate the conclusions of modern biblical exegesis to the assertions of the church's magisterium? For example, how is it possible to claim that Jesus, in his historical ministry, intended to institute a sacrament of "orders" or ministry in the church? Is it reasonable to believe that the priesthood, as we now know and experience it, is somehow rooted in the prophetic, itinerant ministry of Jesus himself? What sort of new community—and new community leadership—did Jesus envisage? And how does that vision correspond to our contemporary understanding of ministry and leadership in the community.

These and related questions will form the focus of this chapter. Our first task will be to explore how the New Testament understood discipleship and ministry. In this connection we will discuss the "discipleship of equals" in New Testament Christianity, as well as the notions of "apostolic" ministry, charism and community order, and the "priesthood" of Jesus and Christians. In a second section we shall examine the Roman Catholic tradition about holy orders as interpreted in light of these biblical orientations. We will need to ask what it means to say that Christians have a "right" to ministry; what the liturgical and theological significance of "ordination" is; how ordained ministry is related to non-ordained service in the church; and why the Catholic tradition has insisted that holy orders is a permanent "state" or "condition" that uniquely "marks" the minister.

I

Biblical Orientations

A DISCIPLESHIP OF EQUALS

Discipleship—faithful following of Jesus and adherence to his message—was a paramount concern for many of the New Testament writers. The word "disciple" (Greek, *mathētēs*) appears nearly two hundred and fifty times in the gospels and the book of Acts. There, the call to discipleship is always attributed to *Jesus'* initiative (see, e.g., Lk 9:57-58). Nor is the invitation to follow Jesus portrayed as something the disciple merits. Among those called are the disreputable, social outcasts like Levi the tax-gatherer (Mk 2:13ff.). In each case the relationship between Jesus and disciple is unique and personal. Jesus himself lays down the conditions for following him and determines the content of the relationship. For their part, the disciples must accept Jesus' authority unconditionally—and they must also expect a share in his suffering (see, e.g., Lk 14:27). In Mark's gospel, especially, following Jesus leads ineluctably to the cross: just as the Master is most truly "Son of God" when he suffers, so the disciple faces the same destiny.[1] Failure is another aspect of the New Testament's portrait of discipleship. The disciples fail to comprehend Jesus' goal and mission, and at the critical moment of his career they flee (see, e.g., Mk 8:31-33; 14:50).[2]

This last point indicates that the word "disciple" is used in both broad and narrower senses by the evangelists. Those fail to comprehend Jesus' purpose are not "the disciples" generally, but those special ones (sometimes identified as "the Twelve") chosen for more intimate association with him.[3] In the more restricted sense, therefore, "the disciples" are those who engage in a special ministry with Jesus—like the Twelve whom Luke calls "apostles" (Lk 6:13). In sum, the New Testament disciples may be either those historically associated with Jesus' public ministry or those who later accepted the church's message about Jesus and became followers of the Christian "way".

An important dimension of discipleship in the New Testament is its egalitarian character. Elisabeth Schüssler Fiorenza has argued that the early Christian movement was a "countercultural-religious" one which, by definition, was "egalitarian and interpersonal."[4] "The circles of followers around Jesus did not belong to the establishment of its society or religion," she writes, "but were a group of outsiders who did not accept the patriarchal values and hierarchial institutions of their society but often stood in opposition to them."[5] Several aspects of the early Christian movement seem to support this view. First, the movement transcended

---

[1] On this point in Mark's gospel see Paul Achtemeier, *Mark*, (Proclamation Commentaries; Philadelphia: Fortress Press, 1975), pp. 82-100.

[2] See K. H. Rengstorf, "*manthanō*', in: Gerhard Kittel, ed., *Theological Dictionary of the New Testament*, translated by Geoffrey Bromiley, (10 vols.; Grand Rapids: Wm. B. Eerdmans Publishing Company, 1964-1976), Vol. 4. pp. 391-461.

[3] See Raymond Brown, *Priest and Bishop*, (New York: Paulist Press, 1970), pp. 21-22.

[4] See Elisabeth Schüssler Fiorenza, "The Biblical Roots for the Discipleship of Equals," *Journal of Pastoral Counselling* 14 (1979), 11; complete article, 7-15.

[5] *Ibid.*, 11.

cultural and religious boundaries; both Jews and Gentiles were invited to membership, thus creating "inter-racial" churches like that of Antioch. Secondly, the Christian community itself became the focus of a new allegiance that surpassed in importance blood-ties with family and relatives.[6] The synoptic tradition can thus represent Jesus as saying "whoever does the will of God is my brother, and sister and mother" (Mk 3:35). Thirdly, women appear to have played an important role in both the Palestinian Jesus-movement and the missionary expansion to hellenistic urban centers. Paul's letters mention many women as "co-workers", while the synoptic gospels name women among Jesus' closest disciples during his ministry.[7] This suggests that, at least in its earliest stages of development, Christians did not attempt to push women into stereotyped cultural roles, but welcomed their leadership.

There are other ways, too, in which the theme of equality surfaces in early Christian literature. Paul, for instance, presents himself as one who has voluntarily surrendered prerogatives he might justly have claimed as an apostle (see I Thess 2:9). These included the right to financial support (1 Cor 9:3-15), as well as the right to issue commands to his congregations (1 Cor 7:6).[8] Similarly, the Christians at Corinth are encouraged to contribute to the collections for the Jerusalem church so that there may be an "equality" among believers (2 Cor 8:13-14). Even more radical is the text in Galatians 3:28: "There is neither Jew nor Greek, there is neither slave nor free, there is neither male nor female; for you are all one in Christ Jesus." Many scholars agree that this strongly egalitarian statement has its source in a very early Christian baptismal liturgy.[9] It expresses the conviction that

[6] *Ibid.*, 12-13.

[7] *Ibid.*

[8] See L. William Countryman, "Christian Equality and the Early Catholic Episcopate," *Anglican Theological Review* 63 (1981), 116-117; complete article, 115-138.

[9] See Fiorenza, "The Biblical Roots for the Discipleship of Equals," 14; Countryman, "Christian Equality and the Early Catholic Episcopate," 118.

among Christian believers all racial, cultural and religious differences have been swept aside. "This egalitarian Christian self-understanding did away with all distinctions and privileges of religion, class and caste," Elisabeth Fiorenza writes, "and thereby allowed not only gentiles and slaves but also women to exercise leadership in the early Christian movement."[10]

If egalitarianism was advocated by Christians in their baptismal liturgy, it was also reflected in the eucharist. One of Paul's complaints against the Corinthians was that they had allowed social distinctions between rich and poor to intrude upon their celebration of the Lord's Supper (see 1 Cor 11:22). Such distinctions, Paul implied, are intolerable at a meal where all should share equally in one loaf and one cup.[11] One could argue further that Paul's view of ministry was similarly egalitarian. Even a slave like Onesimus could be useful to Paul as a "co-worker", a technical term for one who shares in the work and ministry of the missionary apostle (see Philemon 13-14). Here again Paul hinted that one's social status in the Greco-Roman world has no effect on one's place in the Christian community. Baptism, eucharist and ministry thus seem to have been activities wherein the radical equality of all disciples was recognized and affirmed.

Perhaps even more striking evidence for the egalitarian attitude of early Christians can be found in the synoptic tradition's "reversal sayings." Most of these are well-known: "The last shall be first and the first last" (Mt 19:30); "Whoever exalts himself will be humbled and whoever humbles himself will be exalted" (Mt 23:12; Lk 14:11; Lk 18:14); "It is hard for a rich man to enter the kingdom of heaven" (Mk 10:23).[12] These and similar sayings seem deliberately aimed at subverting commonly held assumptions such as "wealth equals power". It is possible that such sayings were shaped and circulated by those "wandering charismatics" in Palestine

---

[10]See Fiorenza, "The Biblical Roots for the Discipleship of Equals," 14.
[11]See the discussion in Countryman, "Christian Equality and the Early Catholic Episcopate," 125.
[12]*Ibid.*, 118.

who, as we noted in Chapter Two, were proponents of an ethical radicalism that emphasized lack of possessions and non-resistance against aggression as conditions for discipleship. Meeting such conditions would naturally have tended to relativize social differences among Christians.[13] Another Palestinian source, the letter of James, insists on this point: no partiality should be shown to the rich, and no distinctions should be allowed to mar the fundamental equality of believers (James 2:1-12).

There is also evidence, however, that egalitarianism was not always practiced in earliest Christianity, despite the emphasis on a discipleship of equals. Conversion to Christianity did not, for example, alter a slave's legal relation to his master, even if both had converted. While Paul could argue that "in the Lord", slaves are freedmen and freedmen are slaves (1 Cor 7:22)—a typical "reversal saying"—the apostle also recognized that Christian masters may retain legal control over their slaves. This is clear from Paul's letter to Philemon. Paul hints that he would *like* to see Philemon free Onesimus, but nowhere does he insist that Philemon's conversion *necessitates* such a course of action.[14] In deutero-Pauline works like Ephesians and Colossians, a similar line of thinking is evident. Masters are exhorted to treat slaves with justice and equity, but they are not commanded to release them (Eph 6:5-9; Col 4:1). As shocking as it seems to modern sensibilities, earliest Christianity does not appear to have regarded slavery as an institution incompatible with faith in Christ. While all may have become "equal" in baptism (Gal 3:28), this equality had tangible limits in everyday social life. Slaves were still slaves, masters still masters.

Nor does Christian egalitarianism appear to have altered attitudes toward marriage, at least not completely. On this subject the much disputed text of 1 Cor 11:2-16 is relevant. According to some scholars the passage is a later insertion not written by Paul; other exegetes accept it as genuinely

---

[13] *Ibid.*, 118-119.
[14] *Ibid.*, 122-123.

Pauline.[15] To complicate matters further, part of this passage
(1 Cor 11:4-10) seems to deal (as we noted in Chapter Two)
with a very limited and specific situation: the conduct of men
and women who belong to a recognized class of "spiritual
specialists" (*pneumatikoi*) and who meet for prayer sessions
distinct from the regular liturgical assemblies of the whole
community. In short, even if the passage is genuinely Pauline,
it cannot be taken as a complete portrait of Paul's attitude
toward women generally or of his opinion about marriage
specifically.

Does this passage, then, reveal anything about early Christian understandings of the man/woman relationship in marriage? The answer is yes, but some careful analysis is
necessary. Many commentators have been troubled by the
apparent conflict between 1 Cor 11:8 and 11. Verses 8 and 9
appear to affirm the old patriarchal viewpoint: women were
created "for men" and so are somehow innately inferior to
males—"for man was not made from woman, but woman
from man. Neither was man created for woman, but woman
for man." In contrast, verse 11 seems to offer an entirely fresh
perspective on the marital relationship. "In the Lord woman
is not independent of man nor man of woman," Paul writes,
"for as woman was made from man, so man is now born of
woman" (1 Cor 11:11-12a). In the text just cited Paul seems to
argue that "in the Lord"—i.e., in the new situation ushered
into the world through Christ—the nuptial relation between
men and women has been transformed. The patriarchal view,
with its emphasis on the subjection of women, has given way,
in Christ, to a new understanding of human existence and
human relationships. In marriage, there is no longer "superior" (male) and "inferior" (female), but rather a mutual
interdependence of equals since "all things are from God" (1
Cor 11:12b).

How can one resolve the seeming conflict between the
patriarchal view (1 Cor 11:8-9) and the new vision of things in

[15]*Ibid.*, 122, note 16. On the entire passage see Jerome Murphy-O'Connor, *First Corinthians,* (New Testament Message, Vol. 10; Wilmington: Michael Glazier, Inc., 1979), pp. 104-109.

the Lord (1 Cor 11:11-12)? A resolution is possible if we recall
that verses 8 and 9 are part of a specific set of instructions for
recognized "charismatics" in the community. In this light,
Paul's insistence that women keep their heads covered when
they prophesy—and his comment that woman was created
"for man"—has to do not with his understanding of marriage, but with his concern for decorum in the restricted
prayer sessions of the charismatics. If this interpretation is
accurate, then one can better understand the parenthetical
comment contained in 1 Cor 11:11-12a. Having spoken
about the *special* requirements of the charismatic prayer
session, Paul reminds his readers that these special arrangements do not overturn the new vision of marital relations
ushered into the world by Christ: *in the Lord,* men and
women are mutually interdependent—even if, at the charismatic prayer sessions, women are asked to accept the ordinary social conventions (e.g., covering the head). In effect,
Paul is speaking about two different situations: 1) the special
prayer meetings of the charismatics, where women are asked
to respect common social conventions; and 2) the general
situation of Christian married people, where he recognizes
that "in the Lord", men and women are interdependent and
equal.[16]

This benign interpretation of Paul's intentions in 1 Cor
11:2-16 does not, however, resolve every problem. In
deutero-Pauline material such as Ephesians and the pastoral
letters, there are hints of continued difficulty in reconciling
the old patriarchal notion of male dominance over women
with the new Christian vision of equality among disciples.
Ephesians attempts to strike a balance by insisting that
though wives should be "subject" to their husbands, husbands should "love their wives as their own bodies." (Eph
5:22, 28). But I Tim 2:9-15 seems to represent a step back-
wards when it suggests that the fall of humankind was
woman's fault: "For Adam was formed first, then Eve; an

---

[16]For a different interpretation of 1 Cor. 11:2-16, see Murphy-O'Connor, *First
Corinthians,* pp. 104-109.

Adam was not deceived, but the woman was deceived and became a transgressor" (1 Tim 2:13-14).[17]

These texts reveal that early Christianity, in its various expressions, did not have a thoroughly coherent view of marriage or of relations between men and women "in the Lord." Paul may have been trying to express a new understanding of marriage in 1 Cor 11:11-12, though in his advice to women charismatics he urges conformity with contemporary social custom. This suggests that Paul himself was not consistently egalitarian in his attitude toward women in the Christian congregation. Later literature like the Pastorals, moreover, seems decidedly negative toward women. One could say, perhaps, that the New Testament recognizes the principle of "equal partnership" in Christian marriage (Paul, Ephesians), but tends to resolve the conflict between this principle and social practice in favor of the traditional cultural customs of the Greco-Roman world.

This conflict between principle and practice is understandable given the culture and society in which most of the New Testament writers worked. As Elisabeth Schüssler Fiorenza notes, these writers were trying to "make the Christian message acceptable to people in the Greco-Roman world and to defend it against attacks from the outside."[18] This could well explain why Paul urged acceptance of cultural convention by women in the special charismatic prayer sessions— and also why the Pastorals counselled submissiveness by wives to their husbands. By giving such advice these writers could forestall objections from outsiders who might charge that Christians were either wild-eyed enthusiasts or enemies of the social order. "The injunctions for women to behave decently and to be submissive to their husbands were formulated," Fiorenza observes, "as a political argument to show that the Christian community does not undermine the Patriarchal social Greco-Roman order."[19] In short, early Chris-

---

[17]See Countryman, "Christian Equality and the Early Catholic Episcopate," 122.
[18]See Fiorenza, "The Biblical Roots for the Discipleship of Equals," 8.
[19]*Ibid.*, 9.

tian writers were attempting to prove that one could be simultaneously a good Christian and a good citizen of the empire.

We may conclude, therefore, that the "discipleship of equals" was a widely recognized principle in primitive Christianity, but that the expression of this principle was modified by the cultural conditions in which the earliest believers found themselves. Writers like Paul were concerned to show that the Christian movement was neither a haven for "crazies" nor a subversive conventicle of fifth-columnists. They thus urged Christians to continue observing customs and laws that were considered important for good citizenship in the Greco-Roman world. Some of these customs are reflected in the lists of "household rules" incorporated into the New Testament letters (e.g., in 1 Tim 2:8-15, Eph 5:21-6:9). These "rules" were derived from the popular philosophy and ethics of the ancient world, and governed relations within a household (e.g., between husbands and wives, parents and children, masters and slaves). By incorporating such rules into their advice for Christian congregations, the New Testament writers again implied that belief in Jesus did not subvert the cultural customs of Greco-Roman society.[20]

DISCIPLESHIP AND APOSTOLIC AUTHORITY

The early church's conviction about the equality of disciples thus had its practical limits. As L. William Countryman notes, "the early Christians expected their converts to continue observing the social distinctions of contemporary culture in a basic way."[21] Within the congregation itself, however, such distinctions appear to have been reversed or

---

[20]For further information on these "household rules", see Joseph A. Fitzmyer, "Pauline Theology," in *The Jerome Biblical Commentary,* edited by Raymond Brown, Joseph Fitzmyer, and Roland Murphy, (Englewood Cliffs, New Jersey: Prentice-Hall, Inc., 1968), II, p. 827 (79:162-166).

[21]See Countryman, "Christian Equality and the Early Catholic Episcopate," 123.

ignored. In baptism all became equal; at the eucharistic meal, all shared common food at a common table. Yet there is one glaring exception to this pattern of equality within the Christian congregation: the *ministry*. Ministers were the only group, Countryman observes, who were accorded "special status in the church—a distinction based not on worldly prestige, but on religious qualities or endowments."[22] This tendency to grant ministers special—even superior—status appears very early in Christian literature, and we must try to explain why this was so.

Paul's letters suggest that many early Christians were eager—perhaps all too eager—to accept certain leaders as authoritative superiors. At Corinth, especially, this seems to have been a problem. Paul accuses the Corinthians of a kind of hero-worship replete with campaign slogans such as "I belong to Paul" or "I belong to Apollos" (1 Cor 3:4). And in 2 Corinthians Paul bitterly attacked those "super-apostles" whose highhanded way of dealing with the congregation was apparently accepted and even admired (2 Cor 11:20-21). Sarcastically, Paul exclaimed that unlike the super-apostles, he had behaved as a weakling, abasing himself for the sake of preaching God's gospel without cost to the Corinthians (2 Cor 11:7-11). In a nutshell, Paul argued that he *could* have claimed privileges as an apostle called by God, but voluntarily renounced such claims because of his love for Christ's people.

Paul was thus *critical* of hero-worshippers and highhanded apostles, yet also *conscious* that an apostle's status in the congregation is somehow privileged. Frequently in his correspondence, he did not hesitate to use his authority to rebuke persons and correct error. Indeed, 2 Corinthians concludes with Paul saying "I write this while I am away from you, in order that when I come I may not have to be severe in my use of the authority which the Lord has given me for building up and not for tearing down." (2 Cor 13:10). Although Paul may have chosen to minimize his status as

[22]*Ibid.*, 127.

apostle and to renounce its privileges (e.g., the right to a wage), he clearly considered his vocation authoritative, God-given and even "superior" to that of the congregation itself. For these reasons he could demand obedience to his decisions (see 2 Cor 13:1-3), insist on the excommunication of an errant Christian (see 1 Cor 5:1-5), and even challenge the authority of other church leaders like Peter (see Gal. 2:11-21).

It can be objected, however, that Paul's view of apostolic authority was not shared by all his contemporaries. For some of them it was too "low-key". Compared to that of this flashy opponents, the super-apostles, Paul's authority seemed weak, wheedling and ineffective. For others, Paul probably came across as an arrogant late-comer whose credentials were suspect. he had, after all, persecuted Christians at an earlier stage of his career, and he had never actually known Jesus in the flesh. Besides, Paul's voluntary renunciation of privilege, his insistence on preaching the gospel without pay and working with his own hands, lent a unique dimension to his apostleship. Though he was an *apostle,* Paul still considered himself *part* of the Christian community.[23] In this connection one can grasp the importance of Paul's calling the church "the body of Christ," for this metaphor provided him with a way to understand the fundamental equality of all Christians while recognizing the distinctive role of those who direct and oversee the body's operations.

Perhaps one could say that Paul had a "high-church" view of the apostle's authority (God-given, indisputable), but a "low-church" view of its exercise (voluntary renunciation of privilege). L. William Countryman is probably accurate when he remarks, "The functional gap between the apostle who evangelized and led the people who received the Gospel and followed was vast. Paul's refusal to formulate a theory of orders does not really mask the reality."[24] Even though Paul considered himself part of the community and avoided

[23]See John Howard Schütz, *Paul and the Anatomy of Apostolic Authority,* (SNTS Monograph Series, no. 26; Cambridge: University Press, 1975).
[24]See Countryman, "Christian Equality and the Early Catholic Episcopate," 129-130.

making himself a financial burden on its members, he clearly believed that his apostlic authority was critical for guaranteeing the authenticity of the tradition he handed on to his congregations.

In this connection it is important to recognize the impact of Paul's eschatological views on both his personal perception of apostleship and his understanding of the Christian message (or "*kerygma*"). Paul understood that Christians live in a era of "eschatological contingency". The resurrection of Jesus is pledge and promise, the "first-fruits", of a destiny that all will share at the "final harvest" when Christ "delivers the kingdom to God the Father." (1 Cor 15:20-24). Resurrection is thus the Christian's *future* destiny, but it has not yet been experienced. We live in hope "between the times", knowing that Christ's resurrection guarantees our future and knowing too that the present order of things in this world will pass away. Meanwhile, our life remains insufficient, incomplete, unfinished—for it is destined to be replaced by the future resurrection. This incompleteness means that we must live totally by grace, trusting fully in God's promise revealed in the death and resurrection of Jesus.

In a word, Paul sees Christians as living on a kind of "contingency plan." Our future (resurrection) is guaranteed by God's act in Christ, but that future has not yet fully arrived. Only its first-fruits (Christ's resurrection) have appeared. This contingency lies at the heart of both Paul's gospel and his work as apostle. If life itself is suspended "between the times," if we experience it as insufficient and incomplete, and if that insufficiency is part of the gospel message itself—then the same things can be said of Paul's apostleship. As apostle, he too is insufficient, a servant who can boast only of weakness (see 1 Cor 2:3, 2 Cor 12:9). This theology of weakness is central to Paul's understanding of God, of God's work in Christ (the gospel), and of the apostolic ministry. God's foolish weakness confounds the world's wisdom (1 Cor 1:25); Jesus was crucified in weakness (2 Cor 13:4); the apostle's preaching is divine folly (1 Cor 1:21). Paradoxically, weakness and fool-ishness become

Paul's proof that he is an apostle called and confirmed by God.

For Paul, then, "apostleship" and "tradition" (the Christian message) are inseparable. Each interprets the other. Paul's autobiography as apostle, with all its folly and weakness, guarantees the truth of his message about a God whose wisdom appears to be folly and whose power seems to be powerlessness. By the same token, the "tradition"—Jesus crucified in weakness and raised by God's power—guarantees the authenticity of Paul's apostleship, which is exercised in lowliness and suffering. This is why Paul could offer his own life as a paradigm of the gospel, an example worthy of imitation (1 Cor 11:1). It also explains why Paul could have a high-church view of apostolic authority and a low-church view of its exercise.[25]

The apostle's superiority in the church is thus validated, according to Paul, by the service rendered—not by any human assessment of power or privilege. The apostle's life proves the tradition true, and the tradition proves the apostle's life true. One can see why early Christianity, faced by a crisis of leadership in the second and third generations, was so concerned to link its message and ministry with the *apostles'* teaching and way of life. This concern is already evident in the Pastoral letters, which attempt to connect "lesser lights" (e.g., Timothy, Titus) with apostolic pioneers like Paul. A similar impulse can be seen in documents like 1 Clement, whose ministers are explicitly linked with the apostles who received the gospel from Christ and subsequently appointed "their first converts . . . to be bishops and deacons of the future believers" (1 Clem 42:1-4).

We are now in a position to understand why the criterion of apostolicity loomed so large in the Christian understanding of ministry during the later-first and early-second centuries. Because apostleship and tradition were so closely interwined—at least in the thinking of Paul—it was vital to

[25]On these points see John Howard Schütz, "Charisma and Social Reality in Primitive Christianity," *Journal of Religion* 54 (1974), 56-57; complete article, 51-70.

maintain the link between later ministers (bishops, deacons, elders, prophets) and those apostles who were witnesses of Jesus' life and resurrection. One can see, too, why the apostle's superior status became attached also to those leaders whose life and service continued to guarantee the community's faith and its identity as the "people of Jesus" (rather than some other human collectivity). For the church's ministers came to be regarded as a living repository of apostolic truth, "personally authorized by the apostles and their heirs."[26]

Despite the principle of egalitarianism, therefore, we must admit that from a very early period onward, the Christian ministry was seen as taking precedence in the congregation. The supreme example of such ministry was the apostle's, since he or she served as guarantor and prime witness of the gospel message. Later leaders were ratified by their own linkage to that aboriginal apostolic witness. Some of these later leaders, as we noted in Chapter Three, performed functional ministries (e.g., the bishops and deacons of 1 Clement or Ignatius of Antioch); others were accorded senior status because their lives and conversion were, like the apostles', outstanding examples of faith worthy of imitation by all (e.g., the presbyters mentioned in second-century sources). By the second century, such "successors of the apostles" clearly possessed high prestige and superior status in the congregation. The ministers of 1 Clement, for instance, are assumed to have lifelong tenure, and can be removed only for serious cause (1 Clem 44). Similarly, the bishop in Ignatius of Antioch's letters receives his power (as the apostles did) directly from God and so can exercise ultimate authority within the church.[27]

CHARISM AND COMMUNITY ORDER

Apostolicity became, then, the central criterion in judging

---

[26]See Countryman, "Christian Equality and the Early Catholic Episcopate, " 132; see I Tim. 4:16; 6:20-21.

[27]*Ibid.*, 132-133.

who was qualified for authoritative ministry in the congregation. This helps explain why "apostolic succession" and "apostolic tradition" were such overwhelming preoccupations for second-century leaders, like Irenaeus of Lyons, who sought to distinguish orthodox teaching from heterodox speculation. When we read apologists like Irenaeus we are sometimes surprised that their arguments include personal attacks against the heretics' way of life. To us, this sounds like yellow journalism or character assassination, an airing of dirty laundry in public. But we need to remember that for these orthodox Christians, "apostolicity" was, above all, a *way of life* that guaranteed teaching rather than assent to dogma or succession in an ecclesiastical office. For Irenaeus, it was the heretics' way of life that clearly betrayed their departure from apostolic teaching—much as, for Paul, it was the super-apostles' very success that called their doctrine into question (see 2 Cor 11:1-14).

Here we are at the heart of Paul's notion of apostolic authority as a "charism." Earlier in this book we observed that charism has a specific meaning in the Pauline vocabulary: it is God's eschatological gift in Christ, the eternal life that takes hold of believers now, in their very history and bodily existence. Charisms are not vague, hazy properties that belong to spiritual experts, but concrete gifts of service exhibited by all Christians. A charismatic is not a Christian who has an uncanny aptitude for the preternatural and the marvelous, but one in whom God's power (spirit, *pneuma*) works to build up the body of Christ. This is why Paul could regard the entire congregation as charismatic, each person endowed with a "manifestation of the Spirit for the common good" (1 Cor 12:7).

Apostleship, as Paul understood it, is one of these charisms. Like all the others, its proof lies in the service rendered and this service is manifest in everyday realities. "The religious life has its most profound expression," John Howard Schütz writes, "in the concrete, everyday reality of human social life visible in the cultically gathered church, a society which therefore can number its administrators among its pneumatics."[28] There is no opposition, in Paul's view, between "charism" and "authority"—or between "prophet" and "apostle". Charisms are not spectacular eruptions of the Spirit, as opposed to the orderly—if uninspired—work of administrators and office-holders. Instead, charism is itself an *ordering* principle: "it orders the common life," writes Schütz, "by establishing priorities and discriminating among competing manifestations of the spirit."[29] The opposite of charism is neither "institution" nor "authority", but disorder and chaos in the everyday life of the congregation.

This notion of charism as an ordering principle is important for understanding Paul's view of mutual ministry, apostolic authority and community order. There is danger in holding, as Paul did, that *all* are endowed with charism, that *all* are possessed by "spirit". For if this is so, the church could collapse into an amorphous blob of competing charismatics, each insisting that his or her gift is "higher", more praiseworthy or more desirable. By insisting that every charism must be anchored in deeds of concrete *service* to the community, Paul avoided two extremes.[30] First, by saying that *each person* has a gift to offer, he prevented the Christian's self from being submerged or absorbed by an abstract "spirit". In a word, Paul believed that the Christian "possessed by the spirit" does not lose self-identity; the *individual* remains distinct from the charismatic gift. Second, Paul avoided the problem of rampant individualism by showing that the Christian's self achieves its true identity only within the larger community, the body of Christ. The Christian's self-identity is shaped *socially,* within a community of persons who possess a common spirit and engage in deeds of mutual service.

Charism thus orders the community, according to Paul, by preventing both excessive enthusiasm and divisive individualism. Unchecked enthusiasm—a frenzied, ecstatic possession by "spirit"—would lead to loss of self; unbounded

[28]See Schütz, "Charisma and Social Reality," 61.
[29]*Ibid.*, 61.
[30]*Ibid.*, 60.

individualism would lead to competition, to invidious comparison of gifts, and to the eventual destruction of unity in the congregation. Rightly understood, charism checks both these impulses. It preserves the individuality of each person in the congregation, while it also prevents that individuality from becoming divisive or destructive. As John Howard Schütz comments, "charisma provides role identity, that crucial item which helps one understand himself by helping him see his place within a larger social network."[31] As Paul understood it, charism preserves a Christian's unique individuality, while it links that individuality to the larger community where all gifts work together for the common good, for building up the body of Christ.

Because charism orders the church by respecting both individual uniqueness and communal need, it permits Paul to discern a kind of "hierarchy" among the congregation's gifts. Prophecy, for example, is superior to speaking in tongues, for, as Paul says, "he who speaks in a tongue edifies himself, but he who prophesies edifies the church" (1 Cor 14:4). At the same time, charism as an "ordering principle" clarifies the apostle's superior status and role. As a missionary and church-founder, the apostle's responsibility transcends the limits of a *local* congregation. He or she must attend not only to the unity of a local church, but to the harmony and communion of numerous congregations scattered here and there. An expression of this broader responsibility can be seen, for example, in Paul's continuing concern for the collection of money on behalf of the "saints in Jerusalem" (see Rom 15:25). To the apostle's broader pastoral mission must be added his or her responsibility for authenticating the tradition as it is handed on and preserved in the local congregations. In a word, the superiority of the apostolic charism is rooted not in a human hunger for power or control over others, but in the God-given call to accept responsibility for "all the churches" (2 Cor 11:28), and for the integrity of the gospel preached in them.

[31] *Ibid.*

A Theology of Holy Orders

Here again we can see why the charism of apostolicity later came to be linked with the ministry of bishops. For bishops were not only pastors of local congregations, they were also, as a "college" of ministers, responsible for the overall well-being of the church catholic. As Karl Rahner has observed, it is because the individual bishop belonged to such a *college,* with its responsibility for "all the churches", that he could be pastor of a local congregation.[32] And this collegiate character of episcopal ministry tells us something further about the meaning of bishops as "successors of the apostles." Succession is not a personal inheritance belonging to each bishop who can trace his ordination back to "one of the Twelve." Rather, the *college* of bishops "succeeds" the *college* of apostles. Succession is a collegiate characteristic that signals the apostolic responsibility of caring for all the churches and insuring their unity.[33] This understanding of episcopal collegiality and succession faithfully reflects Luke's portrait of the apostles as a body responsible for decisions that affect the church as a whole.[34]

THE PRIESTHOOD OF JESUS

In addition to discipleship, apostolic ministry, charism and community order, there is another element that must be considered in our outline of the New Testament's theology of ministry: the "priesthood" of Jesus. In Roman Catholic theology, the idea of Jesus as priest has exerted enormous influence. According to Thomas Aquinas, for instance, baptized and confirmed Catholics are "conformed" to this priesthood through sacramental "character", while the ordained ministry is yet a further "participation" in Jesus' priesthood.[35] Later in this chapter we shall return to these notions

32See Karl Rahner, *Bishops: Their Status and Function,* translated by Edward Quinn, (Baltimore: Helicon Press, 1964), p.22.

[33]*Ibid.,* pp. 19-21.

[34]See Brown, *Priest and Bishop,* pp. 58-59.

[35]See Thomas Aquinas, *Summa Theologiae,* IIIa Pars, Q. 63, arts. 2-3.

of participation in Christ's priesthood, but for the moment our attention will center on what the New Testament has to say about Jesus as a priest.

The most important source in this connection is, of course, the Letter to the Hebrews. Its author outlines a rather unique Christology based on the conviction that Jesus is a "high priest" whose perfect sacrifice of self has rendered all other sacrifices—past and future—obsolete. It will be necessary to analyze how and why the author of Hebrews developed this priestly Christology, but first we need to see how an earlier generation of Christians, like Paul's, perceived Jesus' death as a "sacrifice" that atoned for sin.

In 1 Cor 15:3-11, Paul quotes an established tradition that deals with the Jesus-event. According to this tradition, Jesus' death was neither a tragedy that befell a just man, nor a gross miscarriage of justice, nor a model for imitation by others. Rather, Jesus' death was God's way of effectively dealing with sin.[36] Through the cross and resurrection of the Lord, God did for humankind what it could not do for itself: he reestablished the "right relation" between himself and human beings. That is why Paul could say that Christ died "for our sins" and that this death happened "in accordance with the Scriptures" (1 Cor 15:3). To say such a thing meant, of course, that the Scriptures had to be drastically reinterpreted—for the Bible itself seemed to condemn a man who "dies on a tree" (see Deut 21:23). Paul took up this challenge of reinterpretation, arguing that by "becoming a curse for us", Jesus freed believers from the condemnation brought on by sin (see Gal 3:10-14). Seen in this light, Jesus' death is an act of God's unconditional love that effectively cancels the debt of sin and results in our new relationship with God. Now rightly related to God, believers know they are forgiven through the cross of Christ.[37]

For these reasons, Paul could interpret Jesus' death as a *sacrifice,* an "expiation" for sin (see Rom 3:24-26). It is

---

[36]See Leander Keck, *Paul and His Letters,* (Proclamation Commentaries; Philadelphia: Fortress Press, 1979), p. 34.

[37]*Ibid.,* pp. 36-37.

important to recognize, however, that expiation is something quite different from "propitiation". Propitiation refers to the dissolving of anger, hostility and wrath by placating someone (God) who was aggrieved. But this was not what happened in Jesus' death, because for Paul the anger that needed to be appeased was never God's—it was *ours*. *We* are the ones caught in a vicious cycle of rebellion and impotent rage against God, and that is precisely why *God* had to do for us what we could not do for ourselves. The cross, therefore, was not propitiation, but *expiation;* it expunged the cycle of sin that had caught hold of us, cancelled the debt created by our anger, and restored us to a right relation with God. Paul could thus borrow the language of the Jewish sacrificial system, in Rom 3:24-26, in order to interpret Christ's death as an expiatory sacrifice that deals effectively with sin.

This interpretation—Jesus' death as an expiatory sacrifice that cancels sin—provides the background for understanding the distinctive contribution made to early Christology by the author of the Letter to the Hebrews. This "letter" is actually not a letter at all, but an extended homiletic midrash on Psalm 109 (110).[38] Through the use of Ps 109:4, especially—"Your are a priest forever according to the order of Melchizedek"—the author developed his argument that Jesus is high priest of a new covenant which renders all other sacrifice and priesthood obsolete. The argument unfolds in four basic movements: 1) Just as there was an "interim" period in Israel's history when, during the wandering in the wilderness, God provided priestly leadership under Moses and Joshua, so there is an "interim" period for Christians (between the first and second comings of the Lord) when God has provided definitive priestly leadership through Jesus' sacrificial death (Heb 3:7-4:11). 2) Jesus fulfills all the necessary qualifications for the office of high priest (Heb 4:14-5:14). 3) Jesus' priesthood is like Mechizedek's—eternal and pemanent (Heb 6:19-7:28). 4) Jesus' priesthood is utterly

---

[38]See Reginald Fuller, "Hebrews," in: *Hebrews, James, 1 and 2 Peter, Jude, Revelation,* (Proclamation Commentaries: Philadelphia: Fortress Press 1977), pp. 6-8.

superior to Israel's levitical priesthood (Heb 9:6-10, 11-14). Some comments about this fourfold argument are in order.

The notion of an "interim" period for Israel and for (1) Christians is based on the author's midrashic interpretation of Ps 94 (95):7-11. Under the leadership of Moses and Joshua, Israel sought that "rest" promised by God to those who would "hear his voice" and abandon their rebellious ways. But, the author argues, Israel never attained that rest because she was hard of heart and unbelieving (Heb 3:16-19). This proves that the "priestly" leadership of Moses and Joshua was ineffective, unable to produce what it promised. By contrast, Jesus has opened up a way to that "rest" for those who believe the good news (Heb 4:1-10). That is why God promised, in the Psalms, another "day" ("today": Ps 94 (95):7) for a new "people of God" (Heb 4:8-9).

As pathfinder of this new way to God's sabbath rest, Jesus (2) is qualified for the office of high priest. His qualifications are impressive. Like all high priests, Jesus is chosen from among humans, shares the weakness of those whom he serves, can sympathize with the ignorant and wayward, and is called by God just as Aaron was (Heb 4:14-5:4). We can see here the author's use of Jewish theological interpretations of priesthood that were common in the post-exilic Second Temple period: e.g., the notion that the priesthood is "Aaronic"; the special ritual role of the high priest, especially on the Day of Atonement.

But according to the author of Hebrews, Jesus' high (3) priesthood is one of a very unique type. For Jesus is priest "according to the order of Melchizedek" (Ps 109 (110):4). This point is the heart of the author's argument since, as we shall see, it provides him with a way to argue the utter superiority of Jesus over the levitical priesthood of "Aaron's sons". Like Melchizedek's, Jesus' priesthood has two supreme advantages: it is not based on physical descent (Gen 14:18 provides no priestly genealogy for Melchizedek, and Jesus himself did not come from a priestly family); and it is not based on an "ineffective law" (Melchizedek appears *before* the law was given to Moses, while Jesus is condemned and crucified as one "outside the law"). These two advantages, the author concludes, mean that Jesus' priesthood, like that of Melchizedek's, is eternal and permanent: "Melchizedek is without father or mother or genealogy, and has neither beginning of days nor end of life, but resembling the Son of God he continues a priest for ever" (Heb 7:3).

(4) A high priesthood of this sort, the author asserts in his fourth and clinching argument, needs no daily round of priests and sacrifices (Heb 7:23-25). The author supports his point through a series of four closely-linked comparisons. First, the levitical priests performed their office *on earth,* while Jesus' priesthood is exercised *in heaven* (Heb 8:1-4). Second the levitical priests offered the *blood of animals,* but Jesus offers *his own blood* (Heb 9:13-14). Third, the Israelite high priest entered an *earthly sanctuary* on the Day of Atonement, while Jesus has entered once for all into a *heavenly sanctuary* (Heb 9:11-12). Finally, the levitical sacrifices are effective only for cases of *ritual impurity,* while Jesus' expiatory sacrifice *takes away sin* (Heb 9:9-10,15).

Having unfolded his argument in this way, the author of Hebrews concludes that Jesus is the definitive high priest whose work, done "once for all" (Heb 7:27), is perpetually effective. There is no longer any need for earthly priests with their sacrifices and blood-rites, since the old covenant has been superseded by a new and eternal covenant made in the blood of Christ. Jesus' sacrifice, moreover, was by its very nature an act of supreme obedience, and thus it has established forever the right relation between God and humankind (Heb 10:1-18). In a word, Jesus' priesthood has permanently eliminated the need for earthly priests and sacrifices. Through the obedience of faith we can draw near to God in full confidence, trusting that our sins are forgiven by the obedient self-sacrifice of Jesus offered once for all (Heb 10:19-22).

Two elements are especially prominent in Hebrews' portrait of Jesus as priest: his obedience and his eternal intercession on our behalf. According to the author's theology, Jesus' self-oblation on Calvary was a "once for all" event; what continues eternally is his intercession and appearance in God's presence on our behalf.[39] And because Jesus' sacrifice was a perfect act of obedience, the way of obedience-in-faith has been opened up for us. Jesus the priest is thus the pathfinder, the pioneer who blazes a new trail for us to follow (see Heb 2:10; 12:2). We participate in Jesus' priesthood precisely by following our pathfinder in the obedience of faith (see Heb 11-12).

THE PRIESTHOOD OF CHRISTIANS

According to the New Testament, it is not only Jesus who is priest, all the believers constitute a "royal priesthood" (1 Pet 2:9). This phrase is one of a series of four Old Testament titles for Israel that the author of 1 Peter applies to the Christian community: "chosen race" (Is 43:2); "royal priesthood" (Ex 19:6); "holy nation" (Ex 19:6); "God's own people" (Hos 1:9; 2:23). Taken together, these titles suggest that Christians are the "New Israel" and are thus empowered as priests and living stones of a new temple to offer "sacrifices acceptable to God through Jesus Christ" (1 Pet 2:5).

It is important to note that by appropriating the title "royal priesthood", the author of 1 Peter was not discussing ministry in the church, but rather the relation between Christians and the rest of the world. Israel was a "kingdom of priests" not only because it was a nation dedicated to the service and worship of its king Yahweh, but also because "its conduct among the nations was expected to be such as to manifest them as his royal courtiers and his priestly servants."[40] Similarly, Christians, who live as "exiles" in an unfriendly world, must exhibit God's grace and holiness to that world (1 Pet 2:11-12). That is why the author fills his letter with numerous exhortations to live blamelessly, in such a way that

---

[39] *Ibid.*, pp. 15-16.
[40] See Joseph Fitzmyer, "The First Epistle of Peter," in *The Jerome Biblical Commentary*, II, p. 365 (58:12).

outsiders will be favorably impressed (see 1 Pet 2:13-3:22). Here again we encounter the recommendation that Christians, though "equals" in baptism, observe the customary cultural patterns of social life. Thus, servants are to be submissive to masters, wives submissive to husbands, and all should honor the secular authorities (emperor, govenors: see 1 Pet 2:13-3:6). The author urges a kind of voluntary renunciation of the freedom that the egalitarian principle brings to the congregation—in order that outsiders may not be given the impression that Christians are subverting Greco-Roman ways.

The metaphor of "royal priesthood" thus serves a double function. It identifies who Christians are in the world, and it explains what kind of behaviour is required if that identity is to become known and respected by outsiders. In this sense, royal priesthood is not a ministerial metaphor; its use does not set up an implicit rivalry between the "priestly faithful" and designated ministers who have authoritative status in the church.[41] This is clear from 1 Peter's description of what constitutes this royal priesthood: holy conduct (1:15); the offering of spiritual sacrifices (2:5); the proclamation of God's wonderful deeds (2:9); the offering of prayer (3:7).[42] Believers are priests because they express in their everyday lives and relationships the transcendent grace and holiness of the God who has called them "out of darkness into his marvelous light" (1 Pet 2:9).

Neither Hebrews nor 1 Peter explicitly comments on the relation between the unique priesthood of Jesus and the royal priesthood of Christians. It is possible, nevertheless, to see a connection. According to Hebrews, Jesus' sacrificial death and his entry into God's presence with his own blood have made him our eternal high priest. That death, with its atoning power, is intimately linked to baptism (see 1 Pet 3:18-22). The implication is clear enough: baptism gives Christians participation in Jesus' death and so puts them in contact with the

[41] *Ibid.*

[42] See Gerhard Krodel, "First Peter," in *Hebrews, James, 1 and 2 Peter, Jude, Revelation* (note 38, above), pp. 51-52.

power of his resurrection (1 Pet 1:3-5). Through participation in Jesus' priestly act of sacrifice/death/resurrection, believers themselves become priestly. Just as Jesus became the "great witness" to God's triumphant grace and holiness through his cross and rising, so believers become a royal priesthood called to witness God's holiness in the world.

SUMMARY

We may now summarize the central elements which the New Testament provides for a theology of Christian ministry. We noted, first, an emphasis on the discipleship of equals. Within the Christian community itself there are no first and second-class citizens; all the baptized are united to the same Lord, and so the ordinary social distinctions between Jew and Greek, slave and free, male and female are radically overturned. In their relations with the larger Greco-Roman world, however, Christians still seem bound to observe the common conventions of their culture. Slaves and masters still exist, and women can still be advised to show deferential respect toward their husbands. This apparent discrepancy between principle and practice can perhaps be explained by the New Testament writers' desire to demonstrate that conversion to Christianity does not imply a rejection of Greco-Roman culture or a subversion of its customs.

Second, the egalitarian principle that governs relations with the Christian congregation appears to admit of an exception: the status and role of ministers as superior to that of ordinary believers. While this superiority has not yet been formalized into a definite hierarchy of "superiors" and "subordinates", it is clear that apostles, for instance, possess God-given power to teach, correct abuse, excommunicate errant members, and receive financial recompense for their work. Although an apostle like Paul voluntarily renounced many of these rights, he clearly recognized his authoritative status vis-a-vis the churches he founded. Because the apostle's ministry was so intimately linked with the Christian message itself, apostolicity quickly became a requirement for *all* ministry in the churches.

We have seen, thirdly, that "charism", as interpreted by Paul, is itself an ordering principle within the community. The opposite of charism is neither institution nor structure nor authority, by rather chaos and disorder. Apostleship, with its God-given authority and broad pastoral responsibility for all the churches, is thus the premier example of charismatic ministry. Moreover, Paul' insistence that charism manifest itself in concrete deeds of service that build up the body allowed him to check both excessive enthusiasm and divisive individualism within the congregation. Charism thus orders the community by respecting each individual's unique gifts, while linking those gifts to the larger community where all work togther for the common good.

Finally, the New Testament speaks of Jesus' unique priesthood, as well as the "royal priesthood" of believers. The remote roots of this theology are already present in the conviction (held by Paul and others) that Jesus' death was an expiatory sacrifice, God's effective way of dealing with sin by restoring a right relation between himself and humankind. In the Letter to the Hebrews the theology of Jesus' sacrifice is developed further through a homiletic midrash on Old Testament texts (chiefly, Ps 109 (110)). Like Melchizedek's, Jesus' priesthood is eternal, and so renders all other sacrifices and priestly mediators obsolete. As a supreme act of obedience, moreover, Jesus' self-sacrifice opens the way to a new obedience in faith for believers. By participating in Jesus' atoning death through baptism, Christians also participate in his priesthood. They become a New Israel, called to witness God's victorious grace and holiness in the everyday social life of this world.

While the New Testament does not provide a systematic theology of Christian ministry nor a fully formalized pattern of ministry that is uniform in all churches, it does outline certain elements which later had a decisive impact on the Christian community's understanding of its ministers. These elements include the notion of authoritative status even within the discipleship of equals, the conviction that all ministry must be rooted in the apostles' teaching, the idea of charism as an ordering principle in the congregation's life, and the insight that Jesus' self-sacrifice has permanently altered the meaning of "priesthood". In the section of this chapter which follows, we shall see how these elements have been integrated into—and sometimes altered by—the later theological tradition.

II

The Tradition

Many of the elements that have shaped the Roman Catholic understanding of holy orders were identified and discussed in Chapter Four, on the evolution of a Christian priesthood. There we noted how, historically, the language of orders and priesthood developed, as well as the way in which ordination came to be perceived as one of the seven sacraments. We observed, too, how the liturgical rites of ordination developed, beginning with their earliest full-fledged description in the third-century *Apostolic Tradition* of Hippolytus. Here, our task will be to summarize the central issues that have evolved, over many centuries, in the Roman Catholic theological tradition about orders.

Four such issues can, I think, be rather clearly identified. It will be useful first simply to list them, and then to offer a more detailed discussion of each item.

1. Christians have a fundamental "right" to ministry; indeed, ministerial service is an essential element in the definition of church. Quite simply, there is no ministry without a church and no church without a ministry. Precisely how this ministry is arranged may vary, however, both historically and culturally. Some ordained ministries, for example, were once regarded as "major", but are now suppressed (e.g., the order of subdeacon, eliminated after the II Vatican Council). Or again, the interaction of church and

culture may produce profound changes in the exercise of an ordained ministry. A bishop like Cyprian of Carthage (+258), for instance, was basically the pastor of a local church, while late-medieval bishops were often courtiers who never actually set foot in their dioceses.

2. 2. The designation of ministers in the church, "ordination", is a public process that includes many elements: participation by the people (through choice, election or at least "consent"); fulfillment of canonical conditions (e.g., attachment to a specific church through the "title of ordination"); ritual action (laying on of hands and prayer); and "vocation" (God's choice of the candidate discerned and expressed through the community's call to ministry). No one of these elements, taken in isolation from all the others, is sufficient to constitute what the Roman Catholic tradition has come to understand as "ordination".

3. 3. The sacrament of order (*Sacramentum ordinis*) cannot be reduced, in Roman Catholic tradition, to "priesthood". Nor can ministry itself be reduced to "orders". The ordained are one example within the larger category of ministry, while priesthood is one example within the larger category of sacramental order.

4. 4. As Roman Catholic theology has come to perceive it, the sacrament of order establishes a permanent claim on the ordained person. Theologians have attempted to describe this permanence through metaphors such as "indelible character", a "mark" imprinted on ordained ministers. Often, too, the permanence of sacramental order has been interpreted as resulting from the ordinand's distinctive "conformation to"—or "participation in"—the priesthood of Jesus Christ.

In the paragraphs that follow we shall explore the significance of these four items, especially as they contribute to a theology of the sacrament, and as they relate to the biblical orientations discussed in the preceding section.

CHURCH'S RIGHT TO MINISTRY

In his recent work on *Ministry,* Edward Schillebeeckx has spoken of the "apostolic right" of Christian communities "to a minister or ministers and to the celebration of the eucharist."[43] This right can never be nullified, he argues, by criteria for admission to ministry which the church may legitimately impose at various moments in its history. In principle, for example, it is legitimate for the church to establish disciplinary requirements for admission to ordained ministry (e.g., celibacy). But if such requirements come to mean that a community is threatened by a shortage or absence of ministers, then the apostolic right must take priority. "In that case," writes Schillebeeckx, "this apostolic right has priority over the church order which has in fact grown up and which in other circumstances may have been useful and healthy...."[44] In short, the Christian people's right to ministry is theologically more fundamental than celibacy as a requirement for admission to holy orders.

What Schillebeeckx calls the apostolic right of Christians to ministry is based on two principles. First, ministry itself exists in order to maintain and strengthen the church's identity as the community of Jesus.[45] By being *this* community—and no other—Christians can claim to be "people of God." It is precisely the Christian community's task—and its identity—to keep alive Jesus' distinctive vision of God and of God's kingdom. That vision shows us a God unconditionally dedicated to the well-being of humankind, to its unity and liberation. The eucharist, above all, is the moment when the church ritually recognizes and renews its identity as the community of Jesus, re-commits itself to his message about God's "reign". Working to maintain this uniquely Christian identity is at the heart of all apostolic ministry in the

---

[43]See Edward Schillebeeckx, *Ministry.* Leadership in the Community of Jesus Christ, translated by John Bowden, (New York: Crossroad Publishing Company, 1981), p. 37.

[44]*Ibid.*; cf. pp. 85-99 for fuller discussion.

[45]*Ibid.,* pp. 24, 35-37.

church. The apostles' task—and that of their "successors"—
is thus to help communities discover the gospel of Jesus
within changing historical crcumstances. And since the eucharist is a supremely important element in this discovery, one
can see why, from a very early period, Christians tended to
connect it with the ministry of those who "succeed the
apostles." This connection is never explicitly made in the
New Testament, though, as Schillebeeckx notes, the general
conception seems to be that whoever is competent to lead the
community in one way or another is also competent to
preside at celebrations of the Lord's Supper.[46]

The second principle which underlies the community's
apostolic right to ministry is the notion of service (*diakonia*)
as an essential element in the definition of "church". Richard
McBrien has written that "the Church is the community of
those who confess the Lordship of Jesus Christ, who ratify
that faith in baptism, and who thereby commit themselves to
membership and mission within that sacramental community of faith."[47] The church's mission, McBrien notes further,
is characterized by three New Testament words: *kerygma,*
the proclamation in word and sacrament that God's kingdom
is revealed in Jesus of Nazareth; *koinonia,* the fellowship of
church members that testifies to the transforming action of
God's Spirit; and *diakonia,* the service of God's kingdom in
the socio-political order.[48] All three of these are essential to
the church's self-identity. The church is more than a herald of
glad tidings or a word-and-sacrament organization; like
Jesus, it is also "servant". Nor is this service merely inner-
directed (restricted to community members); it reaches out to
all men and women. This must be so because what the gospel
offers is not merely "religion" for those who happen to like it,
but an interpretation of human existence itself. God's
"cause", revealed in Jesus' proclamation of the kingdom, is
nothing more or less than the human cause in all its

[46] *Ibid.,* p. 30.
[47] See Richard McBrien, *Church: The Continuing Quest*, (Paramus, New Jersey:
Newman Press, 1970), p. 73.
[48] *Ibid.,* pp. 73-85.

dimensions—including the concrete realities of socio-political life. Christian ministry in areas such as human rights and social justice is an intrinsic element of the church's mission and thus of its identity. To abandon such ministry as being merely "secular" would in fact result in a loss of the church's identity as "community of Jesus." For Christians believe that in Jesus the ultimate destiny of all humankind is revealed—a destiny symbolized by "sitting at table with God in the festive banquet of the kingdom."

Both these principles—maintainence of the church's identity and *diakonia* as an essential element in that identity—support Schillebeeckx's conviction about the apostolic right to ministry. This right exists not merely for the community's sake, but for the world's sake. Here once more we can see why the word "apostolic" became such a massively important one in the Christian vocabulary of ministry. We can see too why, in the second century for example, apologists like Irenaeus insisted on "apostolic succession" in the churches (linked, in his view, with each community's list of episcopal leaders). At stake in the matter of apostolicity is not simply continuity with the past, but the church's identity in the present (i.e., in every age of history). "Apostolic" is thus a *defining* term that identifies Christians, with their ministers, as people of God, community of Jesus, servant in and for the world.

It is thus not surprising that the church's theological tradition has regularly used "apostolic" to define both community and ministers. The earliest Christian creeds, for example, confess the church as "one, holy, catholic and apostolic." Documents of the church's official magisterium have emphasized the apostolic nature of the ministry, especially that of the bishop. The Council of Trent, for example, spoke of "the bishops who hold (or succeed to) the place of the apostles."[49] Here we must recognize that the Council was expressing a *theological conviction,* rather than a literal historical fact (though most of the Fathers at Trent probably

[49]See H. Denzinger and A. Schoenmetzer, eds., *Enchiridion Symbolorum*, (33rd edition; Rome: Herder, 1965), n. 1767; my translation.

regarded bishops as historical successors of the apostles.) As we noted in Chapter Two, modern biblical scholars would deny that the apostles "ordained bishops" as their literal and immediate successors. *Theologically,* however, one is justified in viewing bishops as "apostolic" and even as "successors of the apostles"—especially if one recalls that the episcopal ministry is aimed at maintaining the church's unity, preserving its identity as "community of Jesus", guaranteeing the preaching of the gospel, and insuring the presence of a ministry.

But here we seem to be up against a serious problem. How can something be theologically truthful, yet historically inaccurate or even false? In the present case, how can one claim that the church's episcopal ministers "succeed" the apostles—and at the same time claim that the historical origins of the episcopate are not necessarily linked to a deliberate choice by Jesus, by the "Twelve", or by missionary apostles like Paul? A comparison may be useful in answering this question. The biblical stories of creation in the first chapters of Genesis are designed to make a theological statement about the nature and meaning of human existence in the world. Genesis does not pretend to give a precise and scientifically factual account of the origins of the universe—and thus a faithful Christian is not required to choose between the "Bible's truth" and that of "science." The reason for this is rather simple. The questions that concerned the authors of the creation stories were not those of a twentieth-century astrophysicist. The biblical writers were asking questions such as: what does our human condition as "male" and "female" tell us about our relation to God and to one another? why must we die? how can one explain the deep split that divides humans from one another and from God? Struggling with these questions of religious meaning and value, the authors of Genesis affirm that "God created." Understood religiously, creation means that this world, with all its grandeur and stupidity, is the God-willed environment within which we learn to accept our finitude, freedom and responsibility. "To think of the world as God's creation," writes John

Macquarrie, "is not to hold some theory about its origin but to experience it as an environment which one can trust and toward which one can be both free and responsible."[50]

The human language of time is thus used in Genesis for a *theological purpose,* not for the sake of chronological accuracy. A similar use of time can be detected in the New Testament stories of Jesus' resurrection and subsequent appearances. *Theologically,* the paschal mystery is a single event, encompassing Jesus' dying and rising, his exaltation as Lord, and the sending of the Spirit. But this single event is arranged chronologically, especially in sources such as Luke/Acts, where the ascension occurs "forty days" after the resurrection, and Pentecost ten days later (see Acts 1:3, 2:1-4). This "resurrection chronology" has, of course, a theological purpose: it permits Luke to demonstrate, for example, how the earliest nucleus of believers in the Jerusalem church was formed and instructed under the direction of the Risen One.

Such a use of temporal references for theological and symbolic purposes is thus rather evident in the Bible. It is perhaps less evident—but it is nonetheless present—in other theological sources as well. I would suggest that the symbolic use of time also appears in documents of the church's magisterium such as the one from Trent which we were considering above. That is why I indicated that Trent's remarks about the bishops as "successors of the apostles" express a theological conviction rather than a literal historical fact. The point of Trent's assertion is that the relation of bishops to the historical life of Christian communities parallels that of the apostles to the earliest congregations. The parallelism of this relation is the important point, since it indicates that witness and ministry are part of the church's very definition, in its origins and in its ongoing history.

Magisterial documents like those of Trent thus affirm, through symbolic references to time, that ministry is at the

[50]See John Macquarrie, *The Faith of the People of God,* (New York: Charles Scribner's Sons, 1972), p. 82.

heart of the church's identity and definition—and that this ministry must always be "apostolic", an expression of that "original" relationship which existed between Christ, the first-fruits of his preaching (the apostles), and the earliest Christian congregations. This helps to explain why theologians like Schillebeeckx speak of the "apostolic right" of Christians to ministry. Such a right stems directly from the church's origins and identity as the community of Jesus whose mission is to keep alive in the world his unique vision of God and of God's kingdom. Without apostolic ministry, the church would lose its Christ-centered identity and become simply another good-will organization.

And since this ecclesial identity is recognized, expressed and renewed at eucharist, one can understand why theological tradition has so closely linked ministry, eucharist and church. Ignatius of Antioch's formula provides a clear early example of this linkage: one bishop, one eucharist, one church. But it must be remembered that this familiar Ignatian formula did not prevent development and change in the way ministry, church and eucharist were connected. Because of changing circumstances, for instance, presbyters later emerged as the ordinary pastors and presiders at eucharist in local communities, while the bishop became more the "administrator" of a large diocese. Such change was necessary if the Christian right to ministry was to be respected, since increasing numbers made it impossible for the bishop to maintain his role as immediate "local pastor" in the manner envisioned by Ignatius.

Edward Schillebeeckx thus seems quite correct when he argues that the right to ministry has fundamental priority. Ministry is, after all, an historically conditioned reality; it arises and responds to concrete needs of changing communities. Though the link between ministry, eucharist and church remains vital and constant, the church's own history may reveal new needs that require new types of service. A recent example is the restoration of the diaconate as a permanent ministry. But more far-reaching changes are also possible. As Schillebeeckx notes, "even the old and venerable does not enjoy any priority because it is old and venerable."[51] The restoration of an ancient church order such as the diaconate may prove to be valuable, but this does not exclude the possibility that altogether new (and as yet unrecognized) ministries may emerge. As we saw in Chapter Four, it took many centuries for theologians to agree that church order is a "sacrament"—and longer still for them to identify exactly which ministries were part of that sacrament. As an historical institution the church must remain open to the possibility that newly emerging forms of ministry are in fact part of that "holy order" which the church manifests when it lives in fidelity to the apostles' teaching and way of life.

ORDINATION AS PROCESS

Roman Catholics often assume that the only "really necessary" action needed to make one a minister in the "sacramental" sense is the liturgy of ordination. The assumption is understandable, given the historical evolution of Christian priesthood and sacramental orders outlined in Chapter Four. There we noted, for example, how in the late twelfth century the "title" of ordination—originally designed to express the minister's real relation to an actual community—became a kind of legal fiction that merely guaranteed an income. We noted, too, how the people's role in choosing ministers declined until it too was little more than a fiction. Until the reforms of the II Vatican Council, the people's approval of the candidate for orders was sought through a negative question asked (in Latin) by the bishop during the rite of ordination: "Does anyone know of a reason why this man should not be ordained?" The people's role is recognized more positively in the post-conciliar liturgy, where they are invited to express their active approval of the candidate, usually through applause. Still, in many parts of the church today, the notion that the people ought to be consulted in the selection and preparation of ministerial candidates is considered novel or negligible.

In response to this situation it is often pointed out that, according to the church's long-standing tradition, the people's choice or election of ministers has never been considered sufficient, in itself, to "make" one a bishop, presbyter or deacon. In one sense this is true. From at least the beginning of the third century, as we know from sources like the *Apostolic Tradition* of Hippolytus, popular choice must be supplemented by actions reserved to one already ordained (the bishop): laying on of hands and prayer. Although in the early church the community exercized sovereignty in the election of its bishop and in the approval of those chosen for presbyterate, it was not empowered to "ordain".[52] Bishops, presbyters and deacons did not, therefore, receive their ordination from the local church; they were not merely its "representatives" and thus, though they could be deposed, their ordination could not be revoked through a popular referendum.[53]

Here we must ask how these two principles—the right of election by the people and the right of ordination restricted to bishops—can be reconciled. If the people have an apostolic right to ministry, as well as the power to choose ministers, why is an "ordination" needed at all? The reason can perhaps best be sought by reflecting on the source of the church's power. In the church, all power (including the power to choose ministers) comes from Christ and the Spirit.[54] To put it another way, the church's power is not self-generated; Christians live by grace, and grace is precisely a gift from a Source different from ourselves. Empowered by grace, the church must confess that the Lord whom it serves is transcendent—greater than the church and greater than the

[51]See Schillebeeckx, *Ministry,* p. 84.
[52]See Cyrille Vogel, *Ordinations inconsistantes et Caractere inamissible,* (Études d'Histoire du culte et des institutions chrétiennes, I; Turin: Bottega d'Erasmo, 1978), p. (132).
[53]*Ibid.*
[54]See David Power, *Gifts That Differ.* Lay Ministries Established and Unestablished, (Studies in the Reformed Rites of the Catholic Church, Vol. VIII; New York: Pueblo Publishing Company, 1980), p. 116.

world. The transcendent Lordship of Christ and the free grace of the Spirit are recognized especially when the church gathers for worship. There, above all, the church confesses that grace and power are gifts from Another who alone is holy and "most high".

The liturgy of ordination is thus designed to express the transcendent source, the giftedness, of all ministry in the church. Ministry is *discerned* by the community (thus the ancient right of choice or election), but it is not given by the community. *God* gives the gift, the community discerns its presence and declares itself ready to incorporate this ministry into its life and mission.[55] And in the liturgy of ordination the community witnesses to this ministry's source in the transcendent power of God and in the free grace of the Spirit. The earliest ordination prayers make it clear that God is the One who inspires the service, gives the gift, and chooses ministers, as these two examples show:

> *Apostolic Tradition* (ca. 215): Prayer for Bishops
> God and Father of our Lord Jesus Christ,
> Father of mercies and God of all comfort....
> You foreordained from the beginning a race of righteous
> men....
> You appointed princes and priest,
> and did not leave your sanctuary without a ministry.
> From the beginning of the age it was your good pleasure
> to be glorified in those whom you have chosen:
> Now pour forth that power which is from you,
> of the princely Spirit which you granted
> through your beloved Son Jesus Christ to your holy
> apostles
> who established the Church in every place as your
> sanctuary.
> You who know the hearts of all,
> bestow upon this your servant,
> whom you have chosen for the episcopate,

[55]*Ibid.,* p. 128.

to feed your holy flock and to exercise the high-priesthood before you. . . .[56]

Verona Sacramentary (5/6 cent.): Prayer for Presbyters
Lord, Holy Father, almighty and everlasting God,
You bestow all the honors and all the worthy ranks
which do you service. . . .
When you set up high priests to rule over your people,
You chose men of a lesser order and a secondary dignity
to be their companions and help them in their work. . .
Therefore we ask you, Lord,
to grant us, in our weakness, these assistants . . . .
Grant these your servants, Father, the dignity of the
presbyterate.
Renew in their inmost parts the Spirit of holiness.
May they obtain and receive from you, God,
the office of second dignity. . . .[57]

These prayers explicitly acknowledge God as the source of all ministry in the church. They view ordination as an expression of the Spirit's sovereign grace at work for the community's upbuilding, its nourishment and growth. While the community has the power to discern the Spirit's grace at work, it cannot create that grace and thus it cannot make a minister. God's power alone can transform human beings into Spirit-filled servants of the community. That is why the prayers of ordination characteristically take the form of an "epiclesis", i.e., a calling down of the Spirit to transform the candidate through the power of grace.

Our discussion thus far helps explain why, in the church's tradition, ordination cannot be reduced simply to one element (e.g., to a liturgical rite or to election by the people). Ministry is not merely a function aimed at "getting a job

[56]Text cited from Geoffrey J. Cuming, trans., *Hippolytus: A Text for Students,* (Grove Liturgical Study No. 8; Bramcote Notts., England: Grove Books, 1976), p. 9.

[57]Latin text in Leo Cunibert Mohlberg, ed., *Sacramentarium Veronense,* (Rerum Ecclesiasticarum Documenta, Series Maior, Fontes, I; Rome: Herder, 1956), n. 954, pp. 121-122; my translation.

done," because the church's work is not its own—it is God's work. Paul gave classic expression to this insight in 2 Cor 5:18-20:

> All this is from God, who through Christ reconciled us to himself and gave us the ministry of reconciliation; that is, in Christ God was reconciling the world to himself, not counting their trespasses against them, and entrusting to us the message of reconciliation. So we are ambassadors for Christ, God making his appeal through us.

Apostolic ministry, according to Paul, cannot be invented by either individuals or congregations. It is an expression of God's power at work to reconcile the world, to do for us what we could never do for ourselves. For that reason, Paul did not think of his own ministry as something conceded him by local congregations; he was, instead, "a servant of Jesus Christ, called to be an apostle, set apart for the gospel of God" (Rom 1:1).

To sum it up, ordination to Christian ministry is a process encompassing several elements: vocation (God's gift and call); discernment by the community (expressed through election, choice and approval of candidates); ritual acknowledgement of God's grace (through laying on hands and prayer); and attachment to a specific church for a specific ministry (the "title" of ordination). Although these elements are not fully formalized in the New Testament, their emergence in the church's tradition seems faithful to the biblical sources. It must be admitted, however, that the Roman Catholic tradition has sometimes emphasized one element (the liturgy of ordination) to the virtual exclusion of all the others. This has been due, in part, to a preoccupation among medieval and modern theologians with what is *minimally required* if a sacrament is to be considered "valid".

CHRISTIAN MINISTRY AND "HOLY ORDERS"

Partly because of its preoccupation with sacraments and their validity, the Roman Catholic tradition has sometimes given the impression that the only "real" ministry in the church is that of the ordained, especially that of priests (presbyters and bishops). Since the II Vatican Council, however, it has become increasingly clear that Christian ministry and the sacrament of order are not identical. The very effort to implement the Council's call to renewal has already resulted in the emergence of new ministries, some of them local and transitory, some of them perhaps more permanent.[58] In addition, Pope Paul VI's *motu proprio Ministeria Quaedam* (1972) dismantled, in principle, the old system of clerical offices by opening ministries such as reader and acolyte to laypersons in the congregation.[59] Our recent experience tells us, then, that a shift has occurred in both the practice of Christian ministry and its theological interpretation.

Two rediscoveries underlie this shift. The first concerns baptism itself as not merely admission into the church, but as a continuing call to conversion, prayer and service. Quite often this baptismal call to ministry has been related to the metaphor of "royal priesthood" (the "priesthood of the baptized"). But this can be misleading. As we noted above in our discussion of the priesthood of Christians, the use of the priestly metaphor by the author of 1 Peter was directed not toward ministry but toward the relation between Christians and the rest of the world. "Royal priesthood" is not primarily a ministerial metaphor, nor does it suggest a rivalry between lay ministers and ordained personnel. A more appropriate starting point for understanding the ministerial vocation of the baptized (as well as its relation to orders) is, as David Power suggests, the symbol of the "holy people." Membership in this people is constituted by baptism and regularly celebrated in eucharist. It is this ecclesial reality—membership in God's holy people—that provides the basis for all grace and charism in the church.[60] The *grace* bestowed in baptism makes Christians holy precisely by

---

[58]See Power, *Gifts That Differ*, pp. 3-35.
[59]*Ibid.*, pp. 59-60.
[60]*Ibid.*, p. 125.

making them members of God's People; it also gives them knowledge of Christ and of the world's dependence on Christ.[61] What results from the Christian's ecclesial membership and enlightenment through baptismal grace is *charism,* service and participation in the church's mission.

Understood in this way, baptism is the primary sacrament of ministry in the church. This accords well with Paul's conviction that charisms (concrete gifts of service that manifest the Spirit's working) are characteristic of every Christian. But it also provides a way to distinguish between the minstry of all the baptized and that of Christians who are ordained. Though all possess charisms, not all charisms are alike. Leadership is a baptismal charism, though not all Christians possess it—and it is this charism that the church seeks in candidates for ordained ministry. The charism of leadership thus serves as a link between the baptismal call to ministry and the vocation to ordained ministry.[62]

The reason for this is clear if we recall that in Paul's view charism is an ordering principle in the church. It was precisely on the basis of charism that Paul was able to discern a hierarchy among the congregation's gifts (e.g., the superiority of prophecy over speaking in tongues; the authoritative status of apostle in relation to the churches). Like all charisms, that of leadership is a gift of baptism; it results from membership in a holy people and belongs to that mystery of the church celebrated in eucharist. In the sacrament of order the *baptismal* quality of this charism for leadership is neither denied nor diminished. Rather, it is presupposed and intensified. What the sacrament of order "produces" is not a new charism, but a new role for the expression of that leadership charism. This role involves both pastoral and liturgical responsibility. To quote David Power:

> What the sacrament of order then does is to give the recipient a new role in the life of the church, and as principal expression of this, a special role in the celebration of the eucharist, where the mystery of the church is

[61] *Ibid.*
[62] *Ibid.,* p. 126.

celebrated. His position becomes such that in the celebration of the Lord's Supper the relationship to Christ as founder and source of life, as well as the relationship to the community of apostles and to the communion of all the churches, is expressed and served through his presidency.[63]

In a very precise sense, therefore, the sacrament of order is a consequence that necessarily follows from the Pauline view of charism as an ordering principle in the congregation's life, and from the charism of leadership as one of the gifts which some Christians receive through baptismal membership in a holy people. We can also see why the people's participation is an essential element in the process of ordination. Since leadership is a baptismal charism, the discernment of its presence rightly belongs to the community of the baptized. And because this leadership is *for the church,* not for the personal enhancement of individuals, the primary criterion for assessing it must be the "building up of the body." This too is in line with Paul's thinking about charisms in 1 Corinthians.

The rediscovery of baptism as the root of all mission and ministry in the church does not, therefore, eliminate the need for sacramental order. Indeed, the contrary is true. The baptismal charism of leadership expresses itself in the new role established by order, while order always points back to membership in a holy people as the prime mystery celebrated in baptism and eucharist. The ministerial roles that result from ordination are thus intended to express "holy order" as that phrase was understood by early Christian theologians. For holy order is, in the first instance, neither an office nor a function, but a quality manifested by the entire church when its behavior imitates the Lord's, when its teaching is faithful to the apostles' message, and when its leaders are trusted exemplars worthy of imitation by all.

A second rediscovery has also helped clarify the church's tradition about ministry and ordination. Just as those who

[63]*Ibid.,* p. 127.

have ordained roles in the church cannot monopolize ministry, so priesthood cannot monopolize the sacrament of order. Pope Paul VI's restoration of the diaconate was a recognition, in principle, that ordained leadership in the church cannot be restricted to celibate priesthood. The importance of this recognition, for ecumenism and for the church's future, should not be underestimated, as I hope to show in the paragraphs that follow.

For centuries in Roman Catholic theology and piety, the priest has been viewed above all as the one who has "the power to say Mass." The historical evolution of this view has already been described in Chapter Four. Here we need only note that this almost exclusively sacramental definition of priesthood has had far-reaching effects on both theology and pastoral practice. The pastoral leadership of the priest was seen as quite secondary to his extraordinary sacramental power, a power he personally possessed in virtue of ordination. Indeed, the priest's "power to consecrate the eucharist" came to be regarded as quite independent from pastoral service within an actual community of Christians. He could "say Mass for the living and the dead" without any congregation present, as an act of personal devotion or as a votive offering for another's intentions.

This historical tendency to place sacramental power before pastoral leadership represents a reversal of the pattern one can discern in the New Testament. In the earliest church, as Edward Schillebeeckx observes, ministry grew up not around eucharist or liturgy, but around "the apostolic building up of the community through preaching, admonition and leadership."[64] The New Testament thus never explicitly connects ministry with eucharist, probably because it was assumed that whoever possessed the charism of pastoral leadership would, *ipso facto,* be qualified to preside at the Lord's Supper. In short, the New Testament pattern places pastoral leadership before sacramental power — and assumes, indeed, that this leadership is the

[64]See Schillebeeckx, *Ministry,* p. 30.

essential mark of a minister's authority and status in the church.

By restoring the diaconate as a permanent role within the church's ordained leadership, Paul VI implicitly broke the long-standing connection between ordination and "sacramental power." Although deacons may officiate at some liturgies (e.g., marriage, Christian burial, the liturgy of the hours), presiding at worship is not their principal task. Nor are deacons ordained for the presidency of the eucharist. Theirs is a ministry, rooted like all others in a recognition of baptismal charism, that places pastoral leadership before sacramental power. The diaconate represents, then, those New Testament qualities of ministry which Schillebeeckx has aptly described as "the apostolic building up of the community through preaching, admonition and leadership."[65]

The restoration of the diaconate is thus important not because it resurrects an ancient order that had all but faded in the West, but because it affirms the principle that *recognition of pastoral leadership is the fundamental basis for calling a Christian to ordained ministry*. Ordained service in the church begins not with the acquisition of sacramental powers, but with the baptismal charism of leadership, discerned by the community. Even in the case of priesthood, liturgical presidency is derived from pastoral leadership, not vice versa. For as David Power has remarked, "Presidency of community and presidency of the eucharist require the charism of leadership. They fittingly go together, and history suggests that it was one suited to the former who in fact assumed the later."[66]

This can, I believe, have important repercussions for ecumenical discussions of ministry. If we can agree that the primary qualification for ordination and ministry is the baptismal charism of leadership, other issues (such as "how many ordained ministries shoud there be?" or "who should

[65] *Ibid.*
[66] See Power, *Gifts That Differ*, p. 127.

preside at eucharist?") assume secondary importance. The following outline will help clarify this point.

1 The ministry of order is rooted in the common call to mission and ministry which results from membership in a holy people through baptism.

2 If the Christian churches recognize the authenticity of one another's baptism—as most of them do—then they also implicitly recognize a common basis for the ministry.

3 If the charism of leadership (a baptismal gift) is the basic qualification sought in candidates for ordained ministry, then the churches have a common criterion for deciding who should be called to orders.

4 History reveals a considerable amount of diversity in patterns of church order. Even the Council of Trent appears to have been aware of this variability. Although it insisted that hierarchical ministry and priesthood were "instituted by Christ," it showed extreme delicacy in identifying precisely what arrangement of ministries Jesus intended.[67]

5 Even the notion of "hierarchy" in the ministry can be better understood if one roots it in the Pauline conviction that some charisms are superior to others (insofar as they contribute to the building up of the church more directly). One can argue further that charism is itself an ordering principle in the congregation's life—and that hierarchy among ministers is actually a consequence of diversity among baptismal gifts.

We may say, in summary, that the ministry common to all Christians and the ministry of holy orders both flow from the same source: baptism as membership in a holy people. In this sense, the sacrament of order gives explicit expression to what is already implied by the very structure of the baptized community. All Christians are endowed with gifts of ministry, but not all gifts are alike. The charism of leadership also gives rise to the explicit recognition of roles

[67]See A. Duval, "The Council of Trent and Holy Orders," in *The Sacrament of Holy Orders.* Some papers and Discussions concerning Holy Orders at a Session of the Centre de Pastorale Liturgique, 1955, (Collegeville, Minnesota: The Liturgical Press, 1962), pp. 219-258.

in the community. These roles—pastoral presidency, liturgical leadership—are identified in the liturgy of ordination as God's gifts and as evidence of the Spirit's sovereign grace at work in the community.

4. THE PERMANENCE OF ORDERS

Another sensitive point in ecumenical discussions of ministry has been the question of permanent tenure in ecclesiastical offices. Put most simply, do ministers remain "ordained" even if they retire, resign or are ousted from active service? The Roman Catholic tradition has insisted, at least since the late twelfth century, that ordination establishes a permanent claim on the individual. This claim, technically called the "sacramental character" and often described as "an indelible mark on the soul", is usually interpreted to mean that a bishop, presbyter or deacon radically retains the power of order (though not of jurisdiction) even if he is "reduced to the lay state." According to this view, for example, a laicized priest would still retain the "power" to preside at eucharist—though it would be illegal for him to do so.

Some of the historical reasons for the development of the theology of permanent "character" attached to ordination have already been discussed in Chapter Four. Here our task will be to see if and how this tradition about the permanence of holy orders can be related to the topics we have been discussing in the present chapter. I will suggest that the most fruitful way to understand the permanence of ordained ministry flows from three principles: 1) the permanence of Christian baptism; 2) the permanence of the community's apostolic right to ministry; and 3) the permanence of Jesus' priesthood.

In the preceding section we noted that all Christian service, including that of the ordained, is rooted in the call to mission and ministry which comes from baptism. Significantly, it was in relation to baptism that Augustine first developed his theory of a permanent or indelible "character."[68] By claiming that baptism permanently marks or claims the individual, Augustine was arguing, in effect, that *God* is the one who initiates and sustains all sacramental relationships. It is thus God's unflinching fidelity to human persons that creates the permanent bond between himself and believers in baptism. There was also a strongly ecclesiological sense to Augustine's thinking about character. Baptism brings membership in a holy people, and God's relation to that people (the church) is revealed as unconditionally faithful in Christ, who "loved the church and gave himself up for her" (Eph 5:25). The language of character gave Augustine a way to speak about God as the faithful initiator and sustainer of all sacramental relationships in the church. So great is this faithfulness that it cannot be overcome by human unworthiness or infidelity. For Augustine, even the heretic and apostate are permanently marked and claimed by God's faithful love.

Given this view of character, one can rather easily understand why it was transferred to the ordained ministry. In ordination, too, Augustine perceived a lasting relationship initiated and sustained by God. This makes sense if one remembers that the relation between ordained persons and the community is rooted in baptism, the source of all charisms of leadership in the church. Moreover, since the ordained are responsible for leading those very actions whereby the mystery of the church is constituted and celebrated (baptism, eucharist), ordination points to the uncompromising permanence of God's self-giving love. Like other human beings, Christian ministers may recoil from that love, repudiate and abandon it—but God's offer of self is never withdrawn. God's "yes" to believers—in both baptism and ministry—endures.

To speak of the permanent "character" of ordination is thus to speak, in the first instance, of the permanent cove-

---

[68]See John A. Gurrieri, "Sacramental Validity: The Origins and Use of a Vocabulary," *The Jurist* 41 (1981), 33-34; complete article, 21-58. See also Power, *Gifts That Differ*, p. 126.

nant God establishes with Christians in baptism. And since baptism results precisely in membership among a holy people, a second factor also contributes to the idea that orders create a permanent "mark" or "claim" on the minister. That factor is the community's "apostolic right" to ministry, a point discussed earlier in this chapter. Permanent tenure in an ordained role is not a matter of personal exaltation for the individual; it results, rather, from the community's evangelical right to the pastoral leadership that has been given by God, discerned by God's people, and ritually recognized through the laying on of hands and prayer.

(2)   Approaching this point from a slightly different angle, we can say that the Christian right to ministry flows from the church's definition as a community constituted by *Word, sacrament,* and *service.* Word and sacrament, service and mission, essentially define the church; without them, Christians would lose their identity as the community of Jesus, as the "persisting presence" of the Incarnate Word in space and time.[69] But the Word preached, the sacraments celebrated and the service rendered by Christians are not merely human works; they are perceived by faith as *God's* action in and for the world. For when the church assembles to preach and celebrate, it proclaims not itself but *God* as the saviour of humankind. Christian preaching, sacraments and service always point to the God who celebrates what Karl Rahner has called "the liturgy of the world."[70] "The world and its history," Rahner writes, "are the terrible and sublime liturgy, breathing of death and sacrifice, which God celebrates and causes to be celebrated in and through human history in its freedom . . . ."[71] The sacraments of the Chris-

---

[69]See Karl Rahner, "The Theology of the Symbol," in *Theological Investigations* IV, translated by Kevin Smyth, (Baltimore: Helicon Press, 1966), p. 240; see also Rahner's "The Word and the Eucharist," *ibid.,* pp. 254-255. On service (*diakonia*) and mission as essential elements in the church's definition, see Richard McBrien, *Church: The Continuing Quest,* (Paramus, New Jersey: Newman Press, 1970), pp. 80-85.

[70]See Karl Rahner, "Considerations on the Active Role of the Person in the Sacramental Event," in *Theological Investigations* XIV, translated by David Bourke, (New York: The Seabury Press, 1976), pp. 166-170.

[71]*Ibid.,* p. 169.

tian community are small "landmarks", rough-hewn signs that point to the world itself as the place permeated by God's presence, permanently claimed by his love, and redeemed at its root by the cross of Christ.[72]

Christian ministry exists precisely to remind the church that its preaching, sacraments and service are *God's* work, not its own—and that Christian liturgy is but a humble sign of that larger "liturgy of the world" that throbs throughout human flesh and history. Ministry exists to "keep the church honest," to prevent it from collapsing into that arrogant self-love which tries to incarcerate God within the "sacred precincts" of holy rites and rigid dogmas. When we say, therefore, that the church has a permanent right to ministry—and that ordained ministers are permanently "marked" as such—we are really saying something about the way God relates to the world, its history and its people. The permanence of ordained ministry signals the permanence of the church's need for Word, sacrament and service; at the same time, it signals God's enduring presence within that larger "liturgy of the world," with all its grandeur and greed, selflessness and stupidity. Seen in this light, ordained ministry exists not merely for the church but for the world. The baptismal charism of leadership which a candidate for ordination is expected to exhibit requires more than leading the church in preaching, prayer and sacrament. Ordained leadership also involves discerning God's presence in the thick, tumbling textures of human history—in the cry of the oppressed, in the struggle for justice, in the search for peace. To say that such leadership enjoys permanent tenure in the church is to say that God lives and acts, permanently, in all the world's wounds and wonders. The permanence of ordination is thus a testament to the permanence of God's dangerous intimacy with us and with our world. For the God of Christians is neither a retired deity nor a prisoner of ecclesiastical institutions; he is, rather, a God who identifies himself with our flesh and breath, our living and dying.

[72]*Ibid.*, pp. 169-170.

(3)   This dangerously intimate God was revealed in the "priestly" ministry of Jesus, especially in the "sacrifice" of the cross. We have already investigated, in the first section of this chapter, the New Testament's use of such priestly and sacrificial metaphors as applied both to Jesus and to the Christian people. Suffice it to recall here that Jesus' priesthood is understood, particularly by the Letter to the Hebrews, as eternally effective and as eliminating the need for further sacrifices. The permanence of Jesus' priesthood gave rise, among theologians, to the notion that Christian believers and their ordained ministers somehow "participate" in the Lord's priestly character.

Exactly what is meant by such "participation" is, however, far from clear.[73] J.M.R. Tillard has noted that the word "participation", as used by theologians like Thomas Aquinas, might have four different—though related— meanings. 1) Interpreted along Platonic lines, participation may indicate "the connection between a reality of the higher world and a reality of the lower world. This is a connection in which the second reality depends on the first while it bears deep within its nature a kinship with it."[74] In this sense, for example, human persons are said to be "by participation" what God is "by essence"—living, intelligent, good. Inscribed within the human person is a deep resemblance and kinship with God—a kinship described as "participation" in God's life and goodness. 2) A second and more dynamic meaning stresses action "and centres attention less on the person who acts than on the act which proceeds from the person."[75] Here, participation signifies that *God* is the radical source of all authentically human acts (i.e., acts that are free, intelligent and responsible). 3) Aquinas sometimes used "participation" as a way to describe the contact made between a baptized Christian and the power of Jesus' pas-

[73]See J.M.R. Tillard, "The Ordained 'Ministry' and the 'Priesthood' of Christ," *One in Christ* 14 (1978), 232-234.
[74]*Ibid.,* 232.
[75]*Ibid.,* 232-233.

sion.[76] In this case, to participate means "to have a share in the effects" of the Lord's suffering and death. 4) Finally, participation can refer to the covenant or bonds of friendship that knit human persons to God. Here, the emphasis is placed on the divine/human communion established and sustained by God's freely given grace.

At the Second Vatican Council, the language of participation was used to describe both baptized Christians and their ordained ministers. According to *Lumen Gentium* (Constitution on the Church) 10, "the common priesthood of the faithful and the ministerial or hierarchical priesthood . . . . each in its own proper way shares in the one priesthood of Christ" (*"de uno Christi Sacerdotio participant"*).[77] In *Presbyterorum Ordinis* ("Decree on the Ministry and Life of Priests") 2, bishops—and in a subordinate way, priests—are said to be "sharers in the consecration and mission" of Christ (*"consecrationis missionisque suae participes"*).[78] As our discussion in the preceding paragraph reveals, this language of participation is somewhat ambiguous. It is not quite enough to say that ordained ministers "share" in Christ's priestly consecration and mission. We must also ask *how* such a share is to be understood.

J.M.R. Tillard has offered an interesting response to this question. He notes that, according to the theology of the Letter to the Hebrews, the priesthood of Jesus is constituted not only by his suffering and death but also by his resurrection.[79] As "high priest of a new covenant," Jesus enters God's sanctuary through the resurrection, carrying with him his own life's blood. Jesus' priestly actions of suffering, rising and interceding on our behalf are thus utterly unique. No one except Jesus can be a priest in precisely this sense.

[76]See Thomas Aquinas, *Summa Theologiae,* IIIa Pars, Q. 86, art. 4, ad 3: "A person participates totally in the power of Christ's passion."
[77]See Austin Flannery, ed., *Vatican Council II.* The Conciliar and Post-Conciliar Documents, (Collegeville, Minnesota: The Liturgical Press, 1975, paperback edition), p. 361.
[78]*Ibid.,* p. 864.
[79]See Tillard, "The Ordained 'Ministry' and the 'Priesthood' of Christ," 236-237.

Nor can Christian ministers "repeat" Jesus' priestly action, since they have been done "once-for-all" and are all-sufficient (Heb 10:12).[80] Christian ministry is thus a "priesthood" only insofar as it serves to unfold and apply the unique priesthood of Jesus to believers. In this sense alone can an ordained Christian priest "participate" in the all-sufficient activity of Jesus, our "high priest."

One other point must be added here. The bond that unites the Risen Jesus with believers is the Spirit, who indwells hearts and imparts holiness to the baptized (see, e.g., Rom 8). All Christians are thus called to a common vocation that might be described as "the priesthood of holy life."[81] Just as ordained ministers serve to unfold and apply the unique priesthood of Jesus, so they are also called to serve that "bond" (the Spirit) which unites the Lord with his people. As J.M.R. Tillard has put it:

> The minister is a Christian called to the service of the bond between the glorified Priest and the community of believers . . . . The priestly *consecration* of Jesus is a reality in which he *participates* solely by serving it. Ministry of transparency, its aim is to reveal and radiate the priesthood of the risen Christ.
>
> The Christian minister is only the *doulos* slave or *diakonos* servant of the one Priest.[82]

Through their ordination, Christian ministers are thus permanently commissioned as servants of Jesus' unique priesthood and as servants of that Spirit who imparts holiness and unites believers to the Lord. The "once-for-all" character of Jesus' priesthood creates a permanent claim on the ordained minister—for just as Jesus cannot cease interceding on our behalf as "high priest of a new covenant," so the ordained minister is permanently "marked" as servant. This servantship is accomplished through the power of that same Spirit which overshadowed Jesus at the outset of

[80]*Ibid.*, 237.
[81]*Ibid.*
[82]*Ibid.*, 238.

his ministry, raised him to life, and caused him to enter God's sanctuary with the blood of the cross. That is why, as we noted in Chapter Four, the church's ordination prayers have characteristically taken the form of an "epiclesis," i.e., a prayer that the Spirit may take full possession of the minister and put him, permanently, at the service of Christ's priesthood.

To sum it up, the permanence of holy orders results not from some sacral power mysteriously imparted to the ordained, but from the nature of Christian baptism, the community's right to ministry, and the uniqueness of Jesus' priesthood. Rooted in a recognized baptismal charism of leadership, the call to ordained ministry is discerned by the community and ritualized through the laying on of hands and prayer. The result is lifelong servantship of Christ and of the Spirit who unites believers to Christ.

CONCLUSION

Our final chapter has sought to relate biblical conceptions of ministry to the church's theological tradition of ordination. We began by noting a certain tension between the "discipleship of equals" and the authoritative status accorded ministers in the New Testament. We discovered that the "charism" of apostolic ministry, as interpreted by Paul, is an "ordering principle that respects both individual uniqueness and communal need in the Christian congregation. Our discussion of Jesus' priesthood led to the conclusion that as our "pathfinder and pioneer," he has opened to believers the way of obedience-in-faith. Christians themselves can thus be described as a priestly people who express, through their faith and everyday lives, the transcendent grace and holiness of the God who has called them "out of darkness into his marvelous light" (1 Pet 2:9).

The second part of the chapter examined the church's tradition about holy orders by focusing on four issues: the "apostolic right" of Christians to ministry; ordination as a process; the relation between ordained and non-ordained ministries; and the permanence of ordained ministry in the church. We concluded that the call to ordination is radically rooted in the baptismal vocation common to all Christians. Every believer has a gift of ministry (a "charism") to offer others, but not all possess the charism of leadership. Those who do may be called to serve the unique priesthood of Christ. Ordained ministry is thus a permanent condition of servantship, through which the minister seeks to unfold the priestly activity of Jesus among his people and to strengthen that bond of the Spirit which imparts holiness and unites believers to the Lord.

Recommended Reading

Countryman, L. William, "Christian Equality and the Early Catholic Episcopate," *Anglican Theological Review* 63 (1981), 115-138. An essay that challenges the notion that all believers were considered "equal" in earliest Christianity.

Fiorenza, Elisabeth Schüssler. "The Biblical Roots for the Discipleship of Equals," *Journal of Pastoral Counselling* 14 (1979), 7-15. A valuable discussion of this principle conflicted with cultural conditions in the Greco-Roman world.

Power, David. *Gifts That Differ*. Lay Ministries Established and Unestablished. Studies in the Reformed Rites of the Catholic Church, Vol. VIII. New York: Pueblo Publishing Company, 1980. An important recent study of non-ordained ministries in the church: their history and their prospects for the future.

Tillard, J.M.R. "The Ordained 'Ministry' and the 'Priest-hood' of Christ," *One in Christ* 14 (1978). Contains valuable discussions of the idea of "participation" in the unique priesthood of Christ.

CONCLUSION

Our study of ordained Christian ministry has spanned many centuries and has examined a variety of theological interpretations linked with the sacrament of holy orders. By way of conclusion, it may be helpful to summarize the results of our study:

1. The Israelite priesthood, for all its influence during the Second Temple period, seems to have had little impact on the earliest Christians. While some believers—like the party of James at Jerusalem—may have continued adhering to the Temple and its cult, many Christians appear to have abandoned allegiance to the Temple and its priesthood.

2. The first generation of Christians did not possess a uniform pattern of ministry that was considered "normative" for all the churches. Paul's view of charism, for example, did not find acceptance everywhere, nor did his vision of apostleship match that of later Christian writers such as Luke.

3. Christians of the second and third generations were confronted by a serious crisis of leadership. The fall of Jerusalem, the delay of Jesus' return, and the death of the earliest witnesses to Jesus' ministry and resurrection caused Christians to face the prospect of a "long haul" ahead. One can discern, in documents like the Pastoral Letters, a con-

cern for structures of leadership that would survive the
vicissitudes of an uncertain future.

4. Gradually, Christians began appropriating the language and the theology of their religious ancestors in Israel.
Ministers began, in the second and third centuries, to be
identified with the priests of the Old Covenant. The language of priesthood and sacrifice was associated, especially,
with the liturgical responsibilities of Christian leaders.

5. During the Middle Ages, theologians grew concerned
about the specifically sacramental nature of ordained ministry. From the twelfth century onward, ordination came to
be viewed as a sacrament of the church, permanent in its
effects.

6. In our own day, biblical and theological research has
uncovered a number of items that call into question many of
the traditional assumptions associated with the sacrament
of order. It is clear, for example, that in early Christianity
women assumed positions of leadership which, for centuries, have been regarded as the exclusive prerogative of men.
It is clear, too, that the threefold hierarchy of "deacons,
priests and bishops" is not something that can be "proved"
from the pages of the New Testament.

Today's Christians find themselves, therefore, confronted
by a tension between historical facts and theological
assumptions. This tension need not be destructive; it can,
indeed, lead to a renewal of ministerial service in the church.
Increasingly, Christians at the "grass roots" level are assuming responsibility for the church's ministry and mission in
the world. Perhaps this is the surest sign that the Spirit of the
Lord, who anointed Jesus for his ministry, is still at work,
calling men and women to the service of Jesus, the priest of a
new and lasting covenant.